Study Guide

for

Carson • Butcher • Mineka
Abnormal Psychology and Modern Life
Eleventh Edition

Prepared by
Elizabeth A. Levy

Allyn and Bacon
Boston London Toronto Sydney Tokyo Singapore

ISBN 0-321-05453-9

Printed in the United States of America

10 9 8 7 6 5 4 3 2 1   03 02 01 00 99

TABLE OF CONTENTS

Part Three: ASSESSMENT, TREATMENT, AND PREVENTION

TO THE STUDENT

In many schools, abnormal psychology is often one of the most popular courses offered. Frequently, students enrolled in this course major in quite diverse fields, and many may have taken only an introductory course in psychology. Similarly, some psychology majors will take this course before taking many other psychology courses. These students sometimes feel at a disadvantage in competing with upper-level psychology majors. In addition, the familiarity of the subject matter and its high relevance to real life may give some students the feeling that they "understand" the material when they do not. At examination time, they find out that they do not "know" the material in the way the instructor expected.

This study guide has been developed to assist you in learning the material presented in the textbook. It has been designed to help you overcome any lack of experience you may have in approaching psychological material and to make you familiar with the kind of information it is important to know in order to do well on exams. It is written in a straightforward and serious style, minimizing games and other gimmicks. Most students find the textbook *Abnormal Psychology and Modern Life* so full of case histories, examples, and inherently interesting material, that they become interested in and motivated to learn the material without any outside props. What students often do need is help to decide *what to learn* and an organized place to write down the information that can be used as notes from which to study for examinations.

HOW TO STUDY

Many teachers recommend the following approach to studying course material:

1. Skim major headings and read chapter summaries.

2. Read and highlight (or underline) important sections of the text, giving particular emphasis to key terms.

3. Outline the important points you have highlighted in your reading. (Psychological studies show that putting material into your own words helps you to learn and retain the information better.)

4. Study from your text notes and class notes for exams, as well as review the highlighted material in the text. The former is especially helpful for exam questions requiring recitation (e.g., essays, short answer, fill-in-the-blanks) of the most important points. The latter is especially helpful for multiple-choice questions requiring recognition of a wide range of more detailed points.

This *Study Guide* indicates the terms and concepts many teachers feel are most important in the text. Do you seem to be underlining the same points? If not, the guide will help you pick up on points you may have overlooked rather than have you wait until exam time for this feedback. The most important function of the *Study Guide*, however, is as a substitute for difficult and time-consuming organizing and outlining. In the *Study Guide*, you will find that a lot of the choosing and organizing of the material has been done for you. Also, in some places, charts have been constructed to help you consolidate and learn the material. You have been given the general outlines. Your job is to fill in the specific information so you can prepare a complete and efficient set of notes to use in studying for examinations.

HOW TO USE THIS STUDY GUIDE

The *Study Guide* follows the sequence of the textbook and uses the same chapter headings and section headings. Each *Study Guide* chapter consists of nine sections (with the exception that "Names You Should Know" is deleted from four chapters). It is recommended that you first read the "Overview," then read the chapter summary in the textbook. Next, skim the chapter by reading the major section headings so you get a mental picture of the overall organization of the chapter. Then read the next sections in the *Study Guide* entitled "Chapter Outline" and "Learning Objectives."

After reading the Overview in the *Study Guide*, the major section headings in the text, and the "Chapter Outline" and "Learning Objectives in the *Study Guide*," you should have a general orientation to the chapter and should be ready to begin reading and highlighting the text. As you do, in addition to highlighting material you see as important, you should consult the sections in the *Study Guide* entitled "Terms You Should Know," "Concepts to Master," and "Study Questions" and fill in the correct answers in each. These are the *core sections for mastering the material in the text*. The questions in each of these three sections are arranged in the order in which the material appears in the text and are page-referenced. Thus, you should have little difficulty in finding the correct answers. Finally, you should read the thought-provoking questions in the section entitled "Critical Thinking on Difficult Topics."

Once you have finished reading the text and have finished the relevant sections in the Study Guide, you should have the relevant information secured. Your remaining task is to memorize the material to prepare for examination. After doing this, you should take the "Chapter Quiz" at the end of the *Study Guide* chapter.

A more detailed description of each of the sections in the *Study Guide* follows.

1. Chapter Overview

This short section is designed to prepare you to begin the chapter. The overview attempts to orient you to the purpose and some of the implications of the material you are about to read. It is designed to alert you to the overall importance of the chapter so you will, hopefully, feel motivated to start reading it.

2. Chapter Outline

This is a new section introduced with this edition of the study guide. Each chapter of this study guide has a detailed outline of the textbook chapter. The outline is based directly on the major headings and subheadings, and should be useful for you in organizing your notes. Additionally, this should provide a nice reference to any section in the text. Here it may be useful to pencil in notes beside the outline. After reading the text chapter and completing the study guide chapter, it may also be useful to attempt to attempt to replicate the outline from memory, so as to have a mental map of the material. Ideally, the outline will help provide you with a framework for each chapter's organization.

3. Learning Objectives

This section presents a more detailed overview of the material to be covered in the chapter and an indication of what you should have learned once you have completed the chapter. The listing of the learning objectives generally corresponds to the major headings and subheadings of the chapter but often will more specifically identify the goals of your studying. This section is intended to provide a general orientation to the chapter. You should not try to write out answers to these learning objectives.

4. Terms You Should Know

Here you will find listed all the major terms introduced in the chapter along with a page reference on which to find the definition (and often a discussion) of the term in the textbook. The focus of this section is to build your vocabulary--i.e., to ensure that you are familiar with the terms routinely used in the field of abnormal psychology. Many of the terms can also be found in the glossary at the back of the textbook. It is, however, still a good idea to look up the definition of the term within the chapter to be certain you know the context in which the term appeared. In the space provided, write out a brief definition of each term.

5. Names You Should Know

Textbooks cite hundreds or even thousands of authors. Students often would like to know whose names they should learn. This does not, however, mean that you should have to try to memorize the names of all the authors cited in the text. This section is not intended to identify names to be covered on an exam. It is, on the other hand, probably useful for you to begin to learn the names of prominent people in the field--especially if you intend to go to graduate school or in some other way pursue the field of abnormal psychology.

The task of deciding which names to list was difficult in part because *Abnormal Psychology and Modern Life* is not written to "feature" authors. Consequently, in compiling these names, a conservative strategy was adopted. The intention is that those names that were considered to be identified as major contributors by almost anyone in a given area were included. In order to avoid overwhelming you, the list was compiled on the side of identifying too few rather than too many names. This section was omitted from four chapters where it did not fit the material presented. Overall, it is hoped that this section will help you to begin to learn the names of people who are generally familiar to psychologists who teach and do conduct research in abnormal psychology. Unless your instructor indicates otherwise, these names are not likely to appear exams.

6. Concepts to Master

In this section, you are asked questions that require an essay type of answer. In general, these items focus on conceptual rather than factual material. As a result, they will require the most active learning on your part and will require the greatest amount of time. The rewards in learning will be commensurate with the investment of time. The questions have been worded in such a way as to clearly follow the presentation of the material in the text. By using the page numbers given, you should have little trouble identifying the material addressed by the question. In most cases, you should find that the answer to the question is obvious, though it will require judgment on your part as to how to extract the core information from the material in the text. It is hoped that there is sufficient space after each question for you to write in the correct answer. Although it is impossible to precisely judge how much space a given student will require for each answer, in general more space is provided where answers are likely to be longer.

7. Study Questions

The questions in this section focus on material that is more factual in nature than that covered in the previous section. A variety of formats are used--e.g., short answers, filling in blanks, completing a chart, matching two columns. In general, the wording in the questions has precisely followed that in the text, with the result that by consulting the referenced page(s) you will have no difficulty identifying the correct answer. In order to help you review the organization of the material better, the major headings from the text have been used in this section (in italicized bold print) to divide the individual questions into groups dealing with specific topics. You may want to read the entire section in the text before trying to answer the questions under a given heading.

The Study Questions help you identify much of the factual knowledge you should learn about each topic. To complete the requested information, go to the referenced page, locate the appropriate section and read it over, then write a correct response in the *Study Guide*. In the case of fill-in-the-blanks questions, you should attend to the overall statement, not just to the information entered in the blanks. Your instructor may well ask the question in a different way, and important information is often provided in addition to what you are asked to provide in the blanks.

A word of warning is in order here. Although the coverage of factual material in this section of the *Study Guide* is extensive, it is simply impossible to ask about *all* possible factual material in a text as comprehensive as *Abnormal Psychology and Modern Life*. In order to maximize your learning, you should try to use the Study Questions as a guide to help you pick out important material. Then highlight additional factual material in your text (sparingly, so that you do not end up with most of the text highlighted).

8. Critical Thinking About Difficult Topics

In sharp contrast with the other sections in the *Study Guide*, which focus on mastering material as presented in the text, this section asks you to think more deeply about interesting, difficult, and often unresolved issues in the field. In most--or, at least, many--cases, there are no right or wrong answers, but it is important that you understand the issues involved. The goal of this section is to challenge you to develop a more sophisticated conceptualization of these topics. These questions usually will emphasize points already made in the text, and the relevant pages are cited. In rare cases, these questions will offer an alternative to the perspective offered in the text. Frequently, the suggested alternative is not meant to necessarily imply the "correct answer". Rather, it is a perspective you should understand, but with which you might disagree after weighing all the issues. To struggle with issues over which reasonable people can disagree is part of the interest and excitement of this section. Some of the issues might make excellent topics for class discussion.

9. Chapter Quiz

Each *Study Guide* chapter concludes with a short self-test of multiple-choice items. The self-test to some extent will allow you to assess your mastery of the chapter. Complete the self-test items after you have completed all the other *Study Guide* sections but while you still have time for additional study. Look up the correct answer to each item in the Answer Key at the end of the *Study Guide*. Go back to the referenced page for each item you missed and read over the correct answer. Then try to analyze why you made the mistake. Did you not know the material? Did you misinterpret the item? (Try to read each item very carefully and make sure you know the definitions of all the terms introduced in the chapter.) It is unlikely that you will be able to answer all of them correctly, but if you find you incorrectly answer *a substantial portion*, you may well need to study more. You should be aware, however, that this short self-test can only serve as a rough guide to your knowledge of the text. It does not, of course, assess your response to exam items with other formats (e.g., essay, short answer, definitions) and it is too short to provide a *definitive* assessment of your knowledge of the material in the text.

HOW TO PREPARE FOR EXAMS

Many students become anxious about their performance on tests and this tension becomes greater as exam time grows nearer. Research suggests that the most effective preparation is accomplished under moderate levels of anxiety. Therefore, do *not* leave all your studying until the last minute when tension renders your behavior disorganized and less effective and when there is simply not enough time to master the material. Use your anxiety to motivate you to study well in advance of the exams. That is, read the text and complete the *Study Guide* on an ongoing basis during the term, and aim to complete these tasks several days before the exam.

Plan to study for a few hours each day on the several days before the scheduled exam. Study from your completed *Study Guide*, your class notes, and from the highlighted portions of your textbook. Re-reading the entire textbook is time-consuming and inefficient. If you've been conscientious in completing the *Study Guide*, it contains most of the material you need to learn. Start with the Terms You Should Know section. Cover the definition and try to recite it from memory. (If you have a private study area, it's likely to be even more effective to say the definition out loud.) Go back over the list and cover each term successively. Read the definition and try to recall the term to which it applies. This general approach is to be used with Concepts to Master and Study Questions, as well. Cover the answers you have written and try to generate them from memory. Continue to review the *Study Guide* until you can reproduce all the correct answers from memory.

Another critical point is to *take good lecture notes* in class. For most students, it is not possible to write down all the important information during the lecture. As soon as you can find the opportunity (ideally, immediately after class but certainly on the day of the lecture), sit down and go over your notes and fill in as much additional material as you can remember from the lecture. Then read over your notes and be sure you understand the instructor's organization and major points. If you have missed material, ask your instructor or teaching assistant to help you fill it in. Almost all instructors will lecture on material they believe is most important and many will emphasize that material on the exams. Thus, your class notes may provide an invaluable guide as to what you should learn. In reading the text and using the *Study Guide*, give an even greater emphasis to any topics covered in lecture. Doing so may be doubly valuable, inasmuch as (a) it may help you answer questions on the exam that refer specifically to the lectures and (b) the instructor may be more likely to write exam questions on the text material that relates to the lectures.

Whether your teacher will be using multiple-choice or essay exams should not greatly affect how you will prepare--both types of testing require a command of the basic facts. Well-prepared students come out on top no matter what form of testing the instructor uses. Some students may argue that memorization is not necessary for multiple-choice tests which only require recognition of the right response. This is untrue. Instructors purposely write the wrong answers to look and sound plausible. If you don't know the facts, you'll be misled by these distracters.

It may be helpful to determine how much time to allocate to studying for this course. The normative expectation for a three-semester-hour course is that students will spend six hours per week (every week) studying for the course. This estimate refers to *actual study time*--i.e., not time spent commuting to class, buying books, talking with the instructor or fellow students about the course, etc. Assuming that all students spend this much time, it is important to understand that doing so will not guarantee an A in the course. Unless you are unusually gifted or well-prepared, you may find that you need to spend more than six hours per week to truly master the material in a demanding course such as Abnormal Psychology, although so can be very difficult. If you are registered for 15 semester hours, it means you may have to spend more than 30 hours per week studying. When you add in the time lost to commuting, everyday activities, and a social life, it is not easy to find extra hours for studying. This is doubly difficult if, for example, you are working to earn money for 15 to 20 hours per week in addition to carrying a full-time academic load. Your time is scarce and valuable. You should give careful thought to how it is used and do all you can to allocate as much time as possible to studying. It is an important discipline to budget your time and use it for things that are most important.

CONCLUSION

It is hoped that the *Study Guide* helps you master the material in this course and, of course, to do well on the exams. However, it is also hoped that learning the material in this course serves you well in the future. The topics studied in abnormal psychology impact on everyone. Having a sophisticated understanding of these topics should help you understand events in your life better and may even help you provide information or help to a friend or relative suffering from some of the problems discussed in the course. For a sizable number of you, this course will provide a foundation for a future career in which knowledge of the material may be of value (e.g., in general medicine, nursing, teaching, etc.) or for a career as a mental health professional.

Whether or not you pursue such a career, I hope the course and the *Study Guide* have been of value to you.

Much credit belongs to the authors of previous editions of this study guide. In particular, much of this edition has been adapted from the work of Don C. Fowles. Thanks to the authors of the text, especially Susan Mineka. Thanks also to Cyndy Taylor and Addison-Wesley Longman, Inc. Above all, my deepest gratitude and love go to Mom, Dad, Alan, and Jason, as well as to the rest of my family and friends.

Elizabeth A. Levy

Chapter 1
Abnormal Behavior in Our Times

◊ OVERVIEW

It has been said that psychology "has a long history but a short past." This is certainly true of abnormal psychology. Although examples of bizarre behavior are seen throughout history, and considerations of why people act as they do have appeared and reappeared in literature and philosophy, the scientific study of abnormal behavior really only began around 1900. Chapter 1 begins with a discussion of the difficulty of defining abnormal behavior and of the importance of developing explanations supported by scientific evidence. Then, the meaning of the term "abnormal" is discussed along with a description of contemporary procedures to classify the different ways psychological disturbance may be expressed. Chapter 1 closes with an emphasis on the importance of obtaining scientific data, and a description of the various research methods used to study behavior.

◊ CHAPTER OUTLINE

I.   What Do We Mean By Abnormal Behavior?
     A. Dilemmas of Definition
     B. The DSM-IV Definition of Mental Disorder
     C. Cultural Influences in Abnormality
     D. Mental Disorder as Maladaptive Behavior

II. Classifying Abnormal Behavior
     A. Reliability and Validity
     B. Differing Models of Classification
          1. The Dimensional Approach
          2. The Prototypal Approach

◊ LEARNING OBJECTIVES

After studying this chapter, you should be able to:

1. Explain why it is so difficult to define abnormal behavior, describe different approaches to such definitions, and examine the strengths and weaknesses of each. (pp. 3-6)

2. Summarize the key concepts associated with the task of classification: define *reliability* and *validity*, discuss differing models of classification and the DSM-IV classification system, and describe the problems associated with labeling. (pp. 6-13)

3. Identify psychological assessment and diagnostic techniques and compare their relative benefits and limitations. (pp. 13-17)

4. Describe the methodologies used to determine the rate of mental disorder in the United States and the results of recent major epidemiological studies. (pp. 17-19)

5. Explicate the different methodologies and the methodological issues involved in research in abnormal psychology. (pp. 19-26)

6. List and discuss the concepts embraced by the authors as the basis of a sound and comprehensive study of abnormal behavior. (pp. 26-27)

7. Discuss the problems associated with use of the medical or disease metaphor in classifying abnormal behavior and describe the major alternative approaches. (pp. 27-29)

◊ TERMS YOU SHOULD KNOW

prognosis (p. 3)

abnormal (p. 3-6)

syndrome (p. 4)

classification (p. 6)

reliability (pp. 6-7)

validity (pp. 6-7)

categorical approach (to classification) (p. 7)

dimensional approach (to classification) (p. 7)

prototype (p. 8)

prototypal approach to classification (p. 8)

Diagnostic and Statistical Manual (DSM-IV) (pp. 8-11)

symptoms versus *signs* (p. 8)

operational criteria (p. 8)

comorbidity (p. 10)

axes (in DSM-IV) (pp. 10-12)

disorders secondary to gross destruction of brain tissue (p. 12)

substance-use disorders (p. 12)

disorders of psychological or sociocultural origin (having no known brain pathology) (p. 12)

disorders usually arising during childhood or adolescence (p. 12)

acute (p. 12)

chronic (p. 12)

episodic or *recurrent* (p. 12)

dysfunction (p. 12)

unstructured interview versus *structured interview* (p. 14)

epidemiology (p. 17)

prevalence (p. 17)

incidence (p. 17)

lifetime prevalence (p. 17)

deinstitutionalization (p. 18)

hypotheses (p. 19)

representative sampling (p. 21)

control group (p. 21)

criterion group (p. 21)

correlation (pp. 21-22)

causation (pp. 21-22)

epidemiological studies (p. 22)

experimental method (p. 23)

independent variable (p. 23)

dependent variable (p. 23)

longitudinal study (p. 23)

statistical control (p.23)

analogue studies (p. 23)

learned helplessness (p. 24)

waiting list control group strategy (pp. 24-25)

clinical case study or *N = 1 experiment* (p. 2425

retrospective research (p. 25)

prospective research (p. 25)

symptom/underlying disease model (p. 27)

◊ CONCEPTS TO MASTER

1. Describe two broad perspectives on the definition of abnormality or a mental disorder. (pp. 4-5)

2. List several reasons why a classification system is needed in abnormal psychology and explain the meaning of reliability and validity in reference to such a system. (pp. 6-7)

3. Why is it correct to assert that "validity presupposes reliability"? (p. 7)

4. List and describe three basic approaches to the classification of abnormal behavior and the general assumptions underlying each approach. (pp. 7-8)

5. Describe the five axes of DSM-IV, and discuss the evolution of the DSM as a diagnostic tool. (pp. 8-9; 10-12)

6. A distinct feature since DSM-III is "operational criteria." What does this mean? (p. 8)

7. Discuss the limitations of DSM classification that arise when these precise definitions are applied to the real problems of real patients. (pp. 9-10)

8. Describe some of the problems associated with labeling. (p. 12-13)

9. Describe the process by which psychologists assess and diagnose patients. Compare and contrast structured and unstructured interviewing techniques. (pp. 13-17)

10. Compare and contrast the concepts of prevalence and incidence, including the associated concepts of point prevalence and lifetime prevalence. (pp. 17-18)

11. Why are hypotheses critical supplements to observations of behavior? (pp. 19-20)

12. Explain why research on groups of people is usually preferred to single case studies and why those groups must be representative of larger populations. (pp. 20-21)

13. Explain why correlational research does not establish cause and effect and yet has been extremely valuable in the form of epidemiological research. (pp. 21-22)

14. A mere correlation does not imply causation. A manic individual exhibits a euphoric mood, a high level of activity without regard for its consequences that may lead to financial bankruptcy, and a loosening of cultural inhibitions that may be associated with crude and inappropriate sexual advances. Mania is also associated with a high rate of divorce--a stressful life event. How might divorce precipitate mania and how might mania lead to divorce--i.e., consider how the direction of causation might go in either direction? (p. 22)

15. If one considers a large number of cities, the number of bars in a city is correlated with the number of churches in the city. What third variable probably accounts for this observation? (p. 22)

16. Explain why some experimental studies are inappropriate for abnormal psychology, and indicate how analogue studies have been used in their place. (pp. 23-25)

17. Describe the clinical case study and explain why it is easy to draw erroneous conclusions from this method of research. (p. 25)

18. Compare the advantages and disadvantages of retrospective and prospective research in abnormal psychology. (pp. 25-26)

19. List and explain three concepts about the study of abnormal psychology on which this text is based. (p. 26)

What do we mean by "abnormal behavior"?

1. What is the literal meaning of the word *abnormal*? (pp. 3-4)

2. The authors of the text maintain that the best criterion for determining the normality of behavior is whether it fosters the well-being of the individual and, ultimately, of the group. According to this view, abnormal behavior is thus defined as _____. (p. 5)

3. How do the authors justify considering promotion of inter-group hostility, destructive assaults on the environment, irrational violence, and political corruption as forms of "abnormal behavior"? (p. 6)

4. What is the explicit value judgment in the "abnormal-behavior-is-maladaptive-behavior" framework? (pp. 5-6)

Classifying abnormal behavior: Differing models of classification

5. What example was used to illustrate the concept of "cognitive prototype"? (p. 6)

6. What is involved in classification within abnormal psychology? (pp. 6-7)

7. There are advantages to a prototype approach over a categorical approach. List the advantages of the prototype approach over a categorical approach and then explain why this approach is not used in the text even though the authors believe it is superior. (pp. 6-7)

Diagnostic and Statistical Manual of Mental Disorders (DSM-IV)

8. DSM-IV is based on symptoms of illness. It is referred to as a categorical model which assumes that all human behavior can be divided into normal and abnormal, and within the abnormal there exist non-overlapping types of behavior. As noted in the text, some observers argue that this is an inadequate model for organizing our observations of behavioral abnormalities. List as many problems with this model as you can. (pp. 9-10).

9. Identify the five axes of DSM-IV (pp. 10-12):

Axis I

Axis II

Axis III

Axis IV

Axis V

10. Why do some clinicians object to the use of Axes IV and V on insurance forms? (p. 12)

11. In what ways do Axes IV and V add significant information to that provided by the other three axes? (pp. 11-12)

12. Axis I and II of DSM-IV list the mental disorders, but for purposes of clarity these disorders may be regarded as fitting into several broad groupings. Match the terms on the left with their appropriate headings on the right. (p. 12)

Term	Category
___ a. mental retardation	A. Disorders secondary to the destruction of brain tissue
___ b. alcohol abuse	B. Substance use disorders
___ c. psychophysiological disorders	
___ d. affective mood disorders	C. Disorders of psychological or sociocultural origin
___ e. Alzheimer's disease	D. Disorders arising during childhood or adolescence
___ f. schizophrenia	
___ g. autism	
___ h. anxiety disorders	

The problem of labeling

13. The authors of the text indicate that the process of labeling, no matter what classification system is used, has drawbacks. When a label has been assigned to a person, what impact may this have on the professionals who are treating the person? (pp. 12-13)

14. How might labels affect the patients themselves? (pp. 12-13)

15. How might labels affect the attitudes of others toward the patient? (p. 13)

Assessment and diagnosis

16. The mental status exam is an example of a(n) _____ interview. (p. 14)

17. Discuss the difference between the two types of interview techniques. What are the limitations of each? (p. 14)

Assessing the extent of abnormal behavior

18. The National Comorbidity Survey (NCS) estimated prevalence of major maladaptive behavior patterns in the United States. What were the findings with regard to the one month prevalence for mental disorder and/or substance abuse? Approximately what percent of the U.S. population between the ages of 15-54 will have had a diagnosable Axis I disorder at some time in their lives? What percent will have had a diagnosable Axis I disorder during any one year? Describe gender differences found in the study, and discuss comorbidity findings. (pp. 17-18)

19. List and discuss two reasons for the substantial decline in mental hospital admissions over the past 45 years. (pp. 18-19)

Research in abnormal psychology: Observation of behavior

20. Verbal reports about inner processes are an important source of information that is both troublesome and interesting. Discuss the limitations of these observations as scientific data, and describe precautions taken to ensure their reliability and validity. (p. 19)

21. To make sense of observed behavior, psychologists generate more or less reasonable _____ to help explain the behavior. For example, a psychologist may observe some symptoms and guess that "schizophrenia" is the entity or hypothetical construct that caused the symptoms. This example demonstrates the process of inference in psychology. (p. 19)

Research in abnormal psychology: Sampling and generalization

22. The strategy of intensively studying a single case might yield important leads, but it suffers from a basic difficulty. What is this difficulty? (p. 20)

23. To overcome the limitations of studying the single case, psychologists usually rely on studies using groups of individuals. Explain why in such studies it is desirable to obtain a representative sample. (p. 21)

Research in abnormal psychology: Experimental strategies

24. Match definitions *a* through *f* below with the terms listed in the box.

   a. Therapist systematically monitors the precise relationships between treatment interventions and patient responses. (p. 25)
   b. Mathematical corrections are made for uncontrolled group differences. (p. 23)
   c. The study of behavior that is not actually pathological but is similar to it. (p. 23)
   d. Treatment is withheld for a period of time. (p. 24)
   e. All factors are controlled except for the one of interest, which is manipulated. (p. 23)
   f. A study that compares two or more treatments. (p. 23)

Term   **Letter of Definition**

I. Waiting list control   _____

II. N = 1 experiment   _____

III. Experimental method   _____

IV. Statistical control   _____

V. Analogue study   _____

VI. Comparative outcome research   _____

Research in abnormal psychology: Clinical case studies, retrospective/prospective strategies

25. After each of the following clinical research methods, write one strength and one limitation of the approach:

   a. Case study method (p. 25)
      Strength
      Limitation

b. Prospective research (p. 25)
    Strength
    Limitation

c. Retrospective research (p. 25)
    Strength
    Limitation

A scientific approach to abnormal behavior and a critical attitude

26. What is involved in a "scientific approach" to abnormal behavior? (p. 26)

27. What does it mean to "take a critical and evaluative attitude toward research findings"? (p. 26)

28. What sources can help a student develop an awareness of "common human concerns" and what is the limitation of this information compared with that obtained through scientific observation? (p. 26)

Unresolved issues: On the DSM

29. What are some of the limitations of the symptom/underlying disease model of mental disorders? (pp. 27-29)

◊ CRITICAL THINKING ABOUT DIFFICULT TOPICS

1. The authors of the text argue for a definition of abnormal behavior as maladaptive behavior and conclude that their definition would include "destructive assaults on the environment" (p. 10). Consider the case of an executive of a manufacturing company whose factory discharges pollutants into the air or water that are (a) perfectly legal, (b) within the range of common practice, (c) extremely costly to eliminate, but (d) harmful to the health of a significant number of individuals in the long run. Is his or her behavior indicative of a "mental disorder" (pp. 5-6)? Try to think of other instances in which there is a conflict between "rational" reward-seeking behavior that is not in violation of cultural norms, yet which is "in serious degree contrary to the continued well-being . . . of the human community of which the individual is a member" (pp. 5-6). Similarly, consider the case of the "subcultural delinquent" who acts entirely in keeping with the values, norms, and personal loyalties of his or her gang in committing various delinquent acts that are harmful to many members of the larger society. In what sense does such a person have a mental disorder?

2. How can the problems associated with labeling be prevented?

3. The text refers to three basic approaches to classifying abnormal behavior (categorical, dimensional, and prototypal), and it seems to suggest that the prototypal combines the best features of the categorical and dimensional approaches while avoiding some of their problems. The text used "dog," "cat," "beaver," and "donkey" as examples of cognitive prototypes. In these examples, the distinctions are relatively clear--e.g., there is not a continuum of critical features along which a dog blends into a cat. In contrast, in abnormal behavior there often is such blending, as suggested by the text. For example, anxiety and depressive disorders often blend together, as do schizophrenia and affective disorders. Under such conditions, how effective is the prototypal approach? Is it still useful? What etiological models might account for such blending?

4. The text describes a criterion group of depressed individuals and a control group of psychologically normal individuals (p. 21). It also correctly states that the control group should be comparable to the criterion group in all respects except for the presence of the disorder. Assuming differences are found between these groups, can you think of variables other than depression per se that might account for the differences? It may help to think about using a control group of general medical patients (e.g., patients with diabetes) as a *general medical control* group or of patients with an anxiety disorder as a *psychiatric control* group.

5. Do you think that "Road Rage" should be considered a mental disorder? Why or why not? Discuss your answer in reference to conceptual issues of classification.

◊ CHAPTER 1 QUIZ

Circle the best of the four answers provided and check them according to answers provided at the back of this study guide. Be sure you understand why each answer is correct.

1. The word *abnormal* literally means behavior that: (p. 3)
   a. deviates from society's norms.
   b. interferes with the well-being of the individual.
   c. is "away from the normal."
   d. is undesirable.

2. Cultural relativists like Ullmann and Krasner maintain that abnormal behavior is that which is: (p. 5)
   a. deviant from social expectations.
   b. illegal according to the law of the land.
   c. immoral by religious standards.
   d. psychologically maladaptive.

3. The authors of the textbook maintain that the best criteria for determining the normality of behavior is: (pp. 5-6)
   a. deviance from the norm.
   b. adaptivity of the behavior in furthering individual and group well-being.
   c. variance from societal expectations.
   d. the operational criteria listed in the DSM-IV.

4. When different observers agree on the classification of certain abnormal behaviors, the system is said to be: (p. 6)
   a. diagnostic.   c. standardized.
   b. reliable.   d. valid.

5. Widiger and Frances described three basic approaches currently possible for classifying abnormal behavior. Which of the following is *not* one of them? (pp. 7-8)
   a. categorical   c. prototypal
   b. dimensional   d. configural

6. A distinctive innovation since the DSM-III of 1980 has been the use of "operational" criteria for defining disorders. This means that the DSM now: (pp. 8-9)
   a. clearly specifies the causes or etiological factors.
   b. specifies the theoretical interpretation of the symptoms.
   c. identifies the adaptive function of the symptoms.
   d. specifies the exact behaviors that must be observed.

7. DSM-IV has changed since DSM-I in all of the following ways *except*: (pp. 8-9)
   a. It contains more elaborate differentiation of subtypes of disorders.
   b. Prototypal classification has been eliminated.
   c. There is an increase in the number of diagnoses.
   d. There are stricter diagnostic criteria.

8. There is strong evidence for significant overlap between anxiety and depression. Still a patient receives two diagnoses: one for anxiety and one for depression. This is an example of: (p. 10)
   a. synthesis.   c. convergence.
   b. concurrence.   d. comorbidity.

9. The first three axes of the DSM-IV assess: (p. 10)
   a. how well the individual is coping.
   b. stressors that may have contributed to the disorder.
   c. the person's present condition.
   d. the prognosis of the disorder.

10. In DSM-IV, personality disorders are entered on: (pp. 10-11)
    a. Axis I   c. Axis III
    b. Axis II   d. Axis IV

11 Multiple diagnoses are permissible on: (pp. 10-11)
    a. Axis I   c. Axis III
    b. Axis II   d. all of the above

12. Many clinicians object to the inclusion of a(n) _____ diagnosis on insurance forms because it violates the client's confidentiality. (p. 12)
    a. Axis I   c. Axis III
    b. Axis II   d. Axis IV

13. DSM-IV's major categories or *broad groupings* of mental disorders include: (p. 12)
    a. disorders secondary to gross destruction and malfunctioning of brain tissue.
    b. schizophrenic disorders.
    c. adjustment disorders.
    d. psychosexual disorders.

14. Which of the following terms refers to a mental condition of relatively short duration? (p. 12)
    a. episodic   c. chronic
    b. acute   d. factitious

15. Why do the authors believe it is important to gather epidemiological data? (p. 17)
    a. To help researchers identify causal mechanisms.
    b. To allocate mental health resources effectively.
    c. To help researchers improve treatment.
    d. All of the above.

16. The proportion of those living in a population who ever had a particular disorder (including recovered cases) is known as: (p. 17)
    a. lifetime prevalence.   c. lifetime incidence.
    b. point incidence.   d. lifetime comorbidity.

17. According to the National Comorbidity Survey, the frequency of most diagnosable mental disorders tends to decrease with: (p. 18)
    a. high socioeconomic status and younger age.
    b. high socioeconomic status and older age.
    c. low socioeconomic status and younger age.
    d. low socioeconomic status and older age.

18. In order to make sense of observed behavior, psychologists generate more or less plausible ideas called: (p. 19)
    a. constructs.   c. principles.
    b. hypotheses.   d. theories.

19. The purpose of _____ is to ensure, in effect, that each member of the population has an equal chance of being included in the study's sample. (p. 21)
   a. increasing reliability
   b. hypothesis testing
   c. structured set sampling
   d. random selection

20. Seligman induced learned helplessness in animals by subjecting them to repeated inescapable shock. This study is an example of _____ research. (p. 22)
   a. analogue.   c. correlational.
   b. clinical.   d. epidemiological.

21. A psychologist identifies 50 children who have schizophrenic mothers. At adolescence, the researcher compares those who break down with those who don't. This is an example of a _____ study. (p. 25)
   a. clinical case   c. prospective
   b. comparative outcome   d. retrospective

Chapter 2
Historical Views of Abnormal Behavior

◊ OVERVIEW

Abnormal behavior has fascinated humankind from its beginning, and various explanations of the causes of such behavior have developed over the course of history. This chapter presents a chronological overview of the many ways abnormal behavior has been viewed and treated, starting with early man and continuing through the modern era. Mastering this chapter should enable you to learn how these different views of behavior have evolved. In so doing, this chapter aims to help you understand the background for and basis of many of the fundamental issues in our field.

◊ CHAPTER OUTLINE

I.   Abnormal Behavior in Ancient Times
     A. Demonology, Gods, and Magic
     B. Hippocrates's Early Philosophical and Medical Concepts
     C. Early Philosophical Conceptions of Consciousness and Mental Discovery
     D. Later Greek and Roman Thought

II. Views of Abnormality During the Middle Ages
     A. Mass Madness
     B. Exorcism and Witchcraft

III. The Later Middle Ages: Toward Humanitarian Approaches
     A. The Resurgence of Scientific Questioning in Europe
     B. The Establishment of Early Asylums and Shrines
         1. Cultural Variation in Early Asylums
         2. The Geel Shrine
     C. Humanitarian Reform
         1. Pinel's Experiment

    2. Tuke's Work in England
    3. Rush and Moral Management in America
    4. Dix and the Mental Hygiene Movement
  D. Nineteenth Century Views of the Causation and Treatment of Mental Disorders
  E. Changing Attitudes Toward Mental Health in the Early Twentieth Century

IV. The Beginning of the Modern Era
  A. Establishing the Link Between the Brain and Mental Disorder
    1. General Paresis and Syphilis
    2. Brain Pathology as a Causal Factor
    3. The Beginnings of a Classification System
    4. Advances Achieved as a Result of Early Biological Views
  B. Establishing the Psychological Basis of Mental Disorder
    1. Mesmerism
    2. The Nancy School
    3. The Beginnings of Psychoanalysis
  C. The Evolution of the Psychological Research Tradition
    1. The Early Psychological Laboratories
    2. The Behavioral Perspective
      a) Classical Conditioning
      b) Operant Conditioning

V. Unresolved Issues: Interpreting Historical Events

VI. Summary

◊ LEARNING OBJECTIVES

After studying this chapter, you should be able to:

1. Explain why in ancient times abnormal behavior was attributed to possession by a demon or god and describe how exorcism was administered by shamans and priests as the primary type of treatment for demonic possession. (pp. 32-33)

2. Describe the important contributions from 460 B.C. to 200 A.D. of Hippocrates, Plato, Aristotle, and Galen to the conceptualization of the nature and causes of abnormal behavior. (pp. 33-35, 36)

3. Discuss how mental disorders were viewed during the Middle Ages. (pp. 36-39)

4. Give examples of mass madness or mass hysteria and summarize the explanations offered for this unusual phenomenon. (pp. 37-38)

5. Outline the contributions in the late Middle Ages and early Renaissance of Paracelsus, Teresa of Avila, Johan Weyer, Reginald Scot, and St. Vincent de Paul, all of whom argued that those showing abnormal behavior should be seen as mentally ill and treated with humane care. (pp. 39-41)

6. Describe the inhumane treatment that mental patients received in early "insane asylums" in Europe and the United States. (pp. 41-42)

7. Describe the humanitarian reforms in the treatment of mental patients that were instigated by Philippe Pinel, William Tuke, Benjamin Rush, and Dorothea Dix. (pp. 42-47)

8. Explain how both the discovery of a biological basis for general paresis and a handful of other disorders (such as, the senile mental disorders, toxic mental disorders, and certain types of mental retardation), contributed in a major way to the development of a scientific approach to abnormal psychology as well as to the emergence of modern experimental science which was largely biological. (pp. 49-50)

9. Distinguish between biological and non-biological versions of medical-model thinking about psychopathology. (pp. 50-51)

10. Trace the important events in the development of psychoanalysis and the psychodynamic perspective. (pp. 51-55)

11. Contrast the biological and psychodynamic views of abnormal disorders. (pp. 49-55)

12. Describe how the techniques of free association and dream analysis helped both analysts and their patients. (p. 55)

13. List the major features of the behavioral perspective. (pp. 56-57)

14. Discriminate between classical and operant conditioning. (pp. 56-57)

15. Explain the problems associated with interpreting historical events. (pp. 58-60)

◊ TERMS YOU SHOULD KNOW

Edwin Smith papyrus (p. 32)

exorcism (p. 33)

humors (p. 34)

hysteria (p. 34, 52-54)

mass madness (p. 37)

tarantism (p. 37)

St. Vitus's dance (p. 37)

lycanthropy (p. 37)

humanism (p. 39)

bodily magnetism (p. 40)

Bedlam (p. 41)

La Bicêtre (p. 41)

The Geel Shrine (p. 42)

moral management (p. 44)

deinstitutionalization (p. 46)

alienist (p. 47)

neurasthenia (p. 47)

general paresis (pp. 49-50)

psychoanalysis (p. 51, 54-55)

psychoanalytic perspective (p. 51, 54-55)

mesmerism (p. 51)

The Nancy School (pp. 51-53)

catharsis (p. 54)

the "unconscious" (p. 54)

free association (p. 55)

dream analysis (p. 55)

Journal of Abnormal Psychology (p. 56)

behavioral perspective (p. 56)

classical conditioning (p. 56)

behaviorism (p. 56)

instrumental or *operant conditioning* (p. 57)

psychohistory (p. 60)

◊ NAMES YOU SHOULD KNOW

Hippocrates

Plato

Aristotle

Teresa of Avila

Johann Weyer

Philippe Pinel

Benjamin Rush

Dorothea Dix

Clifford Beers

Emil Kraepelin

Sigmund Freud

Josef Breuer

Wilhelm Wundt

Ivan Pavlov

John B. Watson

E. L. Thorndike

B. F. Skinner

◊ CONCEPTS TO MASTER

1. Describe early beliefs in demonology and explain the reasons why exorcism was used as a cure. (pp. 32-33)

2. Hippocrates rejected demonology as a cause of mental disorders. What three aspects of his alternative approach were truly revolutionary? (pp. 33-34)

3. What assumption did Plato make about mentally disturbed individuals who commit criminal acts and how is this assumption relevant to our current legal system? (p. 34)

4. What was Plato's contribution to understanding human motivation? How is this view relevant to current research with animals by psychologists? (p. 34) Plato held several other beliefs that parallel modern ideas of mental disorders. Discuss some of them. (p. 34)

5. Describe early approaches to abnormal behavior in ancient China. How did the concept of Yin and Yang influence the interpretation of treatments? (Highlight 2.2, p. 38)

6. Describe the treatment for mental disorders used by the clergy during the Middle Ages known as exorcism, or the "laying on of hands." (pp. 38-39)

7. Explain the supposed connection between mental illness and witchcraft and comment on the accuracy of this assumption. (p. 39)

8. During the sixteenth century, Teresa of Avila, a Spanish nun who later became a saint, explained hysteria among a group of cloistered nuns as *comas enfermas,* which is translated "as if sick." Explain what she meant by this term. (p. 40)

9. What did Pinel do to provide more humane treatment for the inmates of La Bicêtre in Paris and what was the effect of these measures on the mental patients? Consider the implications of these results for the "demonic possession" versus the "psychological" theories of mental illness--were the results more compatible with one theory versus the other? (pp. 42-43)

10. How did general values and cultural attitudes in the Victorian era influence the interpretation and treatment of what we now call depression? (Highlight 2.4, p. 48)

11. How did Kraepelin classify mental diseases, and what did he think about the types, courses, and outcomes of mental disorders? (p. 50).

12. Hypnosis played an important role in the early stages of psychoanalysis and in establishing psychological factors as important in abnormal behavior. What critical demonstration of the power of hypnosis by Liebeault persuaded Bernheim of its importance and ultimately led to the founding of the Nancy School? (pp. 51-52)

13. The text notes that the Charcot/Nancy School debate was one of the major debates of medical history. What was the nature of the debate? Which side triumphed, and how did the debate influence modern psychology? (pp. 53-54)

14. What technique employed by Sigmund Freud resulted in the discovery of the unconscious, and on what result was this conclusion based? (p. 54)

15. Describe Watson's impact on American psychology. How did his view contrast with the psychoanalysts and biological psychologists of his day? (p. 56)

16. The of attitudes and treatment of mentally disordered persons in former eras is difficult. A primary difficulty is that we cannot rely on direct observation but have only historical documents from the period to study. List and explain several weaknesses of the kind of retrospective research that attempts to produce an accurate history of mental illness and its treatment. (pp. 58-60)

Demonology, gods, and magic

1. What, according to the earliest known written references, was the most frequent cause of abnormal behavior? (p. 32)

2. What was the primary type of treatment used by ancient peoples and which members of the community were charged with carrying out the treatment? (p. 33)

Early philosophical and medical concepts (400 B.C. to 200 A.D.)

3. Hippocrates is considered the "father of modern medicine" and is credited in your text with five important new ideas that contributed to the development of abnormal psychology. Complete this listing of his important contributions. (pp. 33-34)

   a. He saw the _____ as the central organ of _____ and viewed mental disorders as due to _____. (p. 33)

   b. He emphasized the importance of heredity, predispositions, and head injuries as causes of _____ . (p. 33)

   c. He classified all mental disorders into three general categories: mania, _____, and phrentis--which means "brain fever." (p. 33)

   d. He considered _____ to be important in understanding the patient's personality. (p. 33)

   e. He advocated treatment methods that were far advanced over the exorcistic practices of his time. For the treatment of _____ he prescribed a regular and tranquil life, sobriety, abstinence from all excesses, a vegetable diet, celibacy, and exercise. (pp. 33-34)

4. Hippocrates wrongly believed that hysteria (the appearance of physical illness in the absence of organic pathology) was restricted to _____ and was caused by the _____ wandering to various parts of the body. (p. 34)

5. What was the mental health/legal issue addressed by Plato with which we are still grappling today? (p. 34)

6. What did Aristotle conclude were two important motivational influences on thinking? (p. 34)

7. The Greek physician Galen used dissections of animals to make important original contributions concerning the _____. (pp. 34, 36)

8. The "Dark Ages" in the history of abnormal psychology began with the death of _____ in A.D. _____, after which the contributions of the Greek and Roman physicians were lost and replaced by a resurgence of belief in demonology as the cause of abnormal behavior. (p. 36)

***Views of abnormality during the Middle Ages* (6th to 15th centuries)**

9. List the mental disorders described by Avicenna in *The Canon of Medicine*. (p. 36)

10. The Middle Ages in Europe lasted from about 500-1500 A.D. The Middle Ages can be characterized as _____ with respect to scientific thinking about the causes of abnormal behavior or enlightened treatment of mentally disordered persons. (p. 37)

11. How were the dancing manias, which were considered "abnormal behavior," related to ancient Greek religious practices? Why were these behaviors attributed to symptoms of a spider bite rather than being viewed as religious practices? (p. 37)

12. The occurrence of mass madness peaked in the 14th and 15th centuries. Why, according to the text, was mass madness so common during these years? (p. 37)

Early views of mental disorders in China

13. Around 200 A.D., Chung Ching, who has been called the Hippocrates of China, wrote two well-known medical works. Complete the following description of the views he expressed in these works. (Highlight 2.2, p. 38)

    a. What did Ching believe to be the primary cause of mental disorders?

    b. What, in turn, did he believe that organ pathology can also be caused by?

    c. How did he believe emotional balance can be regained?

14. How did the "Dark Ages" for the mentally ill in China compare to the "Dark Ages" in Europe? (Highlight 2.2, p. 38)

Witchcraft and mental illness: fact or fiction? **(15th and 16th centuries)**

15. Historians have suggested that the typical woman accused of being a witch was not mentally ill. Explain how the belief in two types of demonic possession may have led other historians to over-emphasize the "possessed" theory of witchcraft. (p. 39)

The resurgence of scientific questioning in Europe **(16th and 17th centuries)**

16. Paracelsus, a Swiss physician in the early 16th century, postulated a conflict between the what two "natures?" What treatment did he advocate for mental illness? (p. 40).

17. Several key people during the 16th century facilitated the reappearance of humane treatment for the mentally disturbed. Most notably were _____, a Swiss physician who spoke out against superstitious beliefs about possession; _____, who suggested that the mind can be sick just like the body; _____, who was scorned by his peers and whose step-by-step rebuttal of witchcraft was banned by the church; and, finally, _____, who wrote that witches were but victims of melancholy. (p. 40)

18. King James I of England came to the rescue of demonology, but by that time many of the clergy also were beginning to question the practice. One of these clergy was St. _____, who said, "Mental disease is no different to bodily disease and Christianity demands of the humane and powerful to protect, and the skillful to relieve the one as well as the other." (p. 41)

Establishment of early asylums and shrines (16th and 17th centuries, England and the U. S.)

19. Henry VIII of England established a mental hospital in 1545 called St. Mary of Bethlehem, which soon became known as _____, adding a new word to our language. (p. 41)

20. Describe the atmosphere and treatment methods of these early "hospitals" as illustrated by La Bicêtre in Paris (note: before Pinel's reform in 1792). (p. 41)

21. The first hospital in the United States devoted exclusively to the mentally ill was _____ _____, which was constructed in Williamsburg, Virginia, in 1773. (p. 41)

22. The _____ shrine was one of the few enlightened settings where humane care of disturbed persons was practiced during this period. This colony has continued their work to the present day. Describe their current activities. (p. 42)

Humanitarian reform (19th century)

23. Humanitarian reform of mental hospitals received its first great impetus from the work of _____ of France in 1792. Why is his work referred to as an "experiment"? (p. 42)

24. Pinel's work was begun at _____ hospital and later at _____ hospital, which have become known as the first "modern" hospitals for the care of the insane. (pp. 42-43)

25. Describe the innovations made by William Tuke and Samuel Hitch. (p. 43)

26. _____ was a famous American physician who wrote the first textbook on psychiatry in the United States. He encouraged more human treatment of the mentally ill. (pp. 43-44)

27. What five reasons does the text list for the abandonment of moral management by the late 1800s? (pp. 44-45)

28. The tireless work of Dorothea Dix was honored by the United States Congress with a resolution in 1901 labeling her as "among the noblest examples of humanity in all history." What type of conditions did she find in state institutions at the beginning of her career and how did she attempt to change them? (p. 45, 47)

Changing attitudes toward mental health (20th century)

29. What was the subject of Clifford Beers' book, *A Mind That Found Itself?* (pp. 48-49)

30. What was Clifford Beers' contribution to changing the general public's attitudes toward the treatment of mental patients? (pp. 48-49)

Events leading to the discovery of organic factors in general paresis

31. What was the crucial experiment reported by Krafft-Ebing in 1897 concerning paresis? (pp. 49-50)

32. What was the significance of the development of a blood test for syphillis by von Wasserman in 1906? (p. 50)

Establishment of brain pathology as a causal factor

33. How did the emergence of modern experimental science ultimately help to establish brain pathology as a causal factor in mental disorders? (p. 50)

34. What specific examples of mental disorders were determined to reflect brain pathology? (p. 50)

Kraepelin and the beginnings of a classification system

35. In addition to an emphasis on the importance of brain pathology in mental disorders, the most important contribution of Kraepelin's 1883 textbook was his system of _____, which became the forerunner of today's DSM-IV. (p. 50)

36. Describe Kraepelin's process of distinguishing the mental disorders. How did he view their course? (p. 50)

Advances achieved as a result of early biological views

37. How did the discovery of the cause of general paresis lead to the development of false expectations among researchers? (p. 51)

The psychodynamic viewpoint and psychoanalysis

38. Although Mesmer appears largely to have held incorrect theories about his technique known as mesmerism, he was reportedly able to remove _____ and _____. In this respect, he predated the successful work of the Nancy School. (p. 51)

39. In disagreement with the Nancy School, Charcot insisted that _____ _____ led to hysteria. (p. 53)

40. The Nancy School finally triumphed in their dispute with Charcot, representing the first recognition of a _____ caused mental disorder. (p. 53)

41. In an important development, Sigmund Freud directed his patients to _____ _____ while under hypnosis, during which they usually displayed considerable emotion. This method was called _____. The patients, upon awakening, saw no relationship between their problems and their hysterical symptoms, leading to the discovery of the unconscious and the conclusion that processes _____ can play an important role in the determination of behavior. (pp. 54-55)

42. Freud soon discovered that he could dispense with hypnosis by substituting two methods. What were they? (p. 55)

Advances in psychological research

43. The first clinic to treat behavior disorders from a psychological perspective was founded by _____ at the University of Pennsylvania in 1896. (p. 56)

44. The psychodynamic approach views abnormal behavior as the result of inner psychological problems. In contrast, William Healy was the first to describe juvenile delinquency as a symptom of _____. (p. 56)

45. In so doing, Healy was among the first to argue in favor of _____ or _____ factors as the cause of abnormal behavior. (p. 56)

46. According to the behavioral perspective, only the study of _____ behavior and the stimuli and reinforcing conditions that control it are appropriate for formulating scientific principles of human behavior. (p. 56)

47. The behavioral perspective is organized around a central theme: the role of _____ in human behavior. (p. 56)

◆

◊ CRITICAL THINKING ABOUT DIFFICULT TOPICS

1. In Concepts to Master Question 1 you were asked to describe early beliefs in demonology and explain the reasons why exorcism was used as a cure. Think about these beliefs as an example of the general point that a broad theoretical context (about the causes of lightning, thunder, etc.) influences our interpretation of abnormal behavior (attributed to possession) and leads to a theoretically driven method of treatment (exorcism). A similar point is made clearly in Highlight 2.4 (p. 46) in terms of the influence of Victorian attitudes and values on the interpretation of the symptoms of anxiety and depression and of the causes of these symptoms in women. Later in the text you will see the same phenomenon for psychodynamic, behavioral, and biological approaches to abnormal behavior. That is, each theoretical approach will influence the interpretation of abnormal behavior and the type of treatment offered. All of these examples illustrate the powerful influence of theories on our interpretation of abnormal behavior.

2. To what degree do differing views of abnormal behavior across history contrast "free will" versus "determinism"? That is, in some cases the person showing abnormal behavior is said to have acted wickedly (presumably by choice) and/or *willingly* signed a pact with the devil and, therefore, deserves to be punished. In the other case, an illness is something that happens to a person through natural forces over which the person has no control (determinism) and for which, therefore, the person is not responsible. This contrast is seen throughout this chapter (e.g., in Pinel's argument on pages 42-43 that "mental patients should be treated with kindness and consideration--as sick people and not as vicious beasts or criminals"), and it can been seen in many discussions of mental illness today. At present, the issue is, perhaps, most clearly observed in the current debate over alcoholism. Think through the arguments and issues surrounding the opposing views that alcoholism reflects a free choice for which the individual is responsible versus the deterministic view that alcoholism is an illness

that happens to the person and for which he or she bears no moral responsibility. This example shows a considerable continuity between the issue in the Middle Ages concerning free choice/blame/punishment versus determinism/humane care and current debates concerning the nature of abnormal behavior.

3. The text comments that the vague symptoms of low mood, lack of energy, and physical symptoms, "viewed by the alienists [psychiatrists] as a definable medical condition, were then *considered treatable by medical men* of the times" (p. 47). This statement clearly indicates that labeling a set of behaviors as a disease (a definable medical condition) serves the function of defining physicians as the appropriate group for dealing with the problem and, in this case, controlling hospitals. Consider the possibility that the use of the term "disease" carries little specific scientific meaning in the study of abnormal behavior, but it clearly asserts that the topic is of relevance for physicians. This issue applies generally to the phenomena of abnormal behavior today, and it is centrally involved in arguments between psychologists and psychiatrists as to the nature of abnormal behavior and in professional rivalry regarding the delivery of services.

4. The text describes the beneficial effects of Pinel's reforms (pp. 42-43), of the implementation of moral management (pp. 44-45), and the contrast for Clifford Beers between institutional care and his recovery in the home of a friendly attendant (pp. 48-49). These examples all show the beneficial effects of humane treatment compared with inhumane treatment. Do you think that these examples are best interpreted as evidence that humane treatment is effective in treating mental disorders, or are they more accurately interpreted as evidence that some types of treatment (in this case, inhumane treatment) can make mental illness worse? This question arises in the current literature on psychotherapy, where it is asked whether some treatments may actually be harmful. (Note that in either interpretation, the evidence points to the responsiveness of the abnormal behavior to the environment.)

5. Kraepelin, like most psychiatrists today, "noted that certain symptom patterns occurred regularly enough to be regarded as specific types of mental disease" (p. 50) and the medical model sees these "symptoms" as reflecting an underlying, internal pathology (p. 51). Thus, according to medical models, the ability to describe a "symptom syndrome" or a group of symptoms is often taken as evidence in favor of a disease model. Consider the validity of this argument. There are, after all, many examples of clusters or groups of co-varying features that in no way imply a disease process. For example, consider that differences in family income affect many aspects of the family's life: where the family lives, how large their house is, what types of furniture and appliances they own, what types of vacations they take, what type of medical care they receive, how they dress, etc. The point here is that a cluster or group of co-varying features does not, per se, indicate a disease process. The disease model also tends to assume a categorical approach, as embodied in DSM-IV

and most medical approaches to diagnosis--i.e., the disease is either present or absent and is not viewed as falling along a continuous dimension of illness. The example of differences in income shows that a cluster of co-varying features can be associated with a dimensional phenomenon, since income is a continuous rather than categorical variable. (For example, one is not either rich or poor but rather has a specific income that falls somewhere on the continuous distribution of income in the population). Keep this issue in mind throughout your reading of the text as the medical model is employed in talking about "mental disease" and "mental illness." Do not allow this language usage to make you assume that abnormal behavior does, in fact, fit a disease model.

◊ CHAPTER 2 QUIZ

Circle the best of the four answers provided and check them according to answers provided at the back of this study guide. Be sure you understand why each answer is correct.

1. Which of the following was from the sixteenth century B. C. and recognized the brain as the site of mental functions? (p. 32)
   a. the Ebers papyrus   c. the Old Testament
   b. the Edwin Smith papyrus   d. the Rosetta Stone

2. Hippocrates erroneously held which of the following beliefs? (p. 34)
   a. The brain is the central organ of intellectual activity.
   b. Head injuries may cause sensory and motor disorders.
   c. The environment is important in mental disorders.
   d. There are basically four types of body fluids.

3. Plato and Aristotle anticipated Freud in their emphasis on: (p. 34)
   a. humane treatment.
   b. the influence on thinking and/or behavior of "natural appetites" and the desire to eliminate pain and attain pleasure.
   c. the use of insanity as an excuse for crime.
   d. psychological factors, such as frustration and conflict, as causes of disturbed behavior.

4. The Greek physician Galen's most important contribution to abnormal psychology was his description of: (pp. 34, 36)
   a. the anatomy of the nervous system.
   b. medicinal herbs that could soothe mental patients.
   c. new treatments for the mentally disturbed.
   d. symptoms of common mental disorders.

5. The "Dark Ages" in the history of abnormal psychology began with the: (p. 36)
   a. "Black Death" of the fifteenth century A.D.
   b. death of Galen in 200 A.D.
   c. fall of Rome in the fifth century A.D.
   d. Roman monarchs around 100 A.D.

6. The physician who kept Greek and Roman medical concepts alive in Islamic countries after the fall of Rome was: (p. 36)
   a. Agrippa.
   b. Aristotle.
   c. Asclepiades.
   d. Avicenna.

7. The key concept emphasizing the balance of positive and negative forces in Chinese medicine is: (Highlight 2.2, p. 38)
   a. equilibrium.
   b. homeostasis.
   c. Sun and Earth principle.
   d. Yin and Yang.

8. Which of the following individuals did not argue that those showing abnormal behavior should be seen as mentally ill and treated with humane care? (p. 40)
   a. Paracelsus
   b. Teresa of Avila
   c. King James I of England
   d. Johan Weyer

9. The manual that was a complete guide to the detection and punishment of witches was called the: (p. 40)
   a. *Summes Deciderantes Affectibus.*
   b. *Malleus Maleficarum.*
   c. *Deception of Demons.*
   d. *Discovery of Witchcraft.*

10. In 1584, Oxford-educated Reginald Scot wrote *Discovery of Witchcraft* in which he stated that: (p. 40)
    a. demons, devils and evil spirits did not cause mental disorders.
    b. mental disorders were caused by witches.
    c. the clergy invented witchcraft.
    d. witchcraft was discovered by Galen.

11. The word *bedlam* originated from a(an): (p. 41)
    a. ancient Greek term for "disturbance of biles."
    b. contraction for St. Mary of Bethlehem mental hospital.
    c. description of mass madness in the Middle Ages.
    d. practice of burning witches in their beds.

12. Treatment of mental patients at the Public Hospital of Williamsburg, Virginia, was designed to: (p. 41)
    a. force patients to leave.   c. save inmates' souls from hell.
    b. intimidate patients.   d. surround inmates with love.

13. An institution noted for kindness and humanity in the care of the mentally ill was: (p. 42)
    a. The Geel Shrine, Belgium.   c. St. Mary of Bethlehem, London.
    b. La Maison de Charenton, Paris.   d. San Hipolito, Mexico.

14. In 1805, Pierre was sent to La Bicêtre mental hospital because of his bizarre delusions. Because this hospital was then administered by Philippe Pinel, he was probably treated: (pp. 42-43)
    a. as a beast or prisoner.   c. by letting out his red bile.
    b. by clerical exorcists.   d. in a humanitarian fashion.

15. The founder of American psychiatry is: (pp. 43-44)
    a. William Tuke.   c. Benjamin Rush.
    b. Lightner Witmer.   d. Dorothea Dix.

16. Pinel's and Tuke's moral management in mental hospitals was based on the idea that abnormal behavior is: (p. 44)
    a. a result of sinful living.
    b. due to possession of the devil.
    c. related to an immoral balance of the humors.
    d. the result of severe psychological stress.

17. All of the following are reasons that have been offered as explanations for the abandonment of moral therapy in the latter part of the nineteenth century *except:* (p. 45)
    a. a rising tide of racial and ethnic prejudice.
    b. overextension of hospital facilities.
    c. general loss of faith among the general population.
    d. belief that mental disorders would yield to physical solutions.

18. In the Victorian era a person manifesting symptoms of depression would most likely be diagnosed as suffering from: (Highlight 2.4, p. 48)
    a. oligophrenia.
    b. dysthymia.
    c. neurasthenia.
    d. demoralization.

19. Dorothea Dix is noted for her highly successful campaign to do something about the: (p. 45)
    a. inhuman treatment accorded the mentally ill.
    b. problem of heroin abuse during the Civil War.
    c. view that women were biologically inferior.
    d. overcrowded conditions in large mental hospitals in rural areas.

20. In 1917, Wagner-Jauregg introduced a treatment for general paresis involving: (p. 50)
    a. prescribing laudanum.
    b. prescribing specific wild herbs.
    c. prescribing lithium.
    d. infecting the sufferer with malaria.

21. The Nancy School centered around the use of hypnosis to treat: (p. 52)
    a. tarantism.
    b. hysteria.
    c. neurasthenia.
    d. depression.

22. Sigmund Freud directed his patients to talk freely about their problems while under hypnosis--a method that was called: (p. 54)
    a. mesmerism.
    b. free association.
    c. catharsis.
    d. emotional desensitization.

23. Classical and operant conditioning differ primarily with respect to: (pp. 56-57)
    a. the types of reinforcers involved.
    b. an emphasis on animal versus human subjects.
    c. the number of trials to reach criterion performance.
    d. whether the outcome (reinforcer) is dependent on the animal's behavior.

Chapter 3
Causal Factors and Viewpoints in
Abnormal Psychology

◊ OVERVIEW

This chapter discusses modern viewpoints and causal models of abnormal behavior. Within the biological viewpoint, several broad physiological causal factors are reviewed, ranging from brain and biochemical functioning to genetic/constitutional vulnerabilities. The psychosocial viewpoint encompasses the psychodynamic, behavioral, and cognitive-behavioral models. The chapter then focuses on the importance of early psychosocial factors as powerful causes of abnormal behavior. The sociocultural viewpoint reminds us that humans are part of larger social contexts, and our behavior cannot be fully understood without reference to the influences of the society in which we live. It is now widely recognized that no one model adequately explains every aspect of every form of abnormal behavior. Consequently, one needs to assess and deal with the interaction of biological, psychosocial, and sociocultural factors to develop the total clinical picture.

◊ CHAPTER OUTLINE

I. Causes and Risk Factors for Abnormal Behavior
    A. Necessary, Sufficient, and Contributory Causes
    B. Feedback and Circularity in Abnormal Behavior
    C. Diathesis-Stress Models

II. Models or Viewpoints for Understanding Abnormal Behavior
    A. The Value of Viewpoints
    B. Multidimensional, Eclectic, and Integrative Approaches

III. The Biological Viewpoints

IV. Biological Causal Factors
    A. Neurotransmitter and Hormonal Imbalances

1. Imbalances of Neurotransmitters
2. Hormonal Imbalances
B. Genetic Vulnerabilities
   1. Chromosomal Abnormalities
   2. The Relationship of Genotypes to Phenotypes
   3. Genotype-Environment Correlations
   4. Genotype-Environment Interactions
   5. Methods for Studying Genetic Influences
C. Constitutional Liabilities
   1. Physical Handicaps
   2. Temperament
D. Brain Dysfunction and Neural Plasticity
E. Physical Deprivation or Disruption
   1. Deprivation of Basic Physiological Needs
   2. Stimulation and Activity
F. The Impact of the Biological Viewpoint

V. The Psychosocial Viewpoints
A. The Psychodynamic Perspective
   1. The Structure of Personality: Id, Ego, and Superego
   2. Anxiety, Defense Mechanisms, and the Unconscious
   3. Psychosexual Stages of Development
   4. The Oedipus Complex and Electra Complex
   5. Newer Psychodynamic Perspectives
      a) Object-Relations Theory
      b) The Interpersonal Perspective
      c) Interpersonal Accomodation and Attachment
   6. Impact of the Psychodynamic Perspectives
      a) Impact of Freud's Original Psychoanalytic Perspective
      b) Impact of Newer Psychodynamic Perspectives
B. The Behavioral Perspective
   1. Classical Conditioning
   2. Instrumental Conditioning
   3. Generalization/Discrimination
   4. Observational Learning
   5. Impact of the Behavioral Perspective
C. The Cognitive-Behavioral Perspective
   1. Attributions, Attributional Style, and Psychopathology

    2. Cognitive Therapy
    3. The Impact of the Cognitive-Behavioral Perspective
  D. What the Adoption of a Perspective Does and Does Not Do

VI. Psychosocial Causal Factors
  A. Our Views of the World and of Ourselves: Schemas and Self-Schemas
    1. Variations in Schemas and Personal Growth
    2. Predictability and Controllability
  B. Early Deprivation or Trauma
    1. Institutionalization
    2. Deprivation and Abuse in the Home
    3. Other Childhood Traumas
      a) Separation
  C. Inadequate Parenting Styles
    1. Parental Psychopathology
    2. Parenting Styles: Warmth and Control
      a) Authoritative Parenting
      b) Authoritarian Parenting
      c) Permissive-Indulgent Parenting
      d) Neglectful-Uninvolved Parenting
    3. Inadequate, Irrational, and Angry Communication
  D. Marital Discord and Divorce
    1. Marital Discord
    2. Divorced Families
      a) Effects of Divorce on Parents
      b) Effects of Divorce on Children
  E. Maladaptive Peer Relationships
    1. Sources of Popularity Versus Rejection

VII. The Sociocultural Viewpoint
  A. Uncovering Sociocultural Factors Though Cross-Cultural Studies
    1. Cultural Differences in Which Disorders Develop and How They Are Experienced
    2. Culture and Over-and Under-Controlled Behavior
    3. The Need for More Cross-Cultural Study
  B. Sociocultural Influences in Our Own Society

VIII. Sociocultural Causal Factors
  A. The Sociocultural Environment

B. Pathological Societal Influences
   1. Low Socioeconomic Status and Unemployment
   2. Disorder-Engendering Social Roles
   3. Prejudice and Discrimination in Race, Gender, and Culture
   4. Social Change and Uncertainty

IX. Unresolved Issues: Theoretical Viewpoints and the Causes of Abnormal Behavior
   A. Advantages of Having a Theoretical Viewpoint
   B. The Eclectic Approach
   C. The Biopsychosocial Unified Approach

X. Summary

◊ LEARNING OBJECTIVES

After studying this chapter, you should be able to:

1. Discuss the different conceptual approaches to understanding the causes of abnormal behavior. These approaches will include (a) necessary, sufficient, and contributory causes; (b) feedback and circularity models; and (c) the diathesis-stress model. (pp. 63-67)

2. Summarize the biological theories of abnormal behavior, including neurotransmitter/hormonal imbalances, genetic and constitutional influences, and physical damage to brain structures. (pp. 68-80)

3. Outline the major psychosocial theoretical approaches to abnormal behavior, including the psychodynamic, behavioral, and cognitive-behavioral perspectives. (pp. 81-97)

4. Discuss the substantive contributions of the psychosocial factors of deviant cognitions (schemas and self-schemas), early deprivation or trauma (e.g., parental deprivation, institutionalization, abuse, etc.), inadequate parenting and pathogenic family structures, and problems with peer relationships. (pp. 97-108)

5. Describe the sociocultural perspective and its contributions to understanding abnormal behavior. (pp. 108-115)

6. Explain why the field needs a unified viewpoint and how the biopsychosocial viewpoint may fulfill that need. (pp. 116-117)

◊ TERMS YOU SHOULD KNOW

---

etiology (p. 63)

necessary cause (p. 63)

sufficient cause (p. 63)

contributory cause (p. 64)

distal causal factors (p. 64)

proximal causal factors (p. 64)

reinforcing cause (p. 64)

causal pattern (p. 64)

diathesis (p. 65)

diathesis-stress models (p. 65)

stress (p. 66)

protective factors (p. 65)

resilience (p. 66)

paradigm shifts (p. 67)

eclectic (pp. 67-68)

biopsychological viewpoint (p. 68)

synapse and *synaptic cleft* (p. 69; Highlight 3.1, p. 70)

neurotransmitters (pp. 69, 71; Highlight 3.1, p. 70)

presynaptic and *postsynaptic neurons* (p. 69; Highlight 3.1, p. 70)

neurotransmitter imbalance (p. 69)

re-uptake (p. 69; Highlight 3.1, p. 70)

excitatory and *inhibitory neural transmission* (Highlight 3.1, p. 70)

receptor sites (Highlight 3.1, p. 70)

hormones (p. 71)

hypothalamus-pituitary-adrenal-cortical axis (p. 71)

chromosomes (p. 72)

chromosomal abnormalities (p. 72)

autosomes (p. 72)

sex chromosomes (p. 72)

trisomy (p. 72)

genotype (p. 72)

phenotype (p. 72)

genotype-environment correlation (p. 73)

genotype-environment interaction (p. 73)

polygenically (p. 74)

behavior genetics (p. 74)

pedigree or *family history method* (p. 74)

proband or *index case* (p. 74)

twin method (p. 74)

monozygotic vs. *dizygotic twins* (p. 74)

concordance rate (p. 74)

adoption method (p. 75)

shared and *nonshared environmental influences* (p. 75)

constitutional liability (pp. 75, 77)

temperament (p. 77)

developmental systems approach (p. 78)

id, *ego*, and *superego* (p. 81, 84)

humanistic perspective (Highlight 3.3, p. 82)

self-concept (Highlight 3.3, p. 82)

self-actualizing (Highlight 3.3, pp. 82-83)

existential perspective (Highlight 3.3, p. 83)

life and death instincts (p. 84)

primary and *secondary process thinking* (p. 84)

libido (p. 84)

intrapsychic conflicts (p. 84)

ego defense mechanisms (p. 84; Table 3.1, 85)

psychosexual stages of development (pp. 84-85)

Oedpius complex/Electra Complex (pp. 85-86)

castration anxiety (p. 85)

object relations theory (pp. 86-88)

introjection (pp. 86-87)

interpersonal perspective (pp. 88-90)

classical conditioning (pp. 91-92)

unconditioned stimulus (p. 91)

unconditioned response (p. 91)

conditioned stimulus (p. 91)

conditioned response (p. 91)

extinction (p. 92)

spontaneous recovery (p. 92)

operant conditioning (p. 92)

reinforcement (p. 92)

response-outcome expectancy (p. 92)

conditioned avoidance response (p. 93)

generalization (p. 93)

discrimination (p. 93)

observational learning (p. 93)

cognitive-behavioral perspective (pp. 95-97)

internal reinforcement (p. 95)

attributions (p. 95)

attributional style (p. 95)

schema (pp. 95, 98)

self-schema (pp. 95, 98)

assimilation (p. 99)

accommodation (p. 99)

failure to thrive (p. 101)

psychic trauma (p. 102)

parental warmth (pp. 104-105)

parental control (pp. 104-105)

◊ NAMES YOU SHOULD KNOW

Jerome Kagan

Sigmund Freud

Anna Freud

Margaret Mahler

Otto Kernberg

Alfred Adler

Erich Fromm

Karen Horney

Erik Erikson

Harry Stack Sullivan

John Bowlby

Ivan Pavlov

B. F. Skinner

John Dollard

Neal Miller

Albert Bandura

William James

Aaron Beck

Carl Rogers

Abraham Maslow

1. Contrast the essential features of necessary, sufficient, and contributory causes and distinguish among proximal, distal, and reinforcing causal factors. Which of these types of causes would apply to the statement that smoking cigarettes is a risk factor for lung cancer? (pp. 63-64)

2. When should one use the term "causal pattern"? (p. 64)

3. Simple cause-and-effect sequences are rare in the behavioral sciences. How do the concepts of feedback and mutual, two-way influences differ from simple cause-and-effect sequences? (pp. 64-65).

4. How do the terms proximal, distal, necessary, sufficient, and contributory causes apply to the diathesis-stress model? (pp. 65-66)

5. When does an environmental demand become stressful? (p. 65)

6. What is a "steeling" or "inoculation" effect? (p. 65)

7. What are the three distinct phenomena to which the term *resilience* applies? (p. 66)

8. A patient has the delusion that he is Napoleon. The delusion is the impairment. The specific idea that he is Napoleon is the content of the impairment. How does this delusion reveal that biological causes must interact with experience? (p. 68)

9. List the five categories of biological factors that are especially relevant to the development of abnormal behavior. (p. 68)

10. The concept of biochemical imbalances is one of the basic tenets of the biological perspective today. Outline the sequence of events involved in neurotransmission, identify those mechanisms by which a biochemical imbalance might be produced, and explain how this imbalance might produce abnormal behavior. How do these processes relate to the mechanisms by which medications used to treat various disorders exert their effects? (pp. 69, 71; Highlight 3.1, p. 70)

11. Discuss the genetic approaches to abnormal behavior, including basic genetic concepts (e.g., chromosome, gene, genotype, phenotype, and zygote) and the process of sexual reproduction by which genetic influences are passed from parents to child. (pp. 71-72)

12. What are the three ways in which a genotype may shape his or her environment? Give an example of each. (p. 73)

13. Summarize the various methods (pedigree/family history, twin, and adoption) used in genetic research with humans. (pp. 74-75)

14. What major comparison is involved regarding concordance rates in twin studies and how are the results interpreted? (pp. 74-75)

15. Name the five dimensions of temperament seen at about 2-3 months of age and the three dimensions of adult personality to which they are related. (p. 77)

16. The text states that the temperament of an infant or young child can have profound effects on a variety of important developmental processes. Using the example of a fearful temperament, describe these different effects with respect to classical conditioning of fear, avoidance learning, reaction to environmental stimulation, and forming attachment relationships. (pp. 77-78)

17. Distinguish between gross brain pathology and more subtle deficiencies of brain function, and indicate which applies to only a small percentage of people with abnormal behavior. (p. 78)

18. The text documents the conclusion that dietary deficiencies can have long-term effects on cognitive functioning (well beyond the period of malnutrition) with several examples. Describe the results reported for former World War II and Korean War POWs, and explain the effects of severe malnutrition. (p. 79)

19. Describe the interaction of the id, ego, and superego in Freud's conception of personality. (pp. 81, 84)

20. An important psychoanalytic concept is the unconscious. What types of memories, desires, and experiences exist in the unconscious? (pp. 81, 84-85)

21. Describe three types of anxiety described by Freud, and explain the function of the ego-defense mechanisms. (p. 84)

22. List and describe Freud's five stages of psychosexual development and their effects on personality. (pp. 84-85)

23. Contrast the newer psychodynamic approaches with the earlier Freudian perspective, including the greater emphasis on ego functions and object relations. Summarize some of the newer psychodynamic perspectives developed by Anna Freud, Melanie Klein, Margaret Mahler, and Otto Kernberg. (pp. 86-88)

24. Explain how the work of Alfred Adler, Erich Fromm, Karen Horney, and Erik Erikson became the roots of the interpersonal perspective of psychopathology. (p. 88)

25. Describe the major features of Harry Stack Sullivan's interpersonal theory of personality. (p. 89)

26. Discuss two of Freud's most noteworthy contributions to our understanding of normal and abnormal behavior, and list several criticisms of his approach. (p. 90)

27. Define each of the following, and explain the importance of each to abnormal psychology: classical conditioning, operant conditioning, reinforcement, response-outcome expectancy, conditioned avoidance response, generalization, and discrimination. (pp. 91-93)

28. Describe Albert Bandura's classic experiments and their influence on our understanding of observational learning. Discuss his emphasis on the cognitive aspects of learning. (p. 93)

29. List the major triumphs and criticisms of the behavioral tradition. (p. 94)

30. Discuss the importance of attributions and schemas to cognitive-behavior theory. (pp. 95-96)

31. Contrast the focus of cognitive-behavioral clinicians with that of the behavioristic therapists. (pp. 94-95)

32. How are assimilation and accommodation involved in the processing of new experiences, and which is the basic goal of psychosocial therapies? (p. 99)

33. What are the four categories of psychosocial causal factors that exemplify the psychosocial approach? Explain how each contributes to the development of abnormal behavior. (p. 98, pp. 100-108)

34. How are the variables of parental warmth and parental control related to the authoritative, authoritarian, indulgent, and neglecting parenting styles? (pp. 104-105)

35. Two recent cross-national studies comparing the U.S. and Thailand found no differences in the prevalence of undercontrolled problems but a higher prevalence of overcontrolled problems. However, there were different forms of undercontrolled behavior. What cultural factors account for the differences in prevalence and/or types of problematic behavior? (p. 110)

36. Outline the major sociocultural factors that contribute to abnormal behavior and summarize the evidence in favor of their importance. (pp. 112-115)

37. What are the advantages and disadvantages of adherence to a single, systematic viewpoint? (p. 116)

38. Name and describe one attempt at developing a single, comprehensive, internally consistent viewpoint that accurately reflects what we know empirically about abnormal behavior? (pp. 116-117)

◊ STUDY QUESTIONS

Necessary, sufficient, and contributory causes

1. A _____ cause is one that *must* exist for a disorder to occur, but it is not always a sufficient cause. (p. 63)

2. A _____ cause guarantees the occurrence of a disorder, but it may not be necessary for the disorder to occur. (p. 63)

3. A _____ cause increases the probability of a disorder but is neither necessary nor sufficient. (p. 64)

4. Causal factors occurring relatively early in life that do not show their effects for many years are considered _____ causal factors that may contribute to a _____ to develop a disorder. (p. 64)

5. Causal factors that operate shortly before the occurrence of symptom onset would be considered _____ causal factors that in some cases may be no more than the "straw that breaks the camel's back." (p. 64)

6. A condition that tends to maintain maladaptive behavior that is already present is a _____ cause--e.g., the extra attention, sympathy, and removal from unwanted responsibility that may be secondary to becoming ill. (p. 64)

7. Being raised by a parent who is warm and supportive is an example of a _____ factor.

Models for understanding abnormal behavior

8. Thomas Kuhn noted that theoretical orientations in science typically remain strong even in the face of evidence or alternate explanations. A theory typically lasts until a fundamental insight is achieved that appears to resolve problems left unsolved by existing theories. The new insights, also called _____ shifts, are complete reorganizations of the way people think about a particular issue or field of science. (p. 67)

9. In the study of abnormal psychology, we are still awaiting a new fundamental insight. In the meanwhile, competing viewpoints exist. Therefore, many researchers and practitioners choose to take an _____ approach, which means to select what appears to be best from various viewpoints. It is up to each student to select a particular preference, if any, after he or she becomes more knowledgeable about the field. (pp. 67-68)

Biological viewpoints

10. The extreme biological viewpoint, held by many medical practitioners, states that abnormal behavior is the product of _____ of the central nervous system, the autonomic nervous system, or the endocrine system. In such a viewpoint, neither psychological factors nor the psychosocial environment of the individual are believed to contribute to the causes of mental disorder. (p. 68)

11. The electrical nerve impulse travels from the cell body of a neuron to the terminal buttons via the _____. (Highlight 3.1, p. 70)

12. The _____ or _____ are the sites where neurotransmitter substances are stored until needed. When the nerve impulse reaches the axon endings, the transmitter is released into the _____, a tiny fluid-filled gap between the axon endings of the _____ neuron and the _____ of the postsynaptic neuron. (Highlight 3.1, p. 70)

13. The neurotransmitter substances act on the dendrite of the postsynaptic neuron at specialized places called _____ sites. (Highlight 3.1, p. 70)

14. The effect of the neurotransmitter on the postsynaptic neuron can be either _____, which means it increases the probability that the neuron will fire, or _____, which means that it decreases the probability that the neuron will fire. (p. 69; Highlight 3.1, p. 70)

15. The action of the neurotransmitter substance is time-limited either by deactivation by an _____, such as monoamine oxidase, in the synaptic cleft or by a process called _____, which takes it back into the presynaptic neuron and stores it in the synaptic storage vesicles. (p. 69; Highlight 3.1, p. 70)

16. What is phenylketonuria (PKU), and what causes it? (p. 72)

17. Explain why Down syndrome is also known as Trisomy 21. (p. 72)

18. Highly intelligent parents provide an intellectually stimulating environment. This is an example of what has been termed a(n) _____ effect of the child's genotype on the environment, resulting from the genetic similarity of parents and children. (p. 73)

19. Happy babies evoke more positive responses from others than do passive, unresponsive infants. This is an example of a(n) _____ effect of the child's genotype from the social and physical environment. (p. 73)

20. Extraverted children may seek the company of others, thereby enhancing their own tendencies to be sociable. This is an example in which the child's genotype plays a more _____ _____ in shaping the environment. (p. 73)

21. If a given disorder were completely heritable, the _____ _____ for identical twins with the disorder would be 100%. (p. 74)

22. Those factors that would affect all children in a family similarly are known as _____ _____ _____. (p. 75)

Nature, nurture, and psychopathology: A new look at an old topic

23. One's potential can change if one's environment changes. This conclusion is supported by the example that children born to _____ biological parents who are adopted and reared with _____ parents have a mean IQ about 12 points higher than those reared in the environment of the biological parents. (Highlight 3.2, p. 76)

24. Babies born with the genetic defect causing phenylketonuria only develop the disease if they are exposed to diets with phenylalanine. This example illustrates that the following is a misconception: nature and nurture are _____. (Highlight 3.2, p. 76)

25. Dizygotic twins are more alike than monozygotic twins at birth for height, weight, and IQ, but over time dizygotic twins show greater differences than monozygotic twins. This example illustrates that the following is a misconception: genetic effects _____ with age. (Highlight 3.2, p. 76)

26. Give an example of a disorder that tends to run in families but does not seem to be due primarily to genetic factors. (Highlight 3.2, p. 76)

27. What are the two general types of physical deprivation or disruption that may contribute to abnormal behavior? (pp. 78-80)

28. According to the text, there is a general stereotype that strong genetic effects mean that environmental influences are unimportant. Give an example that illustrates this to be a misconception. (pp. 80-81; also p. 68)

Basics of the psychodynamic perspective

29. The id operates according to the _____ principle. (p. 84)

30. The id generates mental images and fantasies referred to as _____ thinking. (p. 84)

31. The id is the source of two instinctual drives: a) _____ and b) _____. (p. 84)

32. _____ anxiety is caused by the id's impulses, which, if expressed, would be punished in some way. (p. 84)

33. The ego operates according to the _____ principle. (p. 84)

34. The ego uses reason and intellectual resources to deal with the external world, which is referred to as _____ thinking. (p. 84)

35. The ego mediates between the demands of the _____ and _____ in such a way as to insure that needs are met and survival assured. (p. 84)

36. The superego is the outgrowth of internalizing the _____ and _____ of society. (p. 84)

37. The superego operates through the _____ to inhibit desires that are considered wrong or immoral. (p. 84)

38. The superego generates _____ anxiety, which arises from action in conflict with the superego and arouses feelings of guilt. (p. 84)

39. Anxiety is a warning of impending danger as well as a painful experience, so it motivates people to do something about it. The ego can cope with anxiety in basically two ways. First, the ego can cope with anxiety by rational measures. If these are not effective or sufficient, the ego resorts to _____. These alleviate the painful anxiety, but they do so by pushing painful ideas out of consciousness, which leads to a distorted view of reality. (p. 84)

40. List Freud's stages of psychosexual development. At what age does each occur, and what is the source of gratification for each stage? (pp. 84-85)

41. Define and give an example of each of the following defense mechanisms: (Table 3.1, p. 85)

Defense Mechanism	Definition	Example
acting out		
denial of reality		
displacement		
fixation		
projection		
rationalization		

reaction formation

regression

repression

sublimation

undoing.

42. Differentiate the Electra complex from the Oedipus complex. What is the role of castration anxiety, and what is considered to be its proper resolution given normal development? (pp. 85-86)

Newer psychodynamic perspectives

43. What three directions did newer (that is, post-Freud) psychodynamic theorists take? (p. 86)

44. In object relations theory, the focus is not on the ego or on the id. Rather it is on the _____. (pp. 86-87)

45. Object-relations theory is based on the concept of _____ which refers to the incorporation into memory of symbols that represent images and memories of persons the child viewed with strong emotions. (pp. 86-87)

46. Describe the general notions of object-relations theory as developed by Melanie Klein and others in England. (p. 87)

47. The work of Margaret Mahler in the United States added insights to object-relations theory. Describe her concept of separation-individuation that is said to be essential for the achievement of a mature personality. (p. 87)

48. Otto Kernberg describes the result of poor early relationships, which he labels the "borderline personality." The chief characteristic of the borderline personality is _____, an inability to achieve a full and _____ personal identity because of an inability to integrate and reconcile _____. (pp. 87-88)

The interpersonal perspective

49. Theorists who share an interpersonal perspective believe that abnormal behavior is best understood by analyzing a person's _____ both past and present. (p. 88)

50. Match each of the following interpersonal theorists with their most notable viewpoint or achievement: (pp. 88-89)

    a. Karen Horney   _____ believed that people are inherently social beings motivated primarily by the desire to belong to and participate in a group.

    b. Harry Stack Sullivan _____ focused on dispositions that people adopt in their interactions.

    c. Erik Erikson   _____ vigorously rejected Freud's demeaning female psychology.

    d. Erich Fromm   _____ broadened Freud's psychosexual stages into more s socially-oriented concepts.

    e. Alfred Adler   _____ maintained that the term *personality* was best defined in terms of an individual's characteristic way of relating to others.

51. When two persons evolve patterns of communication and interaction that enable them to attain common goals and meet mutual needs, the process is called _____ _____. (p. 89)

52. Bowlby emphasized the importance of the quality of _____ _____ to the development of secure attachments, but also saw the importance of the _____ as playing a more active role in shaping the course of his/her own development than had most earlier theorists. (pp. 89-90)

Impact of the psychodynamic perspective

53. _____ can be seen as the first systematic approach showing how human psychological processes can result in mental disorders. (p. 90)

54. Freud's views replaced brain pathology with intrapsychic conflict and exaggerated ego defenses against anxiety as the cause of at least some mental disorders. One of his most noteworthy contributions was to emphasize the extent to which _____ motives and _____ mechanisms affect behavior, the importance of _____ experiences in later personality adjustment and maladjustment, and the importance of _____ factors in human behavior and mental disorders. The second particularly noteworthy contribution was the realization that the same psychological principles apply to both _____ and _____ behavior. (p. 90)

55. Two important criticisms of psychoanalytic theory have been offered. First, it fails to recognize the scientific limits of _____ as the primary mode of obtaining information. Second, there is a lack of _____ _____ to support many of its explanatory assumptions or the effectiveness of its therapy. (p. 90)

56. What is the focus of therapy from the interpersonal perspective? (p. 91)

The behavioral perspective

57. Behavioral psychologists assert that the data used by psychoanalysts, including material obtained by free association and dream analysis, is unverifiable scientifically. What data do behaviorists prefer? (p. 91)

58. The roots of the behavioristic approach can be traced to the study of _____ _____ by a Russian physiologist named Ivan Pavlov and to the study of _____ by Edward Thorndike. Promotion of the behavioral approach is credited to a young American psychologist named _____. (p. 91)

59. The behaviorists focused on the effects of _____ on the acquisition, modification, and possible elimination of various types of response patterns. (p. 91)

60. Identify the following statements as referring to classical conditioning (C) or operant (instrumental) conditioning (O)--i.e., place a "C" or "O" after each as appropriate. (pp. 91-93)
    a. As we mature, this type of learning becomes more important. _____
    b. Many responses, particularly those related to fear or anxiety, are learned through this type of learning. _____
    c. As we grow up, this type of learning becomes an important mechanism for discriminating the desirable from the undesirable. _____
    d. Consists of simple strengthening of a stimulus-response connection. _____
    e. The person learns a response-outcome expectancy. _____

61. In operant or instrumental conditioning, initially a high rate of reinforcement may be necessary, but thereafter it is especially persistent when reinforcement is _____. (p. 92)

62. A boy who has been bitten by a vicious dog may develop a conditioned avoidance response in which he consistently avoids all dogs. How does his avoidance of dogs lessen his anxiety? Why is his avoidance difficult to extinguish? (p. 93)

63. Match the following terms and examples: (pp. 92-93)

Terms   **Example**

a. Discrimination   _____ A person, previously bitten, avoids dogs.

b. Generalization   _____ An occasional win at gambling keeps the behavior going.

c. Intermittent   _____ A person, beaten as a child by an authority figure, has an
                                    involuntary fear of anyone in authority.

d. Reinforcement   _____ A child performs a response that in the past produced
                                    candy.

e. Avoidance conditioning _____ A child learns that although red and green strawberries look
                                    somewhat similar, only red ones taste good.

Impact of the behavioral perspective

64. Behaviorists believe that maladaptive behavior develops as a result of two things. What are
    they? (p. 94)
    a.
    b.

65. Behaviorism has been praised for its precision and objectivity, its wealth of research, and its
    demonstrated effectiveness in _____ _____ _____. (p.
    94)

66. Behaviorism has been criticized for being concerned only with _____. How is this
    criticism viewed by contemporary behavior therapists? (p. 94)

The cognitive-behavioral approach

67. What does the cognitive-behavioral approach consider that behaviorism does not? (p. 95)

68. According to Beck, different forms of psychopathology are characterized by different _____ _____ that have developed as a function of adverse early _____ _____ and that lead to the _____ of _____, characteristic of certain disorders, such as anxiety, depression, and personality disorders. (p. 95)

69. Cognitive-behavioral clinicians have shifted their focus from overt behavior to the _____ _____ assumed to be producing that behavior. Then the clinican's goal becomes one of altering maladaptive _____. (p. 96)

70. How did B. F. Skinner view the cognitive-behavioral viewpoint? (p. 97)

71. Each psychosocial viewpoint of abnormal behavior depends on _____ from limited observations and research. (p. 97)

72. What is an important consequence of adopting a particular psychosocial perspective? (p. 97)

Psychosocial causal factors: Early deprivation or trauma

73. Two protective factors for children institutionalized at an early age are entering a _____ home and having _____ at school. (p. 100)

74. Which appears to have a more adverse impact on infants: parental abuse or gross neglect? (p. 101)

75. Abused children suffer from many deficits and are at heightened risk for later aggressive behavior, including abuse of their own children. List four other long-term consequences of parental abuse. (pp. 101-102)

76. List four protective factors that decrease the probability of intergenerational transmission of abuse. (p. 102)

77. Bowlby found that, when children age 2 to 5 years are separated from their parents during prolonged periods of hospitalization, the acute effects include significant _____ during the separation and _____ upon reunion. (pp. 102-103)

Psychosocial causal factors: Inadequate parenting

78. Many studies have indicated that parental psychopathology can have profound adverse effects on children, but many children do fine because of protective factors. These include a _____ with the other parent or another adult, having good _____ skills, and being _____ to adults. (pp. 103-104)

79. Match the following parenting styles with child outcomes: (pp. 104-105)

Style	Child Outcome
a. authoritative	_____ impulsive and aggressive; spoiled, selfish, inconsiderate, and demanding; exploit people for their own purposes.
b. authoritarian	_____ disruptions in attachment in childhood; moodiness, low self-esteem, and conduct problems later in childhood; problems with peer relations and academic performance.
c. permissive-indulgent	_____ energetic and friendly, competent in dealing with others and the environment.
d. neglecting-uninvolved	_____ conflicted, irritable, moody; poor social and cognitive skills.

Psychosocial causal factors: Marital discord and divorce

80. In their comprehensive review of the effects of divorce on adults, Amato and Keith concluded that it is a major source of _____, as well as physical illness, _____, _____, and homicide. (p. 106)

81. The effects of divorce on children are often more favorable that the effects of remaining in a home torn by _____ _____ and _____. Amato and Keith found that children living with a stepparent were _____ than children living with a single parent. (p. 106)

Psychosocial causal factors: Maladaptive peer relationships

82. With respect to peer relations, the most consistent correlate of popularity is being seen as _____ and _____. This relationship is probably complexly involved with other variables, such as _____ and physical attractiveness. (p. 107)

83. One large factor associated with being persistently rejected by peers is an excessively _____ or _____ approach to ongoing peer activities. A smaller group of children is apparently rejected because of their own _____. (p. 108)

84. Coie et al. found that _____ toward peers was the best predictor in the fifth grade of juvenile delinquency and school dropout seven years later. One causal pathway suggested by Patterson et al. is that peer rejection often leads a child to associated with _____ several years later, which in turn is associated with a tendency toward juvenile delinquency. (p. 108)

The sociocultural viewpoint

85. How do Italians differ from Swiss, and American patients in response to illness? (p. 109)

86. How does the acute sense of guilt sometimes associated with depression vary across cultures? (pp. 109-110)

Sociocultural influences

87. Factors in the social environment that may increase vulnerability include _____, disorder-engendering social roles, _____, economic and employment problems, and social change and uncertainty. (p. 112)

88. In a longitudinal study of inner-city children in Boston, resilience was best indicated by childhood _____ and having adequate functioning as a child in _____, _____, and _____ relationships. (p. 114)

89. Periods of extensive unemployment are typically accompanied by adverse effects on mental and physical health. In particular, rates of _____, _____, and _____ complaints increase during periods of unemployment, but usually normalize following reemployment. (p. 114)

90. In one prospective study, all the children born on Kauai, Hawaii, in 1955 were followed until age 18. One of the best predictors distinguishing children (especially boys) who experienced significant problems with mental health or delinquency was whether _____. (p. 115)

91. Many more women than men seek treatment for emotional disorders, especially anxiety and depression. List two possible sociocultural factors which might explain this. (p. 115)

◊ CRITICAL THINKING ABOUT DIFFICULT TOPICS

1. Your text states that the belief that biochemical imbalances in the brain can result in abnormal behavior is one of the basic tenets of the biological perspective today (p. 69). It also describes the medical model, which relies heavily on the biological perspective, as in its extreme form using a strictly categorical approach to psychopathology (p. 68). At the same time, it is highly likely that there are naturally-occurring individual differences in each of the many aspects of neuronal functioning. For example, some individuals may naturally produce a larger quantity of a given neurotransmitter that is secreted into the synaptic cleft, others may deactivate this transmitter less well in the synaptic cleft, and still others may show greater receptor reactivity to a given amount of neurotransmitter. Given that such differences in neurotransmitter activity will have significant effects on behavior, temperament theorists will see individual differences of this type as the basis of the genetic influences on temperament (see pp. 77-78). Consider the difference between a disease model approach that emphasizes present-versus-absent categories and the temperament approach that views these differences as continuously distributed normal variations in brain functioning. In coming to an answer, you should see that there are two ways to invoke biological processes in understanding psychopathology. One, the medical model, expects a complete dysfunction (disease) that is either present or absent and makes no distinctions within normal functioning (i.e., when the disease is absent). The other, the temperament model, expects normal variation in brain functioning to affect the development of normal temperament and personality, but also sees these differences as risk factors for psychopathology.

2. Referring to family history, twin, and adoption methods for studying genetic influences, the text says that "although each of these methods alone has its pitfalls of interpretation, if the results from using all three strategies converge, one can draw reasonably strong conclusions about the genetic influence on a disorder" (p. 75). List the weaknesses of each method taken alone and explain why convergence across these methods eliminates alternative interpretations.

3. Some behavior geneticists argue that one's genotype defines a *reaction range* of phenotypic outcomes. For example, in the case of IQ one genotype might restrict phenotypic IQ to the range from IQ = 70 to IQ = 105, whereas another genotype might restrict potential IQs to a range from 90 to 130. An intellectually stimulating environment will facilitate the development of a phenotypic IQ in the upper portion of the range for that person, whereas an unstimulating environment will tend to produce a phenotypic IQ in the lower portion of the individual's range. Your text states that children born to socially disadvantaged parents who were adopted and reared with socially advantaged parents showed a mean IQ about 12 points higher than those children reared in the socially disadvantaged environment. How is this reaction range model consistent with such an adoptive effect on IQ and, at the same time, with the possibility that the differences in IQ between the biological and adoptive parents were attributable in part to genetic factors? If the parental IQ differences were, in fact, partially attributable to genetic influences, what would you expect to find if the IQs of the adopted children were compared with the IQs of biological children of the adoptive parents?

4. Today's society has witnessed a tragic increase in violent mass shootings in high schools. In many cases, these murders are planned and carried out by classmates who are described as "loners" and "outcasts," with a fascination for weapons, etc. List and discuss several biological, psychosocial, and sociocultural factors discussed in Chapter 3 that you believe would adequately explain what motivated these students to commit such horrendous crimes. How did these students get to be this way? Which factors do you believe best account for this? Discuss ways such causal factors may be targeted in order to prevent future crimes from occurring. Save your answer, refer back to it, and revise it if necessary, after you have read the Modern Life section of Chapter 14, which discusses youth violence.

◊ CHAPTER 3 QUIZ

Circle the best of the four answers provided and check them according to answers provided at the back of this study guide. Be sure you understand why each answer is correct.

1. A factor that increases the probability of developing a disorder without being either necessary or sufficient is a _____ cause. (p. 64)
   a. distal
   b. proximal
   c. reinforcing
   d. contributory

2. The specialized structure on the postsynaptic neuron at which the neurotransmitter exerts its effect is the _____. (Highlight 3.1, p. 70)
   a. synaptic cleft
   b. synaptic vesicle
   c. receptor site
   d. enzyme

3. After being released into the synaptic cleft, the neurotransmitter substance may be reabsorbed into the presynaptic axon button, a process called _____. (p. 69)
   a. re-uptake
   b. deactivation
   c. recapture
   d. active transport

4. In genetic studies the subject, or carrier, of the trait or disorder in question who serves as the starting point is known as the: (p. 74)
   a. proband.
   b. zygote.
   c. risk person.
   d. initiation point.

5. According to Freud's psychoanalytic perspective, the source of all instinctual drives is the: (pp. 81, 84)
   a. ego.
   b. id.
   c. libido.
   d. superego.

6. Which type of anxiety is a signal to the ego that the id's unacceptable impulse is threatening to break out? (p. 84)
   a. reality anxiety
   b. neurotic anxiety
   c. moral anxiety
   d. free-floating anxiety

7. Margaret Mahler focused on the process by which children come to understand that they are different from other objects. This process involves a developmental phase called: (p. 87)
   a. assimilation-accommodation.
   b. introjection-identification.
   c. introversion-extroversion.
   d. separation-individuation.

8. Instead of Freud's concept of fixation, Erikson proposed that parental deprivation might interfere with the development of _____. (p. 88)
   a. high self-esteem
   b. tolerance for stimulation
   c. self-control
   d. basic trust

9. The form of learning where an individual learns to achieve a desired goal is: (p. 92)
   a. classical conditioning.
   b. operant conditioning.
   c. modeling.
   d. avoidance conditioning.

10. The ability to discriminate may be brought about by: (p. 93)
    a. classical conditioning.
    b. shaping.
    c. differential reinforcement.
    d. avoidance conditioning.

11. The behavioristic tradition has been criticized for: (p. 94)
    a. its precision and objectivity.
    b. its research orientation.
    c. its failure to demonstrate effectiveness.
    d. its overconcern with symptoms.

12. The tendency to explain one's success as due to luck, as compared to hard work is best categorized as an example of a specific _____: (p. 95)
    a. attributional style
    b. contributory effect
    c. proximal schema
    d. internal representation

13. A basic goal of psychosocial therapies is _____. (p. 96)
    a. accommodation
    b. social skills training
    c. reduction of anxiety
    d. assimilation

14. Bowlby found that when young children were separated from their parents during prolonged periods of hospitalization, their reaction upon reunion was: (p. 103)
    a. strong dependence.
    b. detachment.
    c. joy.
    d. anger.

15. A _____ parental style is likely to produce a child who is impulsive and aggressive, spoiled, selfish, inconsiderate, and demanding and who will exploit people for his/her own purposes. (pp. 104-105)
    a. authoritative
    b. authoritarian
    c. permissive-indulgent
    d. neglecting-uninvolved

16. Which of the following was *not* proposed as a strong factor in popularity among juveniles? (pp. 107-108)
    a. parents' income
    b. intelligence
    c. being seen as friendly and outgoing
    d. physical attractiveness

17. Epidemiological studies that have linked psychopathology with social class are: (p. 113)
    a. based on controlled experimentation.
    b. correlational in nature.
    c. establishing a clear-cut cause-effect relationship.
    d. good examples of analogue studies.

18. According to the authors, the problematic proliferation of diverse viewpoints about psychopathology can best be solved by: (pp. 116-117)
    a. adhering to a single point of view for consistency's sake.
    b. becoming an eclectic.
    c. developing a unified point of view.
    d. divorcing oneself from all major perspectives.

| **Chapter 4** |
| *Stress and Adjustment Disorders* |

◊ OVERVIEW

Chapter 4 begins with a detailed discussion of stress, a topic of increasing concern as modern life becomes more and more pressured. The text discusses the potential sources of stress, the functional equivalence of biological, psychological, and sociocultural sources of stress, and the general strategies for coping with stressful demands. Reactions of individuals to war, concentration camps, and civilian disasters are described and can be viewed as case studies of human functioning under levels of severe stress. The chapter describes: 1) the coping techniques used by individuals in these situations; and 2) the symptoms that arise when coping techniques fail to eliminate the stress--leading in many cases to adjustment disorders. It will seem unbelievable when reading about some of the incidents that there were *any* people who could cope without developing severely abnormal behavior. The practical implications of this chapter are seen in applications such as preparing people to cope more effectively when they face stressful situations.

◊ CHAPTER OUTLINE

I.   What Is Stress?
    A. Categories of Stressors
        1. Frustrations
        2. Conflicts
        3. Pressures
    B. Factors Predisposing a Person to Stress
        1. The Nature of the Stressor
        2. The Experience of Crisis
        3. Life Changes
        4. A Person's Perception of the Stressor
        5. The Individual's Stress Tolerance
        6. A Lack of External Resources and Social Supports
    C. Coping with Stress

1. Task-Oriented Coping
2. Defense-Oriented Coping

II. The Effects of Severe Stress
    A. Biological Effects of Stress
        1. Stress and the Sympathetic Nervous System
        2. Stress and the Immune System
    B. Psychological Effects of Long-Term Stress
        1. Psychological Decompensation
            a) Alarm and Mobilization
            b) Resistance
            c) Exhaustion
        2. Acute and Chronic Post-Traumatic Stress Disorders

III. Adjustment Disorder: Reactions to Common Life Stressors
    A. Stress from Unemployment
    B. Stress from Bereavement
    C. Stress from Divorce or Separation

IV. Post-Traumatic Stress Disorder: Reactions to Catastrophic Events
    A. Distinguishing Between Acute Stress Disorder and Post-Traumatic Stress Disorder
    B. Causal Factors in Post-Traumatic Stress
    C. The Trauma of Rape
        1. Coping With Rape
            a) Anticipatory Phas
            b) Impact Phase
            c) Post-Traumatic Recoil Phase
            d) Reconstitution Phase
        2. Long-Term Effects
        3. Counseling Rape Victims
    D. The Trauma of Military Combat
        1. Clinical Picture in Combat-Related Stress
        2. Prisoners of War and Holocaust Survivors
        3. Causal Factors in Combat Stress Problems
            a) Temperament
            b) Psychosocial Factors
            c) Sociocultural Factors
        4. Long-Term Effects of Post-Traumatic Stress

E. Severe Threats to Personal Safety and Security
   1. The Trauma of Being Held Hostage
   2. Psychological Trauma Among Victims of Torture

V. Treatment and Prevention of Stress Disorders
   A. Stress-Prevention or Reduction
   B. Treatment of Post-Traumatic Stress Symptoms
      1. Medications
      2. Crisis-Intervention Therapy
      3. Direct-Therapeutic Exposure

VI. Unresolved Issues: The Abuse of PTSD Diagnosis

VII. Summary

◊ LEARNING OBJECTIVES

After studying this chapter, you should be able to:

1. Define the concepts of stressor, stress, and coping, describe the basic categories of stressors, and discuss factors that increase or decrease a person's vulnerability to stress. (pp. 120-126)

2. Contrast the two major categories of coping responses and outline the numerous negative consequences of a failure to cope successfully. (pp. 127-132)

3. Characterize the DSM-IV diagnosis of adjustment disorder and describe three major stressors and the consequences that increase the risk of adjustment disorder. (pp. 133-136)

4. List the diagnostic criteria for acute stress disorder and posttraumatic stress disorder, and compare and contrast the two disorders. (pp. 136-139)

5. Summarize what is known about the major features of reactions to catastrophic events. (pp. 139-140)

6. Identify the factors that influence the effects of rape on the victim and describe the typical immediate and long-term consequences of rape. (pp. 140-143)

7. Characterize the phenomenon of combat-related stress and of posttraumatic stress disorder in connection with battlefield stress. (pp. 143-145)

8. List and illustrate the long-term effects of being a prisoner of war or in a concentration camp and note the methodological problems associated with biased sampling. (pp. 145-146)

9. Outline the factors that appear to influence combat-related stress problems, and describe the long-term effects of PTSD. (pp.146-148)

10. Describe the psychological problems associated with being tortured, with being a refugee, and with being held hostage. (pp. 148-151)

11. Summarize the approaches that have been used to treat or to prevent stress disorders and evaluate their effectiveness. (pp. 151-155)

12. Evaluate the pros and cons of using PTSD as a defense in criminal court cases or as a basis of requesting compensation in civil court cases. (p. 155-156)

◊ TERMS YOU SHOULD KNOW

stress (p. 120)

stressor (p. 120)

coping strategies (p. 120)

eustress (p. 120)

distress (p. 120)

frustrations (p. 121)

conflicts (p. 121)

approach-avoidance conflicts (p. 121; Table 4.1, p. 122)

double-approach conflicts (p. 121; Table 4.1, p. 122)

double-avoidance conflicts (p. 121; Table 4.1, p. 122)

pressures (pp. 121-122)

chronic stressors (p. 123)

crisis (p. 123)

crisis intervention (p. 123)

life stress scales (p. 124)

LCU (p. 124)

stress tolerance (p. 125)

task-oriented response (p. 127)

defense-oriented response (pp. 127-128)

decompensation (p. 128)

homeostasis (p. 129)

allostasis (p. 129)

allostatic load (p. 129)

general adaptation syndrome (p. 129; Figure 4.1, p. 130)

alarm reaction (p. 129; Figure 4.1, p. 130; p. 132)

resistance (p. 129; Figure 4.1, p. 130; p. 132)

exhaustion (p. 129; Figure 4.1, p. 130; p. 133)

sympathetic nervous system (p. 129)

challenge study (p. 131)

hypothalamic-pituitary-adrenal dysregulation (p. 131)

psychoneuroimmunology (p. 131)

post-traumatic stress disorder (pp. 133, 136-137; Table 4.3, p. 138)

acute stress disorder (p. 133; 137; Table 4.2, p. 137)

adjustment disorders (p. 133-136)

disaster syndrome (p. 138-140)

shock stage (p. 139)

suggestible stage (p. 139)

recovery stage (p. 139)

conditioned fear (p. 141)

anticipatory phase (p. 142)

impact phase (p. 142)

post-traumatic recoil phase (p. 142)

reconstitution phase (pp. 142-143)

combat-related stress (pp. 143-145)

yohimbine (p. 152)

stress-induced analgesia (SIA) (p. 152)

naloxone (p. 152)

stress inoculation training (p. 153)

direct therapeutic exposure (p. 154)

◊ NAMES YOU SHOULD KNOW

Hans Selye

Scott Monroe

George Brown

◊ CONCEPTS TO MASTER

---

1. Compare and contrast the concepts of stressors, stresses, and coping strategies, noting particularly the interrelation among them. (p. 120)

2. Describe and illustrate three basic categories of stressors. (pp. 121-122).

3. Define an approach-avoidance conflict and list several examples from your own experience. (Table 4.1, p. 122)

4. Discuss the nature and experience of stressors. (pp. 123)

5. The concept of a stressful environment requires attempts to quantify the degree of stress. How did Holmes and his colleagues attempt to measure the cumulative stress associated with life events? What did they find happens as environmental stressfulness increases? (p. 124)

6. Life stress scales are a method to measure the number of life changes currently active in a person's life. Research on life events has been extensive, but the methodology employed in life stress scales has been severely criticized by Monroe and others. Summarize these limitations of life events measurements. (p. 124)

7. Describe how an individual's perception of the stressor, stress tolerance, and external resources and supports can modify the effects of stress. (pp. 124-127)\

8. Differentiate between *task-oriented* and *defense-oriented* reactions to stress, and describe two ego-defense mechanisms that are examples of the latter. (pp. 127-128)

9. Discuss the effect of stress on the sympathetic nervous system and on the hypothalamic-pituitary-adrenal system. (pp. 129-132)

10. List three stages of the "disaster syndrome," indicate at which stage posttraumatic stress disorder may develop, and identify the three intense emotions that may complicate the picture. (pp. 139-140)

11. In the context of predicting who will develop posttraumatic stress disorder in response to traumas of varying severity, compare and contrast the views of Clark, Watson, & Mineka with those of McFarlane. (p. 138)

12. List the four stages of the coping behavior of rape victims and summarize the major features of each stage. (pp. 142-143)

13. Trace the evolution of the concept of combat exhaustion from World War I to the present. (pp. 143)

14. In spite of variations in experience, the general clinical picture of combat stress has been surprisingly uniform for those soldiers who develop it. Describe this common clinical picture, the effects of intermittent versus prolonged periods of shelling, the emotional components of PTSD, and the differences seen between soldiers hospitalized for wounds versus psychiatric problems. (pp. 143-148)

15. Describe the design and results of the study by Laufer, Brett, and Gallops (1985) which evaluated the self-reports of Vietnam veterans, who were grouped according to three levels of experienced stress. (pp. 144-145)

16. Explain how the concept of a representative versus a biased sample is critically important in evaluating the long-term pathogenic effects of the concentration camp experience. (pp. 145-146).

17. What is meant by the concept of *delayed* posttraumatic stress? How severe are the stresses associated with the onset of symptoms? (pp. 147-148)

18. Explain why Turkish political activists developed fewer symptoms of PTSD following torture than did torture victims who were not political activists. (p. 151)

19. Explain why some noradrenergic brain systems are believed to be involved in producing some of the symptoms of PTSD and how the drug yohimbine was used to test this hypothesis. (Highlight 4.4, p. 152)

20. Describe the relationship of uncontrollable stress-induced analgesia (SIA) to symptoms of PTSD, including the use of naloxone to test this theory in patients with PTSD. Explain the roles of unpredictable and uncontrollable stressors in the development of PTSD. (Highlight 4.4, p. 152)

21. Describe a three-stage type of stress inoculation used by cognitive-behavioral therapists. (p. 153)

22. What is "direct therapeutic exposure," when is it used, and what traditional behavior therapy methods may be used in conjunction with it? (p. 154)

23. Describe ways in which the posttraumatic stress syndrome has been used in both criminal and civil court cases. (pp. 155-156)

What is stress?

1. Adjustive demands, also known as _____, create effects within an organism that are known as stress. (p. 120)

2. The following is a list of types of stressors. Match each type with the example that correctly illustrates it. (pp. 120-122)

Example	Type of Stressor
_____	1. Frustration (p. 120)
_____	2. Approach-avoidance conflict (p. 120)
_____	3. Double-approach conflict (p. 121)
_____	4. Double-avoidance conflict (p. 121)
_____	5. Pressures (p. 121)

Example

a. A "mixed blessing dilemma" in which some positive and negative features must be accepted, no matter what the decision--such as an African-American judge who is offered a membership in a discriminatory club.

b. A plus-plus conflict, choosing between two desirable alternatives, such as deciding between a trip to Las Vegas or Reno.

c. Finals week with a part-time job, studying, and social obligations.

d. Finding out that the women's basketball team must travel four to a room, but the men's team has only two per room.

e. A minus-minus conflict, choosing between two undesirable alternatives such as being given the choice to go on a diet or die.

Factors predisposing a person to stress

3. How is the severity of stress gauged or measured? (p. 122)

4. The nature of the stressor is known to influence the degree of disruption that occurs. This impact, in turn, depends on many factors, such as the _____ of the stressor to the person, the _____ of the stress, the _____ of the stressors in the person's life, and whether or not the stressor is seen by the person as within or outside his or her own _____. (p. 123)

Intense stress and the experience of crisis

5. Why are "crises" especially stressful? (p. 123)

6. How can the outcome of a crisis affect a person's subsequent adjustment? (p. 123)

7. The severity of disruption experienced in response to a stressor is related to the individual's perception of the stressor, stress tolerance, and external resources and support. Indicate whether severe or minimal disruption may be expected under the following circumstances:

   a. New adjustive demands that have not been anticipated by the individual and for which no ready-made coping patterns are available. (p. 125)

   b. Adjustive demands placed upon a person who does not handle changing life circumstances well. (p. 125)

   c. Adjustive demands confronted by a person with a supportive spouse, close extended family, and strong religious traditions. (pp. 125-126)

Principles of coping with stress

8. Place the following reactions to stress in the appropriate space to indicate the level at which they operate: (p. 127)

a. Learned coping patterns
b. Immunological defenses against disease
c. Group resources such as religious organizations
d. Self-defenses
e. Damage-repair mechanisms
f. Support from family and friends

Levels of Coping	Reactions to Stress
Biological level	1. _____ 2. _____
Psychological-interpersonal level	1. _____ 2. _____ 3. _____
Sociocultural level	1. _____

9. What are the two challenges with which a person is confronted in coping with stress? (p. 127)

Defense-oriented reaction patterns

10. Two types of defense mechanisms are described in the text. What are they? (p. 128)

1. _____ mechanisms such as crying and repetitive talking.
2. _____ or _____ mechanisms that function to relieve anxiety.

11. In what three ways do defense mechanisms protect the individual from both internal and external threats? (p. 128)

a.

b.

c.

12. Defense mechanisms are learned, automatic, habitual reactions designed to deal with inner hurt and anxiety. As such they may serve useful self-protective functions, but they can also be maladaptive. When are ego-defense mechanisms considered maladaptive? (p. 128)

The effects of severe stress

13. Stress is a fact of life. However, stress can be damaging. Describe how severe stress:

    a. lowers adaptive efficiency. (p. 128)

    b. depletes adaptive resources and lowers tolerance to other stressors. (p. 129)

    c. affects biological responses. (p. 129)

14. Davidson and Baum (1986) studied the effects of stress over a five-year period among residents at Three Mile Island and in a control community. Describe their findings in the follow-up study. (pp. 130-131

15. Numerous studies have suggested that stress associated with grief and separation, as well as examination stress may produce changes in the system that could affect health. How does stress produce these changes? What consequences do these changes bring? (pp. 131-132)

16. Personality decompensation under extreme stress appears to follow a course resembling biological decompensation, which consists of three stages: alarm and mobilization, resistance, exhaustion and disintegration. Provide the missing information below that describes the behavior of the individual during each stage. (pp. 132-133)

Stage   **Behavior of Organism**

Alarm and mobilization

Resistance

Stage of exhaustion

Adjustment disorder: Reactions to common life stressors

17. The DSM-IV provides for the rating of current stress on Axis IV. In addition, it contains three relevant diagnostic categories: adjustment disorder, acute stress disorder, and posttraumatic stress disorder. All three of these disorders occur in response to identifiable stressors. What are the dimensions along which they differ? (pp. 133, 136)

18. List the different stressors associated with adjustment disorders versus posttraumatic stress disorders and indicate the way in which the two groups of stressors differ. (pp. 133, 136)

19. The impact of chronic unemployment on a person's _____, _____, and feeling of belongingness is shattering. (pp. 133-134)

20. Often the first reaction to death of a loved one is _____. Then feelings of _____ frequently overwhelm us. (p. 135)

21. How long does the normal grieving process typically last, and what negative health effects are typically involved? (p. 135).

22. What factors associated with a death often lead to complicated or prolonged bereavement? (p. 135)

23. Many factors make a divorce or separation unpleasant and stressful for everyone concerned. List some of these factors. (p. 136)

Post-traumatic stress disorder

24. Give specific examples of symptoms for the first three and the fifth general symptom categories that typify posttraumatic stress disorder and list the fourth symptom category. (pp. 136-137)

    a. Persistent reexperiencing of the traumatic event
      Example:

    b. Individual avoids stimuli associated with the trauma
      Example:

    c. Persistent symptoms of increased arousal
      Example:

    d. Feelings of depression
      Example:

Distinguishing between acute stress disorder and PTSD

25. What feature distinguishes acute stress disorder from post-traumatic stress disorder? (pp. 137-138)

26. What feature distinguishes between delayed versus acute post-traumatic stress disorder? (pp. 137-138)

Reactions to catastrophic events

27. A "disaster syndrome" has been observed among victims that has been divided into three stages. Fill in the following chart with the behavior that is typical of each stage. (pp. 138-139)

Stage	Behavior Observed
Shock stage	
Suggestible stage	
Recovery stage	

28. Blanchard, Hickling, Barton, and Taylor (1996) initially found that _____ of those motor vehicle accident victims who initially met PTSD criteria had not remitted at a _____-month follow-up. (p. 140)

29. Rubonis and Bickman (1991) concluded that _____ percent of individuals who had experienced disasters showed psychological adjustment problems. (p. 140)

30. What psychological factors can complicated recovery from paralysis in an automobile accident? (p. 140)

Causal factors in post-traumatic stress

31. What factors determine whether someone develops post-traumatic stress disorder or not? (p. 141)

32. What appears to be a key causal factor in all cases of post-traumatic stress? (p. 141)

The trauma of rape

33. Discuss how each of the following variables are thought to affect a woman's response to rape: (pp. 141-142)

    a. Relationship to the offender

    b. Age

    c. Marital status

34. According to McCann (1988), what five areas of a woman's life functioning are affected b the experience of rape? (p. 142)

35. The phase of coping behavior that begins immediately after a rape is known as the _____-_____ _____ phase. (p. 142)

Traumatic reactions to military combat

36. According to the government figures presented in your text, the percent of soldiers who suffered combat exhaustion _____ in each successive war from World War II to Vietnam. (p. 143)

37. According to government claims, _____ percent of soldiers experienced combat exhaustion in Vietnam. (p. 143)

38. What is the relationship between the degree of combat exposure and later development of PTSD? (p. 143)

39. How did the results of studies in Israel strongly support the conclusion that levels of anxiety (and depression, in one case) among civilians were related to exposure to SCUD missile attacks? (p. 144)

40. Laufer, Brett, and Gallops (1985) surveyed 251 Vietnam veterans who varied in combat exposure. Having participated in abusive violence was found to be correlated with what symptoms? (p. 144-145)

41. What are usually the first symptoms of combat exhaustion (combat stress)? (p. 145)

42. What did Merbaum and Hefez (1976) find about the role of previous psychological adjustment in determining a soldier's vulnerability to combat exhaustion? (p. 145)

43. Medical problems are commonly seen in those incarcerated in POW or concentration camps. About _____ of the American prisoners in Japanese POW camps during World War II died during imprisonment, and an even higher number of Nazi concentration camp prisoners died. Interpretation of seemingly psychological symptoms among survivors of Nazi concentration camps is difficult because they may be attributed to biological stressors such as _____, _____, and serious infectious diseases. (pp. 145-146

44. What is the "re-entry" problem for former POWs and concentration camp survivors? (p. 146)

45. Bullman and Kang (1997) found an increased risk of _____ due to _____ _____ associated with PTSD in Vietnam veterans. (p. 146)

46. Clarity and acceptability of war goals, identification with the combat unit, esprit de corps, and quality of leadership are sociocultural factors that play an important part in determining a person's adjustment to combat. Describe how each of these has an effect. (p. 147).

47. What is controversial about assessments of the frequency of diagnosis of delayed posttraumatic stress disorder? (pp. 147-148)

The trauma of forced relocation

48. Refugees face not only the trauma of being uprooted from their home, but also the stress of adapting to a new and unfamiliar culture. Amng those who come to the U.S., the Southeast Asians arriving after 1975 have had the most difficult adjustment. A ten-year longitudinal study of Hmong refugees from Laos found many signs of improvement after ten years in the U.S.: 55% were employed, the percentage on welfare dropped from 53% to 29%, and symptoms of phobia, somatization, and low self-esteem had also improved. On the other hand, considerable problems remained. What were these? (p. 149)

49. Short and Johnston (1997) found that greater adjustment in Chinese parents who immigrated to Canada _____ the degree of stress in their children. (pp. 149-150)

The trauma of torture

50. List and illustrate the array of psychological symptoms experienced after torture. (p. 150)

51. In the study of 55 former Turkish political prisoners who were tortured, what two variables were found by Basoglu & Mineka to have an important impact on the severity of the consequences of torture? (pp. 150-151)

52. What variables appear to have a protective value against PTSD in survivors of torture? (p. 151)

Treatment and prevention of stress disorders?

53. What are the two most important determinants of how stressed an organism is by a stressor? (Highlight 4.4, p. 152)

54. It is known that prior experience with uncontrollable stressors can _____ the organism, that is, make it more susceptible to the negative consequences of later experiences with uncontrollable trauma. (Highlight 4.4, p. 152)

55. Soldiers who had been _____ in childhood were more likely to develop PTSD during the Vietnam War. (Highlight 4.4, p. 152)

56. According to Epstein et al. (1998), how are disaster area workers affected by their work?

57. Describe three treatment approaches for patients with PTSD. (pp. 153-154)

58. What is the most important factor, from the standpoint of legal precedent, in establishing legal justification for the PTSD defense? (p. 155-156)

◊ CRITICAL THINKING ABOUT DIFFICULT TOPICS

1. The text says that the concept of stressors refers to "adjustive demands" and that "all situations, positive and negative, that require adjustment can be stressful" (p. 120). Thus, such events as getting married, being promoted to a better position, graduating from college, and starting a new and attractive job all constitute positive stress or eustress, as opposed to negative stress or distress. Do you think such positive stressors are as pathogenic as negative stressors--e.g., contributing to the onset of depression, ulcers, etc.? Can you imagine a new marriage or a new job having negative consequences without first developing a component of negative stress (e.g., interpersonal conflict in the marriage, inability to cope with new obligations in the job)?

2. Chapter 3 focused on the diathesis portion of the diathesis-stress model, whereas this chapter focuses on "the role of stress as a precipitating causal factor" (p. 120). Psychiatrists with a strong biological orientation are skeptical about the contribution of stress, arguing that the person's stress response reflects greater vulnerability more than the external, objective features of the stressor. Psychologists, in contrast, want to provide unequivocal evidence of the causal contribution of external stressors. The problem arises because, as the text states, often "the severity of stress is gauged by the degree to which it disrupts functioning" (p. 122). The text then goes on to emphasize the importance of "person characteristics" in determining the severity of the stress response. These person characteristics include such factors as the importance of the stressor to a person, the cumulative effect of stressors (which might be secondary to whether or not the person copes adequately with the stressors), chronic difficult life situations (to which the person's personality might contribute), the person's perception of threat and tolerance of stress, and overall vulnerability to stress (p. 123). All of these factors point to the confounding of these person characteristics with the magnitude of the stress response and the degree to which the stressor disrupts functioning. This

perspective is summed up in the statement that "However great a challenge, it creates little stress if a person can easily handle it" (p. 127). In view of this methodological difficulty, how would you prove to a skeptic that the external, objective stress designated in the diathesis-stress model does, in fact, act as a causal factor in the etiology of abnormal behavior? How could you assess the severity of stress without using the degree to which it disrupts functioning?

3. In the previous chapter, biological influences on abnormal behavior and on temperament were emphasized. An important theme of the present chapter is that psychological events in the form of stressors produce physiological changes that contribute to the onset of illness (e.g., heart disease and cancer, p. 131). How does this finding alter the interpretation of biological influences on abnormal behavior and temperament and of the origin of individual differences in biological influences?

4. The text states that in the case of delayed posttraumatic stress disorder "the frequency with which this disorder has recently been diagnosed in some settings suggests that its increased use is as much a result of its plausibility and popularity as of its true incidence" (p. 148). If this assertion is true, what does it tell you about the validity of diagnosis? If a diagnosis can be influenced so strongly by plausibility and popularity, should we view diagnoses with a bit of skepticism?

5. The evidence supporting the relationship between stress and psychopathology is "so substantial that the role of stressors in symptom development is now formally emphasized in diagnostic formulations" in DSM-IV (pp. 131-133). Why did it take very strong evidence to incorporate such a plausible notion in the DSM? In thinking about this problem, consider that (a) the DSM largely reflects psychiatric thinking strongly influenced by the disease model and (b) in the disease model the source of the psychopathology is inside the person, not in the environment. When events such as bereavement over the death of a spouse or anxiety during battlefield conditions elicit emotional problems in a large minority of the population, does it seem right to refer to these individuals as having a psychiatric "disorder"? If not, what does this attitude imply about the cause of psychiatric disorders? Note that even though bereavement often produces the full symptom syndrome of a depressive disorder, DSM-IV excludes the diagnosis of depressive disorder.

6. Developing the point in question 5 further, the text notes that PTSD "bears such a close relationship to the experience of stress" (pp. 131-133) that it is covered in this chapter (on stress) rather than in the chapter on anxiety disorders--implying that stress is a less obvious contributor to other anxiety disorders. What implicit model would allow you to conceptualize this distinction? In finding an answer, think about the concept of underlying liability for a disorder and a threshold (or "breaking point" for appearance of symptoms. For

example, in arbitrary units, it might take 100 points of liability to reach threshold for developing an anxiety disorder. If both diathesis and stress combine additively to produce total liability, what happens as one of these variables becomes more severe?

In the case of the severe traumas reviewed in the present chapter (rape, battlefield stress, incarceration, being held hostage, and forced relocation) would it require less diathesis to reach threshold--e.g., if these potent environmental factors contributed 80 points of liability? In the absence of major stressors, would it take a lot of diathesis to reach threshold? (See the discussion of the contribution of personality factors citing the work of Clark, Watson, & Mineka and of Ursano, Bodystun, & Wheatley on page 141 for a clear statement of this model.) Does this model account for the greater knowledge of environmental factors than of personal characteristics in PTSD (p. 146)? How does this model affect your understanding of the concept of a psychiatric "disorder"? What would you do with intermediate cases, in which the diathesis and the stress each contribute equally?

◊ CHAPTER 4 QUIZ

Circle the best of the four answers provided and check them according to answers provided at the back of this study guide. Be sure you understand why each answer is correct.

1. A wedding is likely to cause which of the following? (p. 120)
   a. distress
   b. stress
   c. stressor
   d. eustress

2. Working at a job that was unfulfilling would probably lead to feelings of: (p. 121)
   a. conflict.
   b. frustration.
   c. pressure.
   d. defensiveness.

3. A person wants to accept a party invitation because he/she is very social but is concerned because there will be a lot of drinking and he/she is a member of AA (Alcoholics Anonymous). He/she is experiencing a(an): (Table 4.1, p. 122)
   a. mixed blessing dilemma.
   b. approach-avoidance conflict.
   c. double-avoidance conflict.
   d. double-approach conflict.

4. Life stress scales have been severely criticized by Monroe (and others) for numerous methodological problems. Which of the following was *not* one of his criticisms? (p. 124)
   a. the subjectivity of the scoring
   b. failure to take into account the relevance of items for the populations studied
   c. they do not assess specific types of disorders
   d. they measure reactions to specific environmental events

5. Which of the following defense-oriented behaviors is of the damage-repair type? (p. 128)
   a. denying
   b. intellectualizing
   c. mourning
   d. repressing

6. When we are faced with a stressor, we need to do two things. One thing is meet the requirements of the stressor, and the other is to: (p. 127)
   a. protect the self from damage and disorganization.
   b. change the way we think about the problem.
   c. protect the self from defense-oriented response.
   d. make sure that we do not face a stressor again.

7. When coping resources are already mobilized against one stressor, they are: (p. 128)
   a. made stronger for coping with others.
   b. less available for coping with others.
   c. shifted immediately to the new stressors.
   d. unaffected by additional stressors.

8. Davidson and Baum found that even five years after people were exposed to the nuclear accident site at Three Mile Island, they showed the presence of: (pp. 130-131)
   a. gastric ulcers.
   b. duodenal ulcers.
   c. urinary noradrenaline.
   d. posttraumatic stress disorder.

9. The alarm and mobilization stage of personality decompensation under excessive stress is characterized by: (p. 132)
   a. emotional arousal, increased tension, and greater alertness.
   b. exaggerated and inappropriate defense measures.
   c. lowering of integration.
   d. rigidity as the individual clings to accustomed defenses.

10. The normal grieving process in bereavement should last no longer than about: (p. 135)
    a. 4 months.   c. 12 months.
    b. 8 months.   d. 18 months.

11. Which of the following is *not* a phase in the coping response of rape victims? (p. 142)
    a. anticipatory phase   c. posttraumatic recoil phase
    b. shock phase   d. reconstitution phase

12. Which of the following causes of combat stress do we know the most about? (p. 146)
    a. constitutional differences in sensitivity
    b. differences in temperament
    c. differences in vigor
    d. the conditions of battle that tax a soldier's stamina

13. Why is it difficult to explicitly relate delayed cases of stress syndrome to combat stress? (p. 147)
    a. The biological effects will be gone.
    b. Clinicians could not do anything anyway.
    c. The psychological effects are not substantial.
    d. There might be other adjustment problems involved.

14. In the study of torture survivors in Turkey, it was suggested that the political activists developed fewer symptoms of PTSD than did those who were not political activists, because political activists: (p. 151)
    a. showed less anxiety before being detained and tortured.
    b. were more prepared by prior experience with stressors, stoicism training, and commitment to a cause.
    c. experienced less severe torture.
    d. received more support and treatment from fellow activists after the torture.

15. According to Vargas and Davidson (1993), which of the following treatments tends to be more effective in improving PTSD symptoms? (p. 153)
    a. both psychotherapy and medications
    b. medications alone without psychotherapy
    c. psychotherapy without medications
    d. both medications and the avoidance of fear-producing situations

16. Definitively proving the existence of PTSD to the satisfaction of the legal system: (pp. 155-156)
    a. would be scientifically unethical.
    b. is exceedingly difficult.
    c. has already been accomplished.
    d. will never be accomplished.

	Chapter 5
	Panic, Anxiety, and Their Disorders

◊ OVERVIEW

Chapter 5 presents a detailed description of the clinical picture, causal pattern, and treatment of the anxiety disorders, each of which is characterized by an unrealistic irrational fear or anxiety of a disabling intensity. Following a general overview of the response patterns of fear and anxiety, the chapter continues with a discussion of the phobic disorders, which includes specific phobias and social phobias. Next is a review of the latest research on panic disorder, both with and without agoraphobia, followed by a discussion of generalized anxiety disorder and obsessive compulsive disorder. Post-traumatic stress disorder - another anxiety disorder - was covered in the preceding chapter rather than this one, because it is largely a prolonged reaction to traumatic stressors. There is also a strong emphasis on the role of unpredictability and uncontrollability in the anxiety disorders. The chapter closes with a discussion of sociocultural causal factors as well as important treatment and outcome issues.

◊ CHAPTER OUTLINE

I.   The Fear and Anxiety Response Patterns

II. Overview of the Anxiety Disorders

III. Phobic Disorders
    A. Specific Phobias
        1. Blood-Injection-Injury Phobia
        2. Age of Onset and Gender Differences in Specific Phobias
        3. Psychosocial Causal Factors
            a) Psychodynamic Viewpoint
            b) Phobias as Learned Behavior
        4. Biological Causal Factors
            a) Genetic and Temperamental Causal Factors

1. The Psychoanalytic Viewpoint
2. Classical Conditioning to Many Stimuli
3. The Role of Unpredictable and Uncontrollable Events
4. A Sense of Mastery: Immunizing Against Anxiety
5. The Content of Anxious Thoughts
6. The Nature and Function of Worry
7. Cognitive Biases for Threatening Information

E. Biological Causal Factors
1. Genetic Factors
2. A Functional Deficiency of GABA
3. Neurobiological Differences Between Anxiety and Panic

F. Treating Generalized Anxiety Disorder

VI. Obsessive Compulsive Disorder (OCD)
A. Prevalence and Age of Onset
B. Characteristics of OCD
1. Types of Obsessive Thoughts
2. Types of Compulsions
3. Consistent Themes
4. Comorbidity With Other Disorders

C. Psychosocial Causal Factors
1. Psychoanalytic Viewpoint
2. The Behavioral Viewpoint
3. OCD and Preparedness
4. The Role of Memory
5. The Effects of Attempting to Suppress Obsessive Thoughts

D. Biological Causal Factors
1. Genetic Influences
2. Abnormalities in Brain Function
3. The Role of Serotonin

E. Treating Obsessive-Compulsive Behavior

VII. General Sociocultural Causal Factors for all Anxiety Disorders
A. Cultural Differences in Sources of Worry
B. Taijin Kyofusho

VIII. General Issues Regarding Treatments and Outcomes

IX. Unresolved Issues: Interdisciplinary Research on the Anxiety Disorders

X. Summary

◊ LEARNING OBJECTIVES

After studying this chapter, you should be able to:

1. Compare and evaluate the merits of Freud's use of the concept of anxiety in the etiology of the neuroses versus the descriptive approach used in DSM since 1980. (p. 159)

2. Distinguish between fear and anxiety. (pp. 160-161)

3. Describe the major features of phobias, identify and differentiate different subtypes of phobia, explicate the major etiological hypotheses, and discuss the most effective treatment approaches. (pp. 161-172)

4. List the diagnostic criteria for panic disorder, contrast panic attacks and other types of anxiety, explain the association with agoraphobia, and summarize the major developments over the last 15 years in theories of etiology. (pp. 172-182)

5. Describe recent findings on a genetic influence for anxiety proneness. Summarize the evidence that anxiety sensitivity constitutes a diathesis for development of panic attacks. (pp. 178, 180; Highlight 5.1, p. 181)

6. Describe how safety behaviors and cognitive biases help to maintain panic. (pp. 180, 182)

7. Compare and contrast the major treatment approaches for panic disorder and agoraphobia. (pp. 182-183)

8. Summarize the central features of generalized anxiety disorder, and distinguish among psychoanalytic, conditioning, and cognitive theories of etiology. (pp. 183-191)

9. Identify the central nervous system processes and structures associated with generalized anxiety disorder, and evaluate treatments for the disorder. (pp. 191-192)

10. Describe the defining features of obsessive-compulsive disorder, summarize theories of etiology along with supporting evidence (or the lack thereof), and outline the treatment of OCD with biological and psychological techniques. (pp. 192-204)

11. Provide several examples of sociocultural effects on anxiety disorders. (pp. 204-205)

12. Critically evaluate the relative merits of treatments for anxiety disorders. (pp. 205)

13. Discuss the issues stemming from the polarization of biological research versus psychological research on the anxiety disorders, and review a possible solution. (p. 206)

◊ TERMS YOU SHOULD KNOW

---

neurotic behavior (p. 159)

neurosis (p. 159)

anxiety (p. 159)

anxious apprehension (pp. 160, 184)

fear/panic (pp. 160-161)

fight or flight response (pp. 161, 173)

anxiety disorder (p. 161)

phobia (p. 161)

specific phobia (pp. 162-168)

social phobia (pp. 162, 168-172)

agoraphobia (pp. 162, 172-183)

secondary gains (p. 163)

blood-injection injury phobia (pp. 163-164)

immunization (p. 166)

inflation effect (p. 166)

behaviorally inhibited (p. 167)

preparedness (p. 167)

exposure (p. 168)

systematic desensitization (p. 168)

participant modeling (p. 168)

specific vs. generalized social phobia (pp. 168-169)

danger schemas (p. 171)

panic disorder (pp. 172-183)

nocturnal panic (p. 172)

true alarms vs. false alarms vs. learned alarms (p. 173)

agoraphobia (pp. 173-183)

suffocation alarm mechanism (p. 176)

biological challenge procedures (p. 176)

panic provocation agents (p. 177)

locus coeruleus (p. 177)

limbic system (p. 177)

kindling (p. 177)

interoceptive fears (p. 178)

interoceptive conditioning (p. 178)

anxiety sensitivity (p. 180; Highlight 5.1, p. 181)

safety behaviors (p. 180, 182)

antidepressants (p. 182)

interoceptive exposure (p. 183; Highlight 5.2, p. 185)

cognitive-behavior therapy (p. 183; Highlight 5.2, p. 184)

generalized anxiety disorder (pp. 183-192)

free-floating anxiety (p. 183)

worry (pp. 183, 189-190)

safety signals (p. 188)

serotonin transporter (p. 191)

GABA (p. 191)

benzodiazepines (p. 192)

obsessive-compulsive disorder (pp. 192-203)

obsessions (p. 194)

compulsions (pp. 194-195)

body dysmorphic disorder (BDD) (Highlight 5.3, p. 196)

striatum (p. 202)

taijin kyofusho (TKS) (pp. 204-205)

◊ NAMES YOU SHOULD KNOW

David Barlow

Peter Lang

Colin MacLeod

Andrew Mathews

Susan Mineka

Jerome Kagan

Joseph Wolpe

Edna Foa

Stanley Rachman

Isaac Marks

Donald Klein

Martin Seligman

Arne Öhman

Jeffrey Gray

David Clark

◊ CONCEPTS TO MASTER

1. Freud's overall views on the nature of neurosis have come under attack as too theoretical. In what way is his use of the concept of anxiety to account for neurosis too theoretical? Why has the decision to adopt a different approach in editions of the DSM since 1980 resulted in greater reliability of diagnosis (with subsequent advances in understanding causes and in treatment)? (p. 159)

2. Compare and contrast the concepts of fear or panic, on the one hand, and anxiety, on the other hand. Be sure to note that both emotions involve cognitive/subjective, physiological, and behavioral components and that the emotions differ with respect to the present versus future orientation. (pp. 160-161)

3. Describe the major manifestations of phobias as a class and differentiate specific phobias and social phobias. (pp. 161-162)

4. Describe the classical conditioning hypothesis of the origin of phobias and explain how observational learning, immunization, and preparedness greatly expand the explanatory power of this hypothesis. (pp. 164-166)

5. Contrast the classical conditioning/vicarious conditioning/preparedness theory of the origin of social phobias with that for specific phobias. (pp. 164-166; 169-170)

6. Explain the importance of a perception of uncontrollability in conditioning models of the acquisition of phobias. (pp. 170-171)

7. Describe cognitive-behavior therapy for social phobia, and discuss its effectiveness as compared to current medications. (p. 172)

8. Define panic disorder according to the DSM-IV definition. (p. 172)

9. Differentiate between panic attacks and other types of anxiety in terms of intensity and the time course. (p. 173)

10. Define agoraphobia and explain its close association with panic disorder. (pp. 173-175)

11. How are the locus coeruleus, the central periaqueductal gray, the limbic system, and the prefrontal cortex involved in the various phenomena of panic disorder? (pp. 177-178)

12. Traditionally a key feature of panic attacks is that they seem to "come out of the blue." Recent evidence, however, suggests that panic attacks are, in fact, triggered by bodily sensations. Compare and contrast the closely related interoceptive conditioning and the cognitive models of panic with respect to the triggering of panic attacks and summarize the extensive evidence supporting the cognitive model. (pp. 178-180)

13. Explain what is meant by the statement that "anxiety sensitivity does seem to serve as a risk factor or diathesis for the development of panic and functional impairment from anxiety symptoms," and describe the way in which two important studies tested this hypothesis. (p. 180; Highlight 5.1, p. 181)

14. Describe the role that safety behaviors and cognitive biases are thought to play in the maintenance of panic disorder. (pp. 180, 182)

15. Discuss current biological and psychological treatments for panic disorder. Which treatment(s) appear to be the most effective? Cite evidence to support your answer. (pp. 182-183)

16. In the diagnosis of generalized anxiety disorder, what symptoms were included in previous DSMs but dropped in DSM-IV and why were they dropped? (p. 183)

17. Describe the attempt to apply a conditioning model to generalized anxiety disorders and indicate why this model has not fared well. Then summarize the more promising cognitive approach emphasizing uncontrollability and unpredictability, including the important study by Mineka et al. with infant rhesus monkeys. (pp. 188-189)

18. What are negative automatic thoughts, and what evidence has shown their presence among patients with GAD? (p. 189)

19. List the five most common benefits of worrying derived by people with GAD, and explain the function of worry. (pp. 189-190)

20. What is the effect of being generally anxious on attending to threat cues, interpreting ambiguous information, and memory for threat cues? (p. 190-191)

21. How are benzodiazepines thought to reduce generalized anxiety, and what neurotransmitters may modulate anxiety? (pp. 191-192)

22. Summarize the major manifestations of obsessive-compulsive disorders, and explain why they are considered maladaptive. (pp. 192-195)

23. Describe the psychoanalytic theory of OCD, and give two reasons why this theory has not been supported. (p. 198)

24. Summarize the behavioral view of OCD and explain how it has been revitalized by the addition of the preparedness hypothesis. (p. 198)

25. To what extent do genetic factors contribute to OCD, and what brain abnormalities have been targeted as possible biological causal factors for OCD? (pp. 201-203)

26. Compare and contrast biological treatments for OCD with the behavior and cognitive-behavior therapies for OCD. (p. 203)

27. Compare and contrast the prevalence and age of onset for each of the anxiety disorders discussed in Chapter 5. (pp. 164, 175, 186, 193-194)

28. How does TKS relate to social phobia? (pp. 204-205)

◊ STUDY QUESTIONS

Introduction

1. What was the original meaning of the term *neurosis* as introduced by Englishman William Cullen? (p. 159)

2. Later, Freud suggested that neurosis stemmed from intrapsychic conflicts. Complete the missing words in Freud's definition. Neurosis is the outcome of an internal conflict between some _____ _____ and prohibitions against its expression. (p. 159)

3. The DSM classification since 1980 is theoretically neutral and abandons the use of the term neurosis. In its place are three general classes of disorders--one of which is anxiety disorders. List the other two classes. (p. 159)

4. Historically, the most common way of distinguishing between fear and anxiety has been whether there is a _____ and _____ source of danger. When the source of danger is _____, the emotion has been called fear. The term anxious apprehension is applied to an unpleasant inner state in which we are _____ some dreadful thing happening that is not predictable from our actual circumstances. (p. 160)

5. Activation of the fight or flight response is associated with the basic emotion of _____ or _____. (p. 160)

6. The basic fear and anxiety response patterns are highly conditionable to previously neutral stimuli. These neutral stimuli may consist not only of external cues, but also of _____ _____. (p. 161)

Anxiety disorders

7. What is the principal manifestation of anxiety disorders? (p. 161)

8. Anxiety disorders are relatively common. According to the results of the National Comorbidity Survey, one form of anxiety disorder was the second most common psychiatric disturbance among women and the fourth most common among men. Which form of anxiety disorder was it? (p. 161)

9. Anxiety disorders, which include generalized anxiety, panic, phobic, and obsessive-compulsive disorders, are thought to have a lifetime prevalence rate of nearly _____ % of U.S. women and _____ % of U.S. men. Twelve-month prevalence rates are: _____ % of U.S. women and _____ % of U.S. men. (p. 161)

10. What percent of those who have ever had a phobic disorder have also had another anxiety disorder? (p. 161)

Phobic disorders

11. A phobia is a persistent fear of some specific object or situation that presents no actual danger to the person, but physiologically and behaviorally the phobic response is often identical to that which would occur in an encounter with an _____ situation. (pp. 161-162)

12. List the five subtypes of specific phobias. (p. 162)

13. Regardless of how they begin, phobias are reinforced in two ways. First, they are reinforced by the reduction in anxiety that occurs each time the individual avoids the feared situation. Second, phobias may be maintained by *secondary gains*. What are secondary gains? Give an example of this. (p. 163)

14. Claustrophobia and agoraphobia tend to begin in _____. (p.164)

15. Experiencing an inescapable and _____ trauma seems to condition fear much more powerfully than the same intensity of trauma that one can to some extent _____. (p. 166)

16. The phenomenon in which a person who acquired a mild conditioned fear then develops a full blown phobia in response to a later traumatic experience even without the conditioned stimulus being present is called the _____ effect. (p. 166)

17. Evidence supporting the contribution of temperament in the etiology of phobias comes from Kagan's finding that _____ children were at higher risk for the development of multiple specific phobias at 7-8 years of age than were _____ children. (p. 167

18. Supporting the _____ theory of phobias, Öhman and his colleagues found that fear was conditioned more effectively to _____-_____ stimuli than to _____-_____ stimuli. (p. 167)

19. _____-based treatments are widely considered to be the treatment of choice for specific phobias. (p. 168)

20. Fear of _____ by others may be the hallmark of social phobias. (p. 168)

21. Specific social phobias involve disabling fears of one or more discrete social situations. Complete the following list of three situations mentioned in the text: (p. 169)
    a. _____
    b. urinating in a public bathroom
    c. _____ or _____ in public

22. Individuals with generalized social phobia have significant fears of most social situations and often also share a diagnosis of _____ personality disorder. (p. 169)

23. What temperamental variable appears to be of greatest importance to social phobia? (p. 170)

24. A distinct advantage that behavioral and cognitive-behavioral therapy techniques have over medication is that they produce much more _____-_____ _____ with very low _____ _____. (p. 172)

Panic disorder and agoraphobia

25. Panic disorder is characterized by the occurrence of _____ panic attacks not triggered by an actual or threatened harm by another person, often seeming to come "out of the blue." (p. 172)

26. To qualify for the diagnosis of panic disorder, an individual must have recurrent, unexpected panic attacks and be persistently concerned about a future attack for a period of at least one month. To qualify as a panic attack, there must be _____ onset of at least _____ of 13 symptoms (such as shortness of breath, etc.). (p. 172)

27. Agoraphobia is a frequent complication of _____ disorder. Cases of agoraphobia without _____ are extremely rare in clinical settings but are not uncommon in _____ studies. The reasons for this discrepancy are unclear. (p. 174)

28. The National Comorbidity Survey found that approximately _____ % of the adult population had panic disorder at some time in their life. (p. 175)

29. Current theory suggests that _____ may have an inhibitory effect on _____ function in the central gray area and/or the _____ _____, acting to inhibit surges of _____ activity that are thought to occur during a panic attack. (p. 177)

30. Panic attacks are only one component of panic disorder. Persons with panic disorder also experience _____ anxiety, and those with agoraphobia also engage in _____ behavior. (p. 177)

31. One possible causal explanation for how bodily sensations come to be catastrophized is that it comes from learning experiences prior to a first attack such as observing parents model _____-_____ behavior or having _____ _____. (p. 178)

32. Two studies demonstrated that anxiety sensitivity is a risk factor for panic symptoms:

    a. Schmidt, Lerew, and Jackson followed young adults undergoing _____ for five weeks. Of those scoring in the top 10% on the Anxiety Sensitivity Index, _____% experienced at least one panic attack, compared with _____% of the remaining study participants. (Highlight 5.1, p. 181)

b. Telch and his colleagues followed for one year 500 _____, half of which were high and half low on anxiety sensitivity. Nearly _____% of the high group compared with only _____% of the low group experienced at least one unexpected panic attack. (Highlight 5.1, p. 181)

33. With panic disorder, if medication withdrawal is not done very gradually, the client is likely to experience what has been called _____ _____. (p. 182)

Generalized anxiety disorder

34. Generalized anxiety disorders are characterized by chronic, unrealistic, excessive worry of at least six months duration that does not appear to be anchored to a specific object or situation. This type of anxiety was traditionally described as _____ anxiety. (p. 183)

35. Complete the following list of the symptoms characteristic of individuals suffering from generalized anxiety disorder, in addition to the core experience of excessive worry. (p. 183)

a. Restlessness or feelings of being _____

b. A sense of being easily _____

c. Difficulty _____ or mind going blank

d. _____

e. Muscle tension

f. _____ disturbance

36. A multi-site study found that patients diagnosed with GAD did not endorse symptoms of autonomic hyperactivity with much frequency, but it was found that they respond to laboratory stressors with high levels of _____ and _____ tension. (pp. 183-184)

37. Although _____ also is part of other anxiety disorders, it is the essence of GAD, leading Barlow to refer to it as the "basic" anxiety disorder. (p. 184)

38. Generalized anxiety disorder is experienced by approximately _____% of the population in any one-year period. (p. 186)

39. According to the psychoanalytic view, the primary difference between simple phobias and free-floating anxiety is that, in the phobias, defense mechanisms of _____ and _____ are operative, whereas in free-floating anxiety these defense mechanisms are not operative. (p. 188)

40. A relative lack of _____ _____ may help account for why people with GAD feel constantly tense and vigilant for possible threats. (p. 189)

41. Experience with _____ and/or _____ life events may promote current anxiety as well as a vulnerability to anxiety in the presence of future stressors. (p. 190)

42. Provide the following information about a newly-discovered gene that likely affects proneness to anxiety: (pp. 191-192)
    a. The gene affects the serotonin transporter. What does this transporter do?

    b. What dimension of human personality is affected, and what does it have to do with anxiety?

    c. This gene accounts for only _____% of the variance on this personality dimension.

Obsessive-compulsive disorder

43. What are the one-year prevalence and lifetime prevalence of obsessive-compulsive disorder? Is there an effect of gender on prevalence? (pp. 193-194)

44. Obsessive thoughts may center around a variety of topics. The content of obsessions consist most often of _____ fears, fears of _____ _____ and _____. (p. 194)

45. What are the three primary types of compulsive acts? (p. 194)

46. What seems consistent across all the different clinical presentations of OCD is: (a) _____ is the affective symptom, (b) people afflicted with OCD fear that something _____ will happen to themselves or others for which they will be responsible; and (c) compulsions usually _____, at least in the short term. (p. 195)

47. Give an example of each of the following forms of obsessive-compulsive symptoms: (Table 5.4, p. 195)
   a. Ruminations
   b. Cognitive rituals
   c. Compulsive motor rituals
   d. Compulsive avoidances

48. Steketee and Foa (1985) describe the treatment of obsessive-compulsive disorder as consisting of two phases: exposure treatment and response prevention. Describe what the therapist did during each phase. (Highlight 5.4, p. 200)

   a. Exposure treatment

   b. Response prevention

Sociocultural causal factors

49. In the Yoruba culture in Nigeria, what are three primary clusters of symptoms associated with generalized anxiety? (p. 204)

Treatment and outcomes

50. What is a major disadvantage of drug treatments for anxiety disorders? (p. 205)

51. Behavior therapies focus on (a) removing specific _____ _____or toward changing . specific negative paterns of thinking that maintain anxiety, but they often seem to have more far-reaching positive results. (p. 205)

Unresolved issues

52. Over the last fifteen years, great progress has been made in both _____ and _____-_____ approaches to the anxiety disorders. It is unfortunate that these two different lines of research have so often proceeded along relatively _____ and _____ paths. What we need to understand is how the events occurring at one level of analysis (_____ or _____) affect events occurring at another level of analysis (_____) and vice versa.   This leads us to the importance of developing a coherent _____ approach to understanding these disorders. (p. 206)

◊ CRITICAL THINKING ABOUT DIFFICULT TOPICS

1. If the causes of two diseases (e.g., cancer and ulcers) are truly independent, the probability of suffering from both of them is the product of their respective prevalences. Thus, if each has a prevalence of 2%, the probability of having both is $.02 \times .02 = .0004$ or .04% (i.e., 4 cases in a population of 10,000). Traditionally, the DSM conceptualized psychiatric disorders as independent diseases. However, in recent years it has become increasingly clear that there is a great deal of co-morbidity--instances of dual diagnoses. For example, in the present chapter the text states that it is "very common for a person diagnosed with one anxiety disorder to be diagnosed with one or more additional anxiety disorders, as well as with a mood disorder" (p. 161) and that individuals with generalized social phobia (an anxiety disorder) "often also share a diagnosis of avoidant personality disorder" (p. 169). What does the phenomenon of comorbidity imply about the conceptualization of these supposedly independent disorders?

2. The text notes that in recent years many prominent researchers have proposed a fundamental distinction between fear or panic, on the one hand, and anxiety, on the other hand (pp. 160, 191). Further, this distinction proves important in understanding differences between phobias and panic, on the one hand, and generalized anxiety, on the other. Have you been making a similar distinction in your everyday usage of the concept of anxiety? If not, how would such a distinction affect your interpretation of your social environment? For example, in terms of personality traits, can you identify some individuals who show more anxiety (worry, preparation for future problems) while others show more fear or panic (acute anxiety)? Do some students worry about and prepare for exams in advance, whereas others do not prepare for them but become very anxious during them? Can a similar distinction be made for public speaking?

3. Both the interoceptive conditioning model and the cognitive model propose that panic attacks are triggered by internal bodily sensations (p. 178). In the cognitive model, it is said that the person has a tendency to catastrophize about the meaning of bodily sensations but that the person is often not aware of making these catastrophic interpretations. The thoughts are often just barely out of the realm of awareness. In comparing the conditioning and the cognitive models, however, the difference between them is that the "cognitive model would predict panic only if this patient makes catastrophic interpretations about what it means that his heart is racing on a particular occasion" (p. 178). How could you test this hypothesized difference between the hypotheses if the catastrophic

interpretations are not always conscious--i.e., how would you know whether the person makes a catastrophic interpretation? In answering this question, it may help to read the evidence supporting the cognitive hypothesis that involves manipulations of perceptions (as opposed to asking subjects about their conscious thoughts).

4. A key feature of the DSM approach to anxiety disorders since 1980 is that people with such disorders must "show prominent symptoms of anxiety" (p. 159). Consider what the following statement implies about the assessment of prominent symptoms of anxiety: Those with generalized anxiety disorder do not have any very effective anxiety-avoidance mechanisms, whereas victims of other anxiety disorders can to some extent allay their anxieties through avoidance behavior (pp. 183-184). For those whose avoidance behavior is successful in allaying anxiety, how are prominent symptoms of anxiety to be demonstrated? Does avoidance behavior alone suffice to infer anxiety? What if the avoidance response is blocked (e.g., among phobics, agoraphobics, or obsessive-compulsives)?

◊ CHAPTER 5 QUIZ

Circle the best of the four answers provided and check them according to answers provided at the back of this study guide. Be sure you understand why each answer is correct.

1. In the National Comorbidity Survey, _____ were the second most common psychiatric disorders reported for women and the fourth-most common for men. (p. 161)
   a. obsessive-compulsive disorders   c. panic disorders
   b. generalized anxiety disorders   d. phobias

2. All phobic behaviors are reinforced by: (p. 163)
   a. increased self-esteem.   c. repetition.
   b. reduction in anxiety.   d. sympathy from others.

3. The concept that explains why phobias often are not learned in spite of the fact that we observe models responding fearfully is: (p. 166)
   a. counter-conditioning.   c. immunization.
   b. stimulus pre-exposure.   d. reciprocal inhibition.

4. In the Cook and Mineka study of the acquisition of phobias through observational learning in rhesus monkeys, it was found that the monkeys did not condition fears to: (pp. 165-166)
   a. toy snakes.
   b. toy crocodiles.
   c. toy rabbits.
   d. live snakes.

5. Fear of urinating in a public bathroom is an example of _____: (p. 169)
   a. panic disorder.
   b. specific social phobia.
   c. generalized social phobia.
   d. generalized anxiety disorder.

6. The two features of panic attacks that distinguish them from other types of anxiety are their characteristic _____ and their _____. (p. 173)
   a. focal stimulus, intensity
   b. brevity, mildness
   c. focal stimulus, constancy
   d. brevity, intensity

7. According to biological psychiatrists, panic disorder is qualitatively different from generalized anxiety because of an apparent finding that a _____ drug appeared to block panic attacks in agoraphobics without affecting their anticipatory anxiety. (p. 176)
   a. minor tranquilizer
   b. tricyclic antidepressant
   c. barbiturate
   d. monoamine oxidase inhibitor

8. The common mechanism underlying the effects of all the various panic provocation agents is that they: (p. 176)
   a. mimic the physiological cues that normally precede a panic attack.
   b. stimulate the locus coeruleus.
   c. interfere with processes that inhibit anxiety.
   d. increase activity in the anxious apprehension system.

9. Which of the following is *not* typically a part of cognitive-behavior therapy for panic disorder? (Highlight 5.2, p. 184)
   a. exposure to feared situations and/or feared bodily sensations
   b. deep muscle relaxation and breathing retraining
   c. identification and modification of logical errors and automatic thoughts
   d. carbon dioxide inhalation and/or lactate infusion

10. Barlow refers to the fundamental process in generalized anxiety disorder as: (p. 184)
    a. the alarm reaction.
    b. the fight or flight response.
    c. anxious apprehension.
    d. prepared focal anxiety.

11. The benzodiazepines, minor tranquilizers that reduce generalized anxiety, probably exert their effects through stimulating the action of: (p. 191)
   a. acetylcholine.
   b. GABA.
   c. serotonin.
   d. norepinephrine.

12. An impulse the person cannot seem to control is called a(an): (p. 194)
   a. compulsion.
   b. delusion.
   c. hallucination.
   d. focal phobia.

13. The personality disorders with which OCD most often occurs are: (pp. 196-197)
   a. narcissistic and antisocial.
   b. borderline and histrionic.
   c. schizoid and schizotypal.
   d. avoidant and dependent.

14. The techniques used by Steketee and Foa in the recommended treatment of obsessive-compulsive disorders are _____ and _____. (Highlight 5.4, p. 200)
   a. counter-conditioning, reciprocal inhibition
   b. exposure treatment, response prevention
   c. implosion, response prevention
   d. cognitive restructuring, exposure treatment

◊ OVERVIEW

Among those who seek psychological help, depression is the most common mood disorder that clinicians encounter. Among the normal population, depression is also widespread. Given its high frequency, there is an important distinction between normal depression - such as that caused by grief over the loss of a loved one - versus depressive mood disorders. Additionally, there are several subcategories of clinical depression ranging from mild (e.g., dysthymia) to severe (e.g., schizoaffective disorder), and from acute to chronic. Moreover, in one subset of mood disorders (i.e., from cyclothymia to bipolar disorders), manic episodes alternate with depressive episodes.

After introducing the clinical picture of these mood disorders, biopsychosocial causal factors and treatment approaches are discussed. Next the text reviews the research on suicide, for which depressed individuals are at constant risk. This section presents information relevant to these questions--asking, for instance, whether all persons who commit suicide are mentally disordered. Data are also presented on the increasing problem of suicide among young people and college students. The section concludes with a discussion of some of the factors that characterize the person who is at high risk for suicide and a brief description of suicide prevention procedures.

◊ CHAPTER OUTLINE

I.   What Are Mood Disorders?
    A. The Prevalence of Mood Disorders
    B. Depression Throughout the Life Cycle

II. Unipolar Mood Disorders
    A. Depressions That Are Not Mood Disorders
        1. Loss and the Grieving Process
        2. Other Normal Mood Variations

B. Mild to Moderate Depressive Disorders
    1. Dysthymia
    2. Adjustment Disorder with Depressed Mood
C. Major Depressive Disorder
    1. Cognitive and Motivational Symptoms
    2. Subtypes of Major Depression
    3. Distinguishing Major Depression
    4. Depression as a Recurrent Disorder
    5. Seasonal Affective Disorder

III. Bipolar Disorders
    A. Cyclothymia
    B. Bipolar Disorders
        1. Features of Bipolar Disorders
    C. Schizoaffective Disorders

IV. Causal Factors in Unipolar Disorders
    A. Biological Causal Factors
        1. Hereditary Factors
        2. Biochemical Factors
        3. Neuroendocrine and Neurophysiological Factors
        4. Sleep and Other Biological Rhythms
            a) Circadian Rhythms
            b) Sunlight and Seasons
        5. Summary of Biological Causal Factors
    B. Psychosocial Causal Factors
        1. Stressful Life Events as Causal Factors
            a) Effects of Life Stressors
            b) Endogenous Depression
            c) Chronic Stressors
            d) Individual Differences in Response to Stressors
            e) Vulnerability and Invulnerability Factors
            f) How Stressors Act
        2. Types of Diathesis-Stress Models for Unipolar Depression
            a) Personality and Cognitive Diatheses
            b) Early Parental Loss as Diathesis
            c) Summary of Diathesis-Stress Models
        3. Psychodynamic Theories

4. Behavioral Theories
5. Beck's Cognitive Theory
   a) Features of Beck's Theory
   b) Personality Variables as Additional Vulnerability Factors
   c) Evaluating Beck's Theory as a Descriptive Theory
   d) Evaluating the Causal Aspects of Beck's Theory
6. The Helplessness and Hopelessness Theories of Depression
   a) Seligman et al.'s Research
   b) Similarities Between Depression and Helplessness
   c) The Role of Attributional Style
   d) The Hopelessness Theory of Depression
7. Interpersonal Effects of Mood Disorders
   a) Lack of Social Support and Social Skills Deficits
   b) The Effects of Depression on Others
   c) Marriage and Family Life
8. Summary of Psychosocial Causal Factors

V. Causal Factors in Bipolar Disorder
   A. Biological Causal Fators
      1. Hereditary Factors
      2. Biochemical Factors
      3. Other Biological Causal Factors
   B. Psychosocial Causal Factors in Bipolar Disorder
      1. Stressful Life Events
      2. Psychodynamic Views

VI. Sociocultural Factors Affecting Unipolar and Bipolar Disorders
   A. Cross-Cultural Differences in Depressive Symptoms
   B. A Belief in Self-Sufficiency
   C. Relieving Losses
   D. Demographic Differences in the United States

VII. Treatments and Outcomes
   A. Pharmacotherapy and Electroconvulsive Therapy
      1. Selective Serotonin Re-Uptake Inhibitors
      2. The Course of Treatment with Antidepressant Drugs
      3. Lithium and Other Mood Stabilizing Drugs
      4. Electroconvulsive Therapy

◊ LEARNING OBJECTIVES

After studying this chapter, you should be able to:

1. Summarize the symptoms associated with normal depression, list the various causes of or contributors to normal depression, and characterize the phases of the grieving process. (pp. 213-214)

2. Compare and contrast the clinical features of dysthymia, adjustment disorder with depressed mood, and major depressive disorder, as well as the various subtypes or subcategories of major depressive disorder. (pp. 214-219)

3. Compare and contrast Bipolar I disorder, Bipolar II disorder, and cyclothymia. (pp. 219-224)

4. List the features of schizoaffective disorder and discuss its relation to mood disorders and schizophrenia. (p. 224)

5. Describe the biological and psychosocial factors that are causally-related to mood disorders. (pp. 224-248)

6. Discuss how sociocultural factors affect the incidence of some of the mood disorders. (pp. 248-249)

7. Review the major hypotheses explaining possible causes for why women are about twice as likely as men to experience clinical depression. (Highlight 6.1, p. 238-239)

8. Outline the evidence supporting a contribution of depressive disorders to domestic violence. (Highlight 6.3, p. 244)

9. Describe biological and psychosocial therapies that have been used to treat mood disorders and evaluate their effectiveness. (pp. 251-255)

10. Characterize the people who are most likely to commit suicide. List some of their motives for ending their lives, and explain how psychosocial and sociocultural variables influence the likelihood of suicide among depressed persons. (pp. 255-264)

11. Evaluate the ethical and legal issues involved in sanctioning and preventing suicide. (pp. 264-265)

◊ TERMS YOU SHOULD KNOW

mood disorders (p. 210)

affect (p. 210)

mania (p. 210)

depression (p. 210)

unipolar disorder or unipolar major depression (pp. 210; Table 6.1, p. 211; p. 212)

bipolar disorder (p. 210; Table 6.1, p. 211; p. 212)

anaclitic depression (p. 212)

normal depression (p. 213)

dysthymia (Table 6.1, p. 211; pp. 214-215)

adjustment disorder with depressed mood (Table 6.1, p. 211; p. 215)

major depressive disorder (Table 6.1, p. 211; pp. 216-219)

melancholic type (p. 217)

endogenous causation (p. 217)

psychotic subtype (p. 217)

severe major depressive episode with psychotic features (p. 217)

mood-congruent (p. 217)

mood-incongruent (p. 218)

double depression (p. 218)

recurrence (p. 218)

relapse (p. 218)

seasonal affective disorder (SAD) (p. 219)

cyclothymia (Table 6.1, p. 211; pp. 219-220)

hypomania (pp. 219-220)

manic-depressive insanity (p. 220)

mixed bipolar disorder (p. 220)

bipolar disorder with a seasonal pattern (p. 221)

Bipolar I versus *Bipolar II disorder* (Table 6.1, p. 211; p. 221)

"flight-of-ideas" (p. 221)

rapid cycling (p. 223)

full recovery (p. 223)

schizoaffective disorder (p. 224)

monoamine hypothesis (p. 225)

hypothalamic-pituitary-adrenal axis (p. 226)

cortisol (p. 226)

dexamethasone (p. 226)

dexamethasone suppression test (DST) (p. 226)

hypothalamic-pituitary-thyroid axis (p. 226)

REM sleep (p. 227)

circadian rhythms (p. 227)

melatonin (p. 228)

endogenous depression (p. 230)

neuroticism (pp. 231-232)

pessimistic attributional style (p. 232)

depressogenic schemas (p. 234)

negative automatic thoughts (p. 235)

negative cognitive triad (p. 235)

dichotomous reasoning (p. 235)

selective abstraction (p. 235)

arbitrary inference (p. 235)

overgeneralization (p. 235)

sociotropy (p. 236)

autonomy (p. 236)

learned helplessness (pp. 236-238)

rumination (Highlight 6.1, pp. 238-239)

reformulated helplessness theory (pp. 237-238)

hopelessness theory (pp. 238-239)

hopelessness expectancy (p. 239)

negative affect vs. *positive affect* (Highlight 6.2, p. 240)

anxious hyperarousal (Highlight 6.2, p. 240)

mixed anxiety/depression syndrome (Highlight 6.2, p. 241)

◊ NAMES YOU SHOULD KNOW

Peter Lewinsohn

Ian Gotlib

John Bowlby

Connie Hammen

George Brown

Scott Monroe

Richard Depue

Hagop Akiskal

Bruce Dohrenwend

E. S. Paykel

Aaron T. Beck

Lynn Abramson

Martin Seligman

Susan Nolen-Hoeksema

◊ CONCEPTS TO MASTER

1. Define "normal depression" and describe how it is related to stress. (pp. 212-214)

2. List eight types of psychological losses in addition to the death of a loved one that may trigger grief. (p. 213)

3. Characterize the four phases of response to the loss of a spouse or close family member (as described by Bowlby) and note when prominent anxiety and prominent depression are likely to appear. (p. 213)

4. Define postpartum depression and note the evidence for and against it. (p. 214)

5. List the two dimensions customarily used to differentiate the mood disorders, and give examples of unipolar mood disorders varying along these two dimensions. (pp. 214-219)

6. How does dysthymia differ from: a) adjustment disorder with depressive mood, and b) major depressive disorder? (pp. 214-215)

7. Describe the clinical manifestations of major depressive disorder, and note the more restricted features of the melancholic type of major depressive disorder. (pp. 216-218)

8. Explain the meaning of the term "double depression." (p. 218)

9. Distinguish between a *recurrence* of depression and a *relapse*. (pp. 218-219)

10. Describe the clinical manifestations of cyclothymia and of bipolar disorder, and note the relation between the two. (pp. 219-224)

11. Explain the difficulty of knowing whether a person showing only depression during an initial episode of affective disorder should be diagnosed as suffering from a bipolar disorder. (p. 223)

12. The text states that "…people with bipolar disorder seem to be more unfortunate than those who suffer from recurrent major depression." List evidence to support this statement. (pp. 223-224)

13. Describe the symptoms of a schizoaffective disorder, and explain why some psychologists find this diagnosis controversial. (p. 224)

14. Summarize the evidence for a genetic contribution to unipolar depression, including the variation in heritability with subtype of depression. (pp. 224-225)

15. Trace the history and current status of the monoamine hypothesis of depression. Note that the antidepressant drugs actually begin to have their clinical effects 2-4 weeks after initial administration and discuss the implications of this consideration for the interpretation of the effects of these drugs. (pp. 225-226)

16. Define the concepts of sleep stages, circadian rhythms, and seasonal variations in basic functions and review their possible involvement in unipolar depression. (pp. 227-228)

17. List the five major facts that support the hypothesis of biological involvement in major depression. (pp. 228-229)

18. List the most frequently encountered precipitating circumstances in depression. (p. 229)

19. Summarize the results of research by Brown et al. and by Dohrenwend et al. on the effects of life events on depression. (p. 230)

20. List the four factors found by Brown and Harris to be associated with *not* becoming depressed among women who experienced a severe life event. (p. 231)

21. Compare and contrast the diathesis-stress theories of depression based on (a) genetic or constitutional diathesis, (b) personality variables, (c) cognitive diathesis, and (d) parental loss or poor parental care. (pp. 231-233)

22. Differentiate between Beck's cognitive theory of depression involving dysfunctional beliefs and Abramson et al.'s reformulated learned helplessness and hopelessness theories involving the concept of a pessimistic attributional style. (pp. 234-236, 236-239)

23. Seligman et al. proposed three deficits produced by learned helplessness. List and discuss them. (p. 237)

24. Discuss the current dominant theoretical approach to understanding the overlap between depressive and anxiety symptoms. (Highlight 6.2, pp. 240-241)

25. Discuss the evidence for the conclusions that interpersonal problems and social skills deficits may play a causal role in depression *and* that depression creates many interpersonal difficulties. (p. 242)

26. Outline the evidence strongly supporting a genetic contribution to the etiology of bipolar disorders. Also, explain the conceptual difficulties created by the finding that among the relatives of bipolar patients there is a higher rate of unipolar than bipolar disorders (pp. 243-245)

27. A person goes on a round of parties to try to forget a broken love affair or tries to escape from a threatening life situation by restless action, occupying every moment with work, athletics, sexual affairs, and countless other activities--all performed with professed gusto but not necessarily with true enjoyment. What psychoanalytic concept do these anecdotes exemplify and what does it have to do with mania? (pp. 247-248)

28. It has been found that even in those nonindustrialized countries where depressive disorders are relatively common, depression generally takes on a form different from that customarily described in our society. Describe these different forms. (pp. 248-249)

29. The two best-known of the depression-specific psychotherapies are Beck's cognitive-behavioral approach and the interpersonal therapy (IPT) developed by Klerman, Weissman, and colleagues. How do these differ from the usual approach in psychodynamic psychotherapy and how effective are these therapies? (p. 254)

30. Summarize the data on the degree to which suicide is communicated directly and indirectly and to whom it is communicated. (pp. 261-262)

31. Define the concept of a "right to suicide" and summarize the vexing ethical and legal issues surrounding the debate on this issue. (pp. 264-265)

◊ STUDY QUESTIONS

Introduction

1. According to recent estimates, depression ranked _____ among 150 health conditions in terms of "disease burden" (i.e., direct and indirect costs) to society. (p. 210)

2. The two key states of mood disorder are depression and _____. (p. 210)

3. Mild depressions are so much a part of our lives that their incidence is difficult to estimate. However, the most recent results from the National Comorbidity Study found lifetime prevalence rates of *major depression* at nearly _____% for males and _____% for females. Fill in the following statements about the incidence of depression. (p. 212)

   a. Bipolar affective disorder is much less common than unipolar depression. Estimates of lifetime risk of bipolar disorder range from _____% to _____%, and there is no discernible sex difference in prevalence rates.

   b. Most mood disorder cases occur during _____ and _____ adulthood. However, about _____ of adults reported the first onset of unipolar depression in childhood or adolescence.

Unipolar mood disorders: Normal depression

4. Everyday depression is unpleasant, but it usually does not last very long and is self-limiting, turning off after a period or a certain intensity level has been reached. Mild depression may even be adaptive because much of its "work" seems to involve _____ images, thoughts, and feelings that would normally be avoided. (p. 212)

5. Normal depression is almost always the result of recent _____. (p. 213)

6. Anger is very common in the _____ phase of grieving. (p. 213)

7. Grief is a psychological process one goes through following the death of a loved one. Clayton (1982) suggests that the process of grieving following bereavement is normally completed within _____. Depression continuing after this period calls for therapeutic intervention. (p. 213)

8. According to O'Hara et al. (1990), post-partum depression is best understood as a(n) _____ disorder, because it tends to be relatively mild and is resolved quickly. Also, the once firmly held notion that women were at especially high risk for depression following childbirth was _____ _____. (p. 214)

Unipolar mood disorders: Mild to moderate depressive disorders

9. The point on the severity continuum at which mood disturbance becomes a mood disorder is a matter of clinical judgment. True or False? (p. 214)

10. The two main depressive disorders of mild to moderate severity recognized by DSM-IV are dysthymia and adjustment disorder with depressed mood. Place these disorders in the blank next to the correct clinical description: (pp. 214-215)

    a. _____ Symptoms essentially similar to major depression, but the nonpsychotic levels of depression last two years or more with no tendency toward hypomanic episodes and with intermittent normal moods lasting from a few days to no more than a few weeks.

    b. _____ Also characterized by nonpsychotic levels of depression developing within three months of an identifiable stressor and lasting no longer than six months.

Unipolar mood disorders: Major depressive disorder

11. To be diagnosed as suffering from major depression, the person must experience either depressed mood or loss of interest in pleasurable activities. In addition, at least four symptoms must have been present all day and nearly every day during two consecutive _____. (p. 216)

12 Few, if any, depressions occur in the absence of another significant affect. This affect is _____. (p.216)

13. The most severe form of major depression is severe major depressive episode with _____ features. (p. 217)

14. The person who has a major depressive disorder may have a loss of contact with reality. Ordinarily, any delusions or hallucinations present are _____; that is, they seem in some sense "appropriate" to serious depression. (p. 217)

15. The term major depression of the _____ type may be used for the person who develops a major depression that includes lost capacity for pleasure and whose other symptoms are likely to include depression being worse in the morning, awakening early in the morning, showing marked psychomotor retardation or agitation, significant loss of appetite and weight, and excessive guilt. Historically, endogenous (internal) causation was thought to be responsible for triggering this form of depression. (p. 217)

16. Major depression may coexist with dysthymia, a condition given the designation _____. (p. 218)

17. The average duration of an untreated episode of major depression is about _____ months, according to DSM-IV. (p. 218)

18. Based on an extensive review of studies done between 1970 and 1993, Piccinelli and Wilkinson estimated that ____% of patients experienced a recurrence of major depression within one year of recovery and ____% experienced a recurrence within 10 years of recovery. Approximately ____% to ____% show persistent depression over five and ten year follow-up. (p. 218)

19. Prevalence rates suggest that winter seasonal affective disorder is more common in people living at _____ _____ and in _____ people. (p. 219)

Bipolar disorder

20. Nondisabling, cyclical mood alterations between depression and elation with no obvious precipitating circumstance and lengthy normal periods between episodes are indicative of _____, a milder variant of bipolar disorder (or, in other words, a subsyndromal form). (p. 219)

21. Bipolar mood disorder is distinguished from major depression by at least one episode of _____. The features of the depressive form of bipolar disorder are clinically _____ from those of major depression. (p. 220)

22. Mixed cases of bipolar disorder are those in which the full symptomatic picture of both manic and major depression occur intermixed or alternating every few hours. True or False? (p. 220)

23. The DSM-IV system contains the implicit assumption that all mania-like behaviors must be part of a _____ or bipolar disorder. (p. 221)

24. The symptoms of mania and depression are compared in the following chart. Fill in the missing information. (pp. 221)

Area of Behavior	Depression	Mania
Activity level	Loss of interest in activities	
Mood	Sad	Euphoric
Mental activity	Diminished cognitive capacity	Flight of ideas
Verbal output	Reduced	
Self-esteem	Self-denunciation and guilt	
Sleeping	Hypersomnia or insomnia	

25. A person with bipolar disorder whose first episode is a depression cannot be correctly diagnosed until the time that a manic episode appears. True or False? (p. 223)

26. Compared to patients with unipolar major depression, patients with bipolar disorder have _____ episodes in the course of their lifetimes, have episodes that tend to be somewhat _____ in duration. Even with lithium maintenance therapy, _____% of bipolar patients had relapsed within six months of recovery, and _____% by seven years, according to Coryell et al. (1995). (pp. 223-224)

Schizoaffective disorder

27. Patients with a diagnosis of schizoaffective disorder have a mood disorder equal to anything seen in major depression or bipolar affective disorder but their _____ and _____ processes are so deranged as to suggest the presence of a schizophrenic psychosis. The latter must include at least _____ major symptoms of schizophrenia. Unlike schizophrenia, the schizoaffective pattern tends to be highly _____ with relatively lucid periods between attacks. (p. 224)

28. The diagnosis of schizoaffective disorder is controversial. Some clinicians believe these persons are basically _____; others believe they have primarily psychotic _____ disorders; and still others consider this disorder a distinct entity. (p. 224)

Causal factors in unipolar disorders: Biological factors

29. One large twin study found that heritability estimates of depression ranged from ____% to ____%, depending on the definition used. However, the evidence for a genetic contribution is much less consistent for milder forms of unipolar depression, such as _____. (p. 225)

30. The most adequate adoption study found that unipolar depression occurred in _____% of the biological relatives of the severely depressed participants and in _____% of the biological relatives of control cases. The actual numbers are probably _____, however, because the study relied exclusively on medical records without direct interviews and family history information. (p. 225)

31. The biological therapies often used to treat severe mood disorders--such as _____ therapy and _____ drugs--may affect the concentrations or the activity of _____ at the synapse. (p. 225)

32. One contemporary hormonal theory of depression has focused on the
_____ _____ axis, and in particular on the hormone cortisol. It
was found that a potent suppressor of plasma cortisol, _____, either
fails to suppress or fails to sustain suppression of cortisol in about ____% of seriously
depressed patients. This gave rise to the widespread use of the
_____ (DST), and it was found that
nonsuppression was correlated with clinical severity and _____ response to drug
treatment. However, recent evidence has called into question the _____ of the
nonsuppression and hence the diagnostic utility of the DST for depression. (p. 226)

33. Studies using brain imaging techniques such as PET suggest that severely depressed patients
show decreased _____ in the _____ regions of the cerebral
hemisphere and especially on the _____ side. (p. 227)

Causal factors in unipolar disorders: Psychosocial factors

34. One of the most frequently enountered precipitating stressors is the _____ of an
important goal or the posing of situations that pose an _____ _____. (p.
229)

35. Brown and Harris concluded that depression often follows severely stressful events, usually
involving some _____ or _____ from one's social sphere. Interestingly, events
signifying danger or threat were found more likely to precede the onset of _____
disorders. (p. 230)

36. Whybrow et al. suggested that psychosocial stressors may play a role in the development of
mood disorders by causing long-term changes in _____ functioning. (p. 231)

37. L. A. Clark et al. (1994) concluded that there is evidence that _____ is
the primary personality variable that serves as a vulnerability factor for depression. There is
also some evidence that low levels of _____ or _____
_____ may also serve as a vulnerability factor for depression. (p. 232)

38. Gotlib and Hammen (1992) concluded that it seems that the contradictory findings regarding
the effects of early parental loss on depression can be resolved if one considers the
_____ of _____ _____ following the loss. (p. 232)

39. Perhaps the most important contribution of the psychodynamic approaches to depression has been to note the importance of _____ (both real, and symbolic or imagined) to the onset of depression and to note the striking similarities between the symptoms of _____ and the symptoms of depression. (p. 233)

40. Lewinsohn et al. proposed that depression can be elicited when a person's behavior no longer brings the accustomed _____ or _____ as, for example, when someone loses a job. (p. 233)

41. Depression-producing beliefs are believed by Beck to develop during childhood and adolescence as a function of one's experiences with one's _____ and with _____ (_____, etc.). (p. 234)

42. A "negative cognitive triad" consists of negative views of the self, world, and the _____. (p. 235)

43. Overlap between measures of anxiety and depression occurs at all levels of analysis. A recent very large twin study by Kendler et al. showed that the liability for generalized anxiety disorder and depression comes from the same _____ _____, and which disorder develops is a result of what _____ _____ occur. (Highlight 6.2, p. 240)

44. In the dominant theoretical approach to understanding the overlap between anxiety and depression, known as the tripartite model, the overlap between anxiety and depression is attributable to the broad mood and personality dimension of _____, depressed persons are specifically low on a second dimension of mood and personality known as _____, and anxious but not depressed individuals show high levels of yet another mood dimension known as _____. (Highlight 6.2, p. 240)

45. Until fairly recently, the finding that mood-disordered persons have an enhanced risk of engaging in family violence was attributed to the dyscontrol and disinhibition associated with _____ or _____ episodes. Recent research has called that explanation into question and implicates _____ disorders in the occurrence of domestic violence. (Highlight 6.3, p. 244)

46. Roberts, Gotlib, & Kassell (1996) demonstrated what appears to be a causal relationship between _____ _____ and the emergence of _____ symptoms, as mediated by self-esteem deficits. (Highlight 6.3, p. 245)

47. According to Gotlib & Hammen (1992) and Murray et al. (1997), depressed mothers have more _____ and have less _____ mutually rewarding interactions with their children. They are also less _____ _____ to their infants and less _____ of their infant's experiences. (p. 243)

Causal factors in bipolar disorders: Biological factors

48. Two reasons that elevated rates of both bipolar and unipolar forms of the disorder are found in the relatives of bipolars are that bipolar disorder does not _____ _____ or that this elevation is not greater than what would be expected due to chance. (p. 243)

49. The early monoamine hypothesis for unipolar disorder was extended to bipolar disorder, suggesting that perhaps mania was caused by an excess of norepinephrine and/or serotonin. Although there is some support for increased _____ during manic episodes, _____ activity appears to be low in both phases of the illness. _____ activity also appears to be elevated during manic episodes. (pp. 245-246)

50. Administration of _____ hormone is known at times to make antidepressant drugs work better. However, this hormone can also precipitate manic episodes. (p. 246)

Causal factors in bipolar disorders: Psychosocial factors

51. In a good prospective study using sophisticated stress measurement techniques, Ellicott and colleagues followed 61 patients with bipolar disorder for one to two years. What did they find regarding the association between high levels of stress and the experience of manic, hypomanic, or depressive episodes? (p. 247)

Causal factors for both unipolar and bipolar disorders: Sociocultural factors

52. As non-Western societies adopt the ways of Western culture, how do the rates of mood disorders change? (p. 249)

53. How do rates of unipolar and bipolar disorders correlate with social class in the U.S.? (pp. 249-250)

54. Traditionally, moderate to serious depression has been treated pharmacologically with a drug such as _____(_____), which is an example of a tricyclic antidepressant. Because of problems with unpleasant side effects and with suicide potential due to high toxicity with the tricyclics, physicians are increasingly prescribing one of the new _____ or SSRIs, such as Prozac (fluoxetine). (pp. 251-252)

55. Early studies indicated that lithium carbonate was considered an effective preventive for approximately ____% of patients suffering repeated bipolar attacks, but one large recent study found only slightly over _____% of patients remained free of episodes over a five-year follow-up. (p. 252)

56. Electroconvulsive therapy is often used with severely depressed, suicidal patients because antidepressants often take _____ to _____ weeks to produce significant improvement. ECT is also used with patients who have not responded to other forms of _____ treatment. When selection criteria are carefully observed, a complete remission of symptoms occurs after about six to twelve treatments. (p. 253)

57. What was the verdict regarding the relative effectiveness for depression of the Beck approach to cognitive-behavioral treatment (CBT) and interpersonal therapy (IPT) according to the carefully designed, multisite study sponsored by the National Institute of Mental Health and reported by Elkin et al.? Circle the correct statement from the choices below: (p. 255)
    1. IPT is more effective than CBT.
    2. CBT is more effective than IPT.
    3. Drugs are more effective than psychotherapy.
    4. Drugs, IPT, and CBT are equally effective for milder cases of major depression.

58. Even without formal therapy, the great majority of manic and depressed patients recover from a given episode within less than _____. At the same time, the mortality rate for depressed patients appears to be significantly higher than that for the general population, partly because of the increased risk of suicide. (p. 255)

59. Fill in the missing information in the following questions about the risk of suicide: (p. 256)
    a. The vast majority of those who commit suicide do so during the _____ phase of depression.
    b. The risk of suicide is just _____ percent during the year a depressive episode occurs but rises to _____ percent over the entire lifetime of an individual who experiences recurrent episodes.
    c. Experts agree that the actual number of suicides is probably _____ times as high as the official number.

60. Women are about three times as likely to attempt suicide as are men, but three times more men than women die by suicide each year. True or False? (p. 256)

61. In recent years, disproportionate increases have occurred in the suicide rates among certain groups. However, the greatest increases have been among _____ year olds, where the rate has tripled. (p. 257)

62. Which is the more frequent precipitant for suicide in college students, poor grades or the breakup of a romance? (Highlight 6.4, p. 259)

63. Suicide rates vary considerably from one society to another. The world's highest rate (more than 40 cases per 100,000) is in _____. The United States has a rate of approximately _____% per 100,000. Among certain groups, such as the Aborigines of the western Australian desert, the rate drops to _____%. (p. 260)

64. The French sociologist Emile Durkheim concluded that suicide rates during times of stress vary according to group _____. The greatest deterrent to suicide is a sense of involvement and identity with other people. (p. 261)

65. Fill in the missing information concerning degree of intent and methods of suicidal behavior: (p. 261)

Feelings About Death	**Method of Suicide**
Do not wish to die	
Intent on dying	
Ambivalent about dying	Tend to choose methods that are moderately slow acting to allow for the possibility of discovery

66. Long-term follow-up of those who have made a suicide attempt show that about _____%
will eventually die by suicide. Moreover, of people who do kill themselves, about _____
% have a history of one or more previous attempts. (p. 261)

67. Which is more common: a person commits suicide and leaves a note, or a person commits
suicide and does not leave a note? (p. 262)

68. The primary objective of crisis intervention therapy is to help the individual with an
immediate life crisis. When persons contemplating suicide are willing to discuss their
problems at a suicide prevention center, it is often possible to avert an actual suicide attempt.
The primary objective is to help individuals regain their ability to cope with their immediate
problems. Emphasis is placed in five areas. Complete the following list of objectives in
suicide crisis intervention: (pp. 262-263)

a. Maintaining contact with the person for one to six contacts
b.
c.
d.
e. Help the person see that the present distress will not be endless

69. Describe the two types of people who come to a suicide prevention center, and indicate the
treatment the two types should receive. (p. 263)

◊ CRITICAL THINKING ABOUT DIFFICULT TOPICS

1. The text states that "many clinicians feel that cyclothymia is but a milder variant of bipolar
disorder, and the evidence for this view has in recent years become quite compelling" (p.
220). This finding that there are milder versions of traditional diagnostic categories is quite
common. What does it imply for the categorical approach to diagnosis, in which the disorder
is viewed as either present or absent?

2. As in earlier chapters, the text indicates that psychosocial stressors "may cause long-term changes in brain functioning" (p. 231). At the same time, person characteristics in the form of distorted cognitions (negative views of self and the world) may cause individuals to perceive the environment to be more stressful than it objectively is (pp. 234-235). Given that environmental events can produce long-term changes in brain functioning and that person characteristics, quite possibly influenced by individual differences in brain functioning, can alter the effects of the environment, how can researchers identify the independent contributions of biological and psychosocial influences in the etiology of psychopathology?

3. A number of psychiatrists advocate the very long-term use of anti-anxiety drugs to correct what they view as a "chemical imbalance" and the recent popularity of the antidepressant drug Prozac has similarly raised questions about the appropriateness and ethics of "prescribing drugs to essentially healthy people because the drugs make them feel more energetic, outgoing, and productive" (p. 252). Consider for yourself under what conditions it would be legitimate to prescribe a psychoactive drug (such as an anxiolytic or an antidepressant) for many years. In reaching an answer, think about the following questions: (a) why is it wrong for an alcoholic to drink alcohol continuously; (b) does your answer depend on whether there are negative "side effects" of the drugs; (c) would it matter whether the drug was obtained "on the street" or via prescription by a physician, (d) is a person on medication fully responsible for what they do, or is there in some sense "diminished capacity" or altered judgment (e.g., it is common for a person who has been drinking to blame the alcoholic state for inadequate or inappropriate behavior), and (e) is the resistance to decriminalizing (legalizing) drugs of abuse based on an assumption that they have serious negative effects or on some other reason?

4. In the pharmacological treatment of depression, the text says that "discontinuing the drugs when symptoms have remitted may result in relapse--probably because the underlying depressive episode is still present and only its symptomatic expression has been suppressed" (p. 252). This statement reflects a typical view of pharmacological treatment of psychiatric disorders: symptoms are treated but the underlying "episode" is not eliminated, and the drug is not expected to reduce the risk of future episodes once it is discontinued (i.e., there is no carry-over benefit of having had the drug in the past). Do you think about psychological treatments in the same way, or do you expect them to have a long-term benefit? How do you conceptualize the processes involved in psychotherapy and how would these relate to continued benefits after therapy is discontinued? For example, you might think of psychotherapy as providing only emotional and moral support that ameliorates a current state of demoralization but does not last beyond active treatment. Alternatively, you might think of psychotherapy as learning more adaptive ways of dealing with problems, which should have benefits in dealing with future problems even though therapy has been discontinued. How does the three year

study by Frank et al. (p. 255) of once per month "maintenance" IPT treatments for prevention of depression fit with your way of thinking about psychological treatments?

5. Why is the DSM assumption that disorders reside exclusively "within" individuals inadequate to conceptualize the processes involved in the relationships among depression, marital distress, and familial violence? (Highlight 6.3, pp. 244-245). If this criticism is valid, how broadly does it apply? In other words, how many disorders involve complex etiologies that do not entirely reside "within" the individual?

6. Your text does an excellent job of discussing the ethical issues involved in the concept of the "right to suicide" (pp. 264-265). If you are like many people who feel some sympathy for the desire to commit suicide in the case of terminal debilitating and painful illnesses, think through your own position with respect to who should be involved in such a decision and what restrictions you would place on the right to suicide. What about a young person who is obviously depressed over some recent perceived failure or rejection? What about a person recently diagnosed as having Alzheimer's (a severe form of dementia) or schizophrenia (a disabling and *often* chronic psychotic disorder), or a person who has become paralyzed from the waist down? Try to articulate the concepts involved in granting or denying the right to suicide in each case.

◊ CHAPTER 6 QUIZ

Circle the best of the four answers provided and check them according to answers provided at the back of this study guide. Be sure you understand why each answer is correct.

1. The lifetime prevalence of major depression among men is 13%. Among women it is: (p. 212)
   a. 4%.
   b. 14%.
   c. 21%.
   d. 27%.

2. Which of the following is *not* one of Bowlby's four phases of response to the loss of a spouse or close family member? (p. 213)
   a. numbing and disbelief
   b. denial and rejection of the dead person
   c. disorganization and despair
   d. some level of reorganization

3. A disorder that involves mood swings between subclinical levels of depression and mania is: (p. 219)
   a. bipolar disorder.
   b. manic depression.
   c. dysthymic disorder.
   d. cyclothymic disorder.

4. Bipolar mood disorder is distinguished from major depression by: (p. 220)
   a. at least one episode of mania.
   b. disturbance of circadian rhythms.
   c. evidence of earlier cyclothymia.
   d. evidence of earlier dysthymia.

5. All of the following are symptoms of the manic phase of bipolar mood disorder *except*: (p. 221)
   a. notable increase in activity.
   b. euphoria.
   c. high levels of verbal output.
   d. deflated self-esteem.

6. In the original monoamine hypothesis, depression was attributed to: (p. 225)
   a. an increase in norepinephrine and/or dopamine.
   b. an increase in acetylcholine.
   c. a depletion of norepinephrine and/or serotonin.
   d. a depletion of acetylcholine and/or GABA.

7. Behaviorists such as Ferster and Lewinsohn assert that depression results when: (p. 233)
   a. angry responses are inhibited by aversive conditioning.
   b. conditioned grief responses are reactivated.
   c. negative reinforcers overwhelm positive reinforcers.
   d. response contingent positive reinforcement is not available.

8. The original learned helplessness theory refers to the depressed patient's perception that: (p. 237)
   a. accustomed reinforcement is no longer forthcoming.
   b. there is no control over aversive events.
   c. reinforcement is inadequate.
   d. the world is a negative place.

9. All of the following have been suggested as biological causes of bipolar affective disorder *except*: (pp. 231-233)
   a. abnormalities of the hypothalamic-pituitary-thyroid axis.
   b. genetic factors.
   c. levels of biogenic amines.
   d. acetylcholine depletion.

10. While lithium therapy is routinely used in the treatment of manic episodes, it is believed that it is effective in treating depression only when: (pp. 252-253)
   a. electroconvulsive therapy has failed.
   b. the disorder is bipolar in nature.
   c. the disorder is melancholic in nature.
   d. used in tandem with psychedelic drugs.

11. In the NIMH multisite study, which of the following treatments has proven most effective in the treatment of milder cases of major depression? (p. 255)
   a. antidepressant drug treatment
   b. Beck's cognitive-behavioral approach
   c. interpersonal therapy
   d. all of the above are equally effective

12. Even without formal therapy, the great majority of manic and depressed patients recover from a given episode within less than: (p. 255)
   a. two weeks.   c. one year
   b. one month   d. two years

13. In suicides associated with depression, most often suicide is committed during the _____ phase of a depressive episode. (p. 256)
   a. early onset   c. peak of depression
   b. late onset   d. recovery

14. A recent review of studies interviewing friends and relatives of people who committed suicide found that ____% had communicated their suicidal intent in very clear and specific terms, and another ____% had communicated a wish to die or a preoccupation with death. (p. 261)
   a. 40, 30   c. 15, 25
   b. 25, 15   d. 10, 20

| Chapter 7
| *Somatoform and Dissociative Disorders*

◊ OVERVIEW

This chapter contains a detailed description of the clinical picture, causal pattern, and treatment of somatoform and dissociative disorders. In the somatoform disorders the central presenting problem is physical complaints or physical disabilities in the absence of any physical pathology, presumably reflecting underlying psychological difficulties. In the dissociative disorders the central problem is a failure of certain aspects of memory due to an active process of dissociation, such as in dissociative amnesia in which individuals cannot remember their names, do not know how old they are or where they live, etc. According to the text, both types of disorders appear to be ways of avoiding psychological stress while denying personal responsibility for doing so. There are suggestions, as well, that both may be associated with traumatic childhood experiences. Whereas our personal experience with anxiety and depression in everyday life aids our understanding of the extreme deviations of these emotions discussed in the last two chapters, the disorders examined in this chapter will likely seem less familiar and less readily grasped as exaggerated forms of everyday psychological phenomena.

◊ CHAPTER OUTLINE

I. Somatoform Disorders
    A. Somatization Disorder
    B. Hypochondriasis
        1. Typical Features
        2. Major Characteristics
        3. More Than Meets the Eye?
    C. Pain Disorder
        1. Clinical Picture
        2. The Subjectivity of Pain
    D. Conversion Disorder

After studying this chapter, you should be able to:

1. Describe the major manifestations of somatoform disorders. (pp. 268-278)

2. List the primary presenting symptoms of somatization disorder and hypochondriasis and note the similarities of and differences between these closely related disorders. (pp. 268-271)

3. Explain what is meant by a pain disorder. Discuss the difficulties of determining that pain is of psychological rather than of physical origin and of reliably assessing an entirely subjective phenomenon. (pp. 271-273)

4. Characterize the symptoms of conversion disorder, trace the history of the concept of "conversion," and describe the likely cause and chain of events in the development of a conversion disorder. (pp. 273-278)

5. Discuss the etiological contributions of biological, psychosocial, and sociocultural factors to the somatoform disorders. (pp. 278-279)

6. Compare and contrast the treatments for the somatoform disorders. What is known regarding their effectiveness, as compared to no treatment at all? (pp. 279-280)

7. Compare the major features of dissociative amnesia and fugue, dissociative identity disorder, and depersonalization disorder. (pp. 280-286)

8. Discuss the causal factors that contribute to the dissociative disorders, and note the critical difficulty caused by the fallibility of memory in determining the contribution of childhood abuse to these disorders. (pp. 286-289)

9. Describe the most appropriate treatments for the dissociative disorders, as well as the limitations of biological and psychological treatments. (pp. 289-290)

10. Describe the conflict between the conflict between the "believers" and the "disbelievers" of the Dissociative Identity Disorder (DID) concept and the related issue of childhood abuse - especially childhood sexual abuse - as a major causal factor. (pp. 290-292)

◊ TERMS YOU SHOULD KNOW

somatoform disorder (pp. 268-280)

dissociative disorder (pp. 268, 280-292)

dissociation (pp. 268, 280)

somatization disorder (p. 268)

hypochondriasis (pp. 269-271)

malingering (pp. 270, 276)

pain disorder (pp. 271-273)

conversion disorder (pp. 273-278)

hysteria (p. 273)

pseudoneurological symptoms (p. 273)

conversion hysteria (p. 273)

secondary gain (p. 274)

analgesia (p. 274)

paresthesia (p. 274)

anesthesia (p. 274)

paralysis conversion reactions (p. 275)

tremors vs. *tics* (p. 275)

astasia-abasia (p. 275)

aphonia (p. 275)

mutism (p. 275)

la belle indifference (p. 276)

factitious disorder (p. 276)

mass hysteria (p. 277)

alexithymia (p. 279)

neurasthenia (p. 279)

automatisms (p. 279)

multitasking (p. 279)

implicit memory and *implicit perception* (p. 280)

amnesia (p. 280)

psychogenic or dissociative amnesia (p. 280)

fugue state (p. 281)

dissociative identity disorder (pp. 282-292)

multiple personality (pp. 282, 283)

host personality (p. 282)

alter personality (pp. 283-284)

depersonalization disorder (pp. 285-286)

derealization (p. 285)

traumatic childhood abuse (p. 286)

iatrogenic (p. 286)

integration and *post-integration therapy* (pp. 289-290

stabilization (p. 290)

false memories (pp. 290-292)

◊ NAMES YOU SHOULD KNOW

J. Kihlstrom

A. Iezzi

H. E. Adams

C. A. Ross

K. Pope

◊ CONCEPTS TO MASTER

---

1. Compare and contrast somatization disorder with hypochondriasis. (pp. 268-271)

2. Explain why hypochondriasis may be viewed as a certain type of interpersonal communication. (p. 271)

3. Describe the clinical features of pain disorder, and explain what the authors of the text mean when they say that people with psychogenic pain disorders may adopt an invalid life style. (pp. 271-273)

4. Describe the major manifestations of a conversion disorder, and describe some sensory, motor, and visceral symptoms that often appear. (pp. 273-276)

5. What are the four criteria that help to distinguish between conversion disorders and organic disturbances? (p. 276)

6. How can you distinguish a person with conversion symptoms from a *malingerer*, that is, a person who is consciously faking an illness? (pp. 276-277)

7. Explain the psychosocial contributions of *neuroticism, childhood abuse*, and *alexithymia* to somatoform disorders. (pp. 278-279)

8. Describe the similarities and differences in the psychological functions of somatoform disorders and dissociative disorders. (p. 280)

9. List and describe four types of psychogenic amnesia, and explain why fugue is considered in the same section. (pp. 280-282)

10. Explain in what way dissociative amnesia and conversion symptoms are similar. (pp. 281-282)

11. Describe the symptoms of dissociative identity disorder (formerly multiple personality disorder), and explain the complexity of determining whether some may be considered genuine and others fraudulent. (pp. 282-285)

12. Explain the nature of alter identities, and list some common alter "roles." (pp. 283-284)

13. Why was the diagnosis of "multiple personality disorder" abandoned for the diagnosis of "dissociative identity disorder?" (p. 283)

14. Review the evidence on the conflict regarding to what extent dissociative identity disorder (DID) is "real." What view do the text's authors hold? (pp. 284-285; 290-292)

15. Describe the symptoms of depersonalization disorder, and note the diagnostic problem that arises because feelings of depersonalization sometimes occur with personality deterioration. (pp. 285-286)

16. List and explain Ross's four causal pathways for DID. (p. 286)

17. Describe Kluft's (1993) three-stage consensus model for the treatment of DID. (p. 290)

◊ STUDY QUESTIONS

Somatoform disorders

1. Sincere somatic symptoms that are thought to represent an expression of psychological difficulties and for which no organic basis can be found are referred to as _____. (p. 268)

2. Complete the following list of the four distinct somatoform patterns covered in the text: (p. 268)
   a. Somatization disorder
   b. Hypochondriasis
   c.
   d.

Somatization disorder

3. This disorder is characterized by multiple complaints of physical ailments over a long period, beginning before age _____, that cannot be attributed to physical disorder, illness, or injury. (p. 268)

4. In making a diagnosis of somatization disorder, the diagnostician need not be convinced that the claimed illnesses actually existed in a patient's background history; the _____ _____ is sufficient. (p. 268)

Hypochondriasis

5. A hypochondriac's visit to the doctor has been humorously called an "organ recital." Describe the characteristic behavior of such individuals. (p. 270)

6. Describe the typical attitude among hypochondriacal patients toward their illnesses. (p. 270)

7. The authors believe that hypochondriasis can be viewed as an interpersonal strategy which results when an individual has learned to view illness as way to obtain special consideration and avoid responsibility. Complete the following statements typical of hypochondriacal adults: (p. 271)

   a. I deserve more of your attention and concern.
   b.

Pain disorder

8. In approaching the phenomenon of pain, it is important to underscore that it is *always* a subjective experience; pain perceived or experienced does not exist in a perfect correlation with _____ or _____. This partial independence of _____ and psychological experience evidently makes it possible to treat real physical pain _____. (p. 270)

9. Pain is also always _____. We have no way of gauging with certainty the actual extent of a patient's pain. However, simply because it is not possible to assess pain with pinpoint accuracy, this does not justify the conclusion that a patient is _____ or _____ his or her pain. (p. 270)

Conversion disorder

10. Freud used the term conversion hysteria because he believed that the symptoms were an expression of repressed sexual energy that was converted into a bodily disturbance. This view is no longer accepted. Rather, the physical symptoms are now viewed as serving a defensive function, enabling the individual to _____ without having to _____. (pp. 273-274)

11. The term _____ _____ is used to refer to any "external" circumstances such as attention from loved ones or financial compensation that would tend to reinforce the maintenance of disability. (p. 274)

12. Compared to the higher incidences in the past, how frequent are conversion disorders today? (p. 274)

13. What is the reason for this change in frequency of conversion disorders? (p. 274)

14. Ironside and Batchelor studied hysterical visual symptoms among airmen in World War II. They found that the symptoms of each airman were closely related to his _____. (p. 275)

15. Hysterical motor symptoms such as paralysis are usually confined to a single limb. True or False (p. 275)

16. Mutism is one of the two most common speech-related conversion disorders. True or False (p. 275)

17. Place the following events in the development of a conversion disorder in the proper causal sequence: (a) Under continued stress, the symptoms of illness appear; (b) a desire to escape an unpleasant situation; (c) a wish to be sick to avoid the situation. (p. 278)
    First   _____
    Second   _____
    Third   _____

18. What determines the particular symptoms the person prone to conversion disorder will develop? (p. 278)

19. Can a conversion reaction occur after an accident in which the victim hopes to obtain compensation? (p. 278)

Causal factors in somatoform disorders

20. Bishop, Mobley, and Farr (1978) reported the observation that somatoform disorders involving _____ _____ and _____ symptoms showed a pronounced tendency to be located on the _____ side of the body. (p. 278)

21. Cultures in which frank expression of emotional distress is unacceptable would also be expected to have a lower prevalence of somatoform disorders. True or False. (p. 279)

Treatment and outcomes in somatoform disorders

22. In many instances, the best treatment for somatoform disorders turns out to be no treatment at all, but rather the provision of _____ _____.
With the exception of conversion disorder and pain syndromes, the prognosis for full recovery from somatoform disorders is _____ . (p. 279)

Dissociative disorders

23. Dissociative disorders, like somatoform disorders, are ways of avoiding anxiety and stress in a manner that permits the person to deny personal _____ for his or her behavior. (p. 280)

Psychogenic amnesia and fugue

24. Amnesia is partial or total inability to recall or identify past experience. If it is due to brain disorder, the amnesia usually involves an actual failure of retention. In such cases, the memories are truly lost. In _____ amnesia, the forgotten material is still there beneath the level of consciousness and can be recalled under hypnosis or narcosis. (p. 280)

25. Label the following descriptions of four forms of dissociative amnesia using the following terms: localized amnesia, selective amnesia, generalized amnesia, continuous amnesia. (pp. 280-281)

Forms of Psychogenic Amnesia	Definition
_____	In this form of amnesia, the individual forgets some but not all of what happened during a given period.
_____	In this form of amnesia, the individual remembers nothing that happened during a specific period--usually the first few hours following some traumatic event.
_____	In this form of amnesia, an individual cannot recall events beyond a certain point in the past.
_____	In this form of amnesia, the individual forgets his or her entire life history.

26. Dissociative amnesia is highly selective. What type of material is most likely to be forgotten? (p. 281)

27. In typical dissociative amnesic reactions, the types of memory that are *not* affected are: (p. 281)
    a. semantic
    b.
    c.
    d. short-term storage

Dissociative identity disorder

28. Dissociative identity disorder (DID) is rare. Until approximately the last quarter century, only about 100 cases had been described, but, oddly, the prevalence of this disorder seems to be increasing. Dissociative identity disorder is a dramatic dissociative pattern, usually due to stress,   in   which   the   individual   manifests   two   or   more   complete _____ _____. (p. 282)

29. Alters are usually strikingly similar to the host or primary personality. True or False. (p. 282)

30. In two substantial series of cases, the average number of alter identities for DID was _____. (p. 283)

Depersonalization disorder

31. Depersonalization, or the loss of the sense of self, is often precipitated by _____ _____ resulting from an infectious illness, an accident, or some other traumatic event. (p. 285)

32. Simeon et al. (1997) noted a widespread occurrence of _____ _____ _____ in 30 cases of depersonalization disorder. (p. 285)

Causal factors, treatments, and outcomes in dissociative disorders

33. Evidence is building impressively in support of the notion that DID is largely a type of _____ - _____ _____ disorder. (p. 287)

34. The incidence and prevalence of dissociative disorders are strongly influenced by the degree to which such phenomena are _____ or _____ as legitimate mental disorders by the surrounding _____ _____. (p. 289)

35. Kluft offered a three-stage "consensus model" for the treatment of DID. These three stages are: (p. 290)
    a.
    b.
    c. Postintegration therapy

Recovered memories of abuse and dissociative disorders: Continuing controversy

36. In the controversy over the link between childhood sexual abuse and DID, the major opponents with seemingly irreconcilable views are the _____, who try to "treat" these conditions, and more _____ mental health professionals, who doubt the validity of both the diagnosis and its alleged source in childhood sexual abuse. (p.290)

37. What three areas of professional competence do Pope and Brown emphasize? Explain each. (p. 291)

    a.

    b.

    c.

◊ CRITICAL THINKING ABOUT DIFFICULT TOPICS

1. There are many phenomena that seem to emphasize the importance of conscious processing of psychologically important stimuli. Two examples will illustrate this point. First, in Chapter 6 you read about cognitive theories of depression from Beck (schemata, dysfunctional beliefs) and from Abramson et al. (internal, stable, and global attributions), both of which might be thought to involve conscious thought processes. Second, in theories about the emotional impact of psychological stimuli (e.g., the difference between "innocent" and "guilty" at the end of a trial or the difference between "I love you" and "I hate you" in an interpersonal context), it is obvious that there must be a process of appraisal of the meaning of the stimuli in order for them to have an emotional impact, and one might think this appraisal involves conscious processing. On the other hand, your text describes the new recognition in experimental psychology "that much (most) mental activity, much processing of information, occurs outside and independent of conscious awareness" (p. 280). How does this new perspective affect your understanding of the theories in the two examples just given? How would this new perspective affect the way in which you might conduct research on these hypotheses--e.g., if people are unaware of these attributional and appraisal processes and cannot tell you about them?

2. Freud found that a number of his female patients reported childhood sexual abuse, and initially he reported this finding as evidence that such events had actually occurred. He received a chilly reception for these reports from his professional colleagues, at least in part because high rates of childhood sexual abuse were unthinkable in the Vienna of his time, and Freud eventually concluded that most such reports by patients "were merely libidinally

inspired fantasies." Now, it is estimated that in the United States there may well be hundreds of thousands of instances of sexual abuse each year (pp. 286-287). Does this information alter your view of the validity of such reports by Freud's patients, or do you think cultural factors may make the incidence and prevalence of sexual abuse vastly higher in the U. S. today than in Freud's Vienna? Do you think there is any way Freud could have ascertained the truth of his patients' reports? If not, what does this tell you about the value of reports by patients in psychotherapy as evidence in support of any given theory?

3. There are several points of overlap within and between the somatoform and the dissociative disorders. Indeed, conversion disorder itself (which is categorized as a somatoform disorder) has been conceived as a form of "psychopathologic dissociation." If there are sound reasons to regard conversion and dissociative disorders as sharing a majority of properties, it would seem unwise to assign them to distinct categories, simply because of their somatic versus nonsomatic manifestations. Are there other reasons for this distinction? Is there similar overlap present for the other somatoform disorders and dissociative disorders? If so, then should these two categories be integrated, using the somatic versus nonsomatic variable as a subtype categorization? Justify your answer. What are the implications for treatment planning and treatment research?

◊ CHAPTER 7 QUIZ

Circle the best of the four answers provided and check them according to answers provided at the back of this study guide. Be sure you understand why each answer is correct.

1. Which of the following is characterized by multiple complaints of physical ailments over a long period that are inadequately explained by independent findings of physical illness? (p. 268)
   a. somatization disorder   c. pain disorder
   b. hypochondriasis   d. conversion disorder

2. A hidden message in the complaints of the hypochondriacal adult is: (p. 271)
   a. "I am terribly anxious about dying."
   b. "I can do things as well as you even though I'm sick."
   c. "I deserve your attention and concern."
   d. "You make me sick."

3. Aphonia is: (p. 275)
   a. inability to speak.
   b. ability to talk only in a whisper.
   c. a grotesque, disorganized walk.
   d. pseudopregnancy.

4. *La belle indifference* would be expected in cases of: (p. 276)
   a. malingering.
   b. hypochondriasis.
   c. conversion disorder.
   d. psychogenic pain disorder.

5. All of the following are part of a chain of events in the development of a conversion disorder *except*: (p. 278)
   a. a conscious plan to use illness as an escape.
   b. a desire to escape from an unpleasant situation.
   c. a fleeting wish to be sick in order to avoid the situation.
   d. the appearance of the symptoms of some physical ailment.

6. Dissociative disorders are methods in which individuals avoid stress by: (p. 280)
   a. escaping from their personal identity.
   b. projecting blame for their "sins" on others.
   c. separating themselves from significant others.
   d. withdrawing from stressful situations.

7. In _____ amnesia, the individual forgets his/her entire life history. (pp. 280-281)
   a. localized   c. generalized
   b. selective   d. continuous

8. Alter personalities would be expected in cases of: (p. 283)
   a. psychogenic pain disorder.   c. conversion disorder.
   b. hypochondriasis.   d. dissociative identity disorder.

9. The strongest evidence implicates _____ as a risk factor for dissociative disorders. (p. 286)
   a. death of a parent during childhood
   b. traumatic childhood abuse
   c. low self-esteem developed during childhood
   d. parental use of strict discipline with excessive punishment

10. Pope and Brown emphasize the importance of "intellectual competence" for therapists involved in the issues of "recovered memories" of childhood abuse. Which of the following is *not* included in the list of basic psychological processes that must be understood by the therapist? (p. 291)
    a. memory functioning.
    b. developmental theory.
    c. theories of emotional functioning.
    d. the nature and consequences of psychological trauma.

Chapter 8
Eating Disorders and Other Psychological Compromises of Physical Health

◊ OVERVIEW

As subspecialties of behavioral medicine and clinical psychology, health psychology explores the many ways that psychological factors influence medical conditions. The field has had a considerable impact on virtually the entire range of clinical medicine. One category of conditions in which health psychology's influence has been realized is the eating disorders. Chapter 8, therefore, opens with the clinical picture, etiology, and treatment of the eating disorders - anorexia nervosa and bulimia nervosa being the most common. This is followed by a discussion of the interrelationships between physical health and attitudes, lifestyle, and coping resources. Next, the chapter explores the functioning of both the autonomic nervous system and the immune system and how these are influenced by psychological factors. In essence, the degree of stress a person is experiencing influences the efficiency with which the individual resists the virus and how rapidly he or she recovers. Then, the chapter reviews specific data on the clinical picture and treatment of diseases such as essential hypertension and coronary heart disease, as well as recurrent headaches. Finally, general etiological issues and methods of treatment are considered.

◊ CHAPTER OUTLINE

I. Introduction

II. Eating Disorders
    A. Definitions and Gender Differences
    B. Clinical Picture and Diagnostic Criteria in Anorexia
    C. Clinical Picture and Diagnostic Criteria in Bulimia
    D. Distinguishing Among Diagnoses
    E. Prevalence of Eating Disorders

F. Generalized Risk and Causal Factors in Eating Disorders
   1. Self-Ideal Body Image Discordance
   2. Biological Considerations
   3. Psychopathologic Vulnerability
   4. Dysfunctional Cognitive Styles
G. Specific Risk and Causal Factors in Anorexia and Bulimia Nervosa
   1. Personality Characteristics
   2. Family Patterns
H. Treatment of Eating Disorders
   1. Treatment of Anorexia Nervosa
   2. Treatment of Bulimia Nervosa
   3. Treatment of Binge-Eating Disorder

III. General Psychological Factors in Health and Disease
A. Health, Attitudes, and Coping Resources
   1. The Two Faces of Optimism
   2. Negative Emotions and Physical Illness
   3. Psychological Factors in Health and Healing
   4. Fight or Flight and Nowhere to Go
B. Psychosocial Factors and the Immune System
   1. Elements of the Human Immune System
   2. Psychosocial Compromise of the Immune Response
   3. Psychoneuroimmunology
      a) Other Neurochemicals and Immune Functions
      b) Conditioned Immunosuppression
      c) Immune Feedback
   4. Stressor Toxicity
C. Lifestyle as a Factor in Health Maintenance

IV. Psychological Factors and Cardiovascular Disease
A. Essential Hypertension
   1. Hypertension and African-Americans
   2. Anger and Hypertension
B. Coronary Heart Disease and the Type A Behavior Pattern
   1. Characteristics of Type A Personalities
   2. Research on Type A and CHD

V. General Causal Factors in Physical Disease
    A. Biological Factors
        1. Genetic Factors
        2. Psychosocial Interaction
        3. Disruption of Physiological Equilibrium
    B. Psychosocial Factors
        1. Personality Characteristics
        2. Interpersonal Relationships as Sources of Protection
        3. The Learning of Illnesses
    C. Sociocultural Factors

VI. Treatments and Outcomes
    A. Biological Measures
    B. Psychosocial Measures
        1. Traditional Psychotherapy
        2. Biofeedback
        3. Behavior Therapy
        4. Cognitive-Behavioral Therapy
    C. Sociocultural Measures

VII. Unresolved Issues: Medical Education and Practice

VIII. Summary

◊ LEARNING OBJECTIVES

After studying this chapter, you should be able to:

1. Describe the field of behavioral medicine and the way in which psychological factors in physical medicine are handled in DSM-IV. (pp. 294-295)

2. Compare and contrast the clinical pictures and diagnostic criteria for each of the following: a) anorexia nervosa (AN), b) bulimia nervosa (BN), c) binge eating disorder (BED), and d) eating disorders, not otherwise specified (ED-NOS). List some of the serious conditions that often result. (pp. 296-298)

3. List several general and specific risk factors for the eating disorders, and discuss possible mechanisms by which these factors might lead to the development of these disorders. (pp. 301-307)

4. Describe the typical personality patterns and cognitive styles of anorexic and bulimic patients. (pp. 304-305)

5. Describe the family dynamics typical of patients with anorexia and bulimia, and discuss how these family patterns might influence the development and maintenance of the eating disorders. (pp. 305-307)

6. Discuss the most effective treatment approach to date for the eating disorders, noting the importance of dietary stabilization prior to psychological intervention. (p. 307-308)

7. Review evidence that the following factors influence the risk of physical illnesses:
   - Health, attitudes and coping resources. (p. 309-311)
   - Cannon's fight/flight response and chronic overarousal of the autonomic nervous system. (p. 310)
   - Effects of psychological stress and depressed mood on the immune system. (pp. 312-316)
   - Various habits and aspects of life-style. (p. 314)

8. Characterize the changes in blood flow that increase blood pressure, define essential hypertension and its consequences, and review the psychological contributors to its development. (p. 316)

9. Describe the three chief clinical manifestations of coronary heart disease and evaluate the evidence for an etiological contribution of Type A personality. (pp. 316-320)

10. Distinguish among migraine, cluster, and tension headaches and both theories of etiology and approaches to treatment. (Highlight 8.4)

11. Explain the "problem of specificity" in psychogenic illness and summarize the biological, psychosocial, and sociocultural factors contributing to these illnesses. (pp. 321-327)

12. Characterize the biological, psychosocial, and sociocultural approaches to treatment of psychogenic illness, as well as sociocultural approaches aimed at prevention. (pp. 325-328)

◊ TERMS YOU SHOULD KNOW

behavioral medicine (p. 294)

psychogenic illnesses (p. 294)

health psychology (p. 294)

eating disorders (p. 295; 296-309)

anorexia nervosa (pp. 296-297; 298-309)

bulimia nervosa (pp. 297-298; 298-309)

binge/purge pattern (p. 298)

Binge Eating Disorder (BED) (pp. 298, 308)

set-point theory (p. 303)

Structural Analysis of Social Behavior (SASB) (p. 306)

atherosclerosis (p. 308)

Type A (p. 316)

placebo effect (p. 310)

flight or fight response (p. 310)

alarm reaction (p. 310)

autonomic nervous system arousal (pp. 310)

immune system (p. 311)

humoral branch (of the immune system) (p. 311)

cellular branch (of the immune system) (p. 311)

B-cells, or humoral immune functioning (p. 311; Figure 8.4, p. 312)

T-cells, or cellular immune functioning (p. 311; Figure 8.4, p. 312)

antigens (p. 311; Figure 8.4, p. 312)

natural killer cells (p. 311)

macrophages (p. 311; Figure 8.4, p. 312)

antibodies (Figure 8.4, p. 311)

HIV-1 (p. 311)

immunocompetence (p. 312)

psychoneuroimmunology (p. 312)

hypothalamus-pituitary-adrenocortical (HPA) *axis* (p. 313)

immunosuppression (p. 313)

essential hypertension (pp. 315-316)

suppressed rage hypothesis (p. 316)

coronary heart disease (CHD) (pp. 316-321)

angina pectoris (p. 317; Highlight 8.2)

myocardial infarction (p. 317, Highlight 8.2)

plaque (p. 316)

Type A behavior pattern (p. 316)

Type B behavior pattern (p. 316)

cardiopulmonary resuscitation (CPR) (Highlight 8.2, p. 317)

Western Collaborative Group Study (p. 320)

Framingham Heart Study (pp. 320-321; Figure 8.5, p. 321)

migraine headache (Highlight 8.4, p. 322)

classic migraine vs. *common migraine* (Highlight 8.4, p. 322)

aura (Highlight 8.4, p. 322)

cluster headaches (Highlight 8.3, p. 322)

simple tension headaches (Highlight 8.4, p. 323)

biofeedback (Highlight 8.4, pp. 323, 328)

hardiness (p. 325)

secondary gains (p. 326)

"managed care" medicine (p. 330)

Walter Cannon

Meyer Friedman and Ray Rosenman

◊ CONCEPTS TO MASTER

1. List the six problem areas targeted by the behavioral medicine approach, and define the relationship between behavioral medicine and health psychology. (pp. 294-295)

2. Distinguish between the Restricting versus the Binge eating/Purging subtypes of anorexia nervosa, and characterize the behavioral patterns of the two subtypes. (pp. 296-297)

3. Explain the difficulty in accurate diagnosis of the eating disorders, noting problems of overlap, heterogeneous and "grab-bag" categories, and comorbidity. (pp. 298-299)

4. Discuss the epidemiology of the eating disorders. What are the overall prevalence rates for AN and BN? How do these estimates vary according to demographic groups, such as socioeconomic status, gender, sexual orientation, and nationality? (pp. 299-301)

5. List several ways that people become susceptible to the development of deviant and self-defeating reactions that apply to eating disorders. (pp. 301-307)

6. Explain the dysfunctional cognitive styles and personality antecedents of AN and BN patients. (pp. 304-305)

7. How do researchers describe the typical parents of pre-AN patients, including how the daughter "rebels?" Define the "hostile-control" quality of parents' interactions with their bulimic daughters. How do AN patients typically describe their own parents? What caution was stressed regarding causal inferences from these observations? (pp. 305-307)

8. How does a person's attitude and outlook on life affect health maintenance and deterioration? Cite evidence from several studies. (pp. 308-310)

9. Describe how the presence of optimism can either help or hinder one's ability to cope with illness, and discuss how a *deficit* in optimism affects health outcomes. (pp. 308-309)

10. What physiological mechanisms are involved in autonomic nervous system arousal? (pp. 310-311)

11. List and describe the component parts of the two main branches (humoral and cellular) of the immune system, and explain the functions of each of the component parts. (pp. 311; Figure 8.4, p. 312)

12. Summarize the research findings that point to psychosocial effects on the immune system, and describe the recent evidence that the relationship between stress and compromised immune function is causal. (pp. 312-313)

13. Explain the field of psychoneuroimmunology and summarize the major evidence supporting its major premise. (pp. 312-313)

14. List several aspects of the way we live that may produce severe physical problems, and explain why healthy individuals find it difficult to change their habits. (p. 314)

15. Define *essential hypertension*, list some physical diseases that it causes, and explain McClelland's variation of the suppressed-rage hypothesis about the cause of essential hypertension. (pp. 315-316)

16. Describe the chief clinical manifestations of coronary heart disease, and list several potential risk factors for CHD. (p. 316)

17. What is meant by the Type A personality? Summarize the evidence linking it to coronary heart disease (CHD). (pp. 316-319; Highlight 8.2, p. 317)

18. Differentiate between the physical causes of migraine and simple tension headaches, and summarize the research findings more strongly implicating psychosocial factors in tension headaches. (Highlight 8.4, p. 322-323)

19. Describe the psychological treatments for tension headaches. (Highlight 8.4, p. 323)

20. Define the "problem of specificity" in the etiology of psychogenic illnesses. (p. 322)

21. Discuss the complexities of differentiating the genetic contributions to diseases of psychogenic origins, as well as potential discoveries via genetic mapping. (pp. 323-324)

22. Liljefors and Rahe's (1970) classic study led to an important separation of genetic and psychological influences. Discuss the study and its theoretical importance. (p. 324)

23. Given the available research, what personality characteristics appear to be associated with the development of: disease resistance and disease progression? (pp. 325-326)

24. What theoretical explanation for the high rate of heart disease in industrialized societies is offered in the book, *The Broken Heart*? (p. 326)

25. How important is a good social support system to good health maintenance? Cite relevant research supporting your answer. (p. 326)

26. Compare and contrast the effectiveness of the various psychosocial approaches to treating psychogenic disorders. (pp. 328-329)

27. Indicate the major objectives of sociocultural efforts to reduce psychogenic diseases. (pp. 329-330)

28. List two external factors that appear to force physicians to become technicians who administer to objectified patients. (p. 330)

◊ STUDY QUESTIONS

Introduction

1. Although an illness may be primarily physical or primarily psychological, it is always a disorder of the whole person, not just of the body or the psyche. The interdisciplinary approach to treatment of physical disorders thought to have psychosocial factors as major aspects of their causal patterns and maintenance is known as _____. Psychologists who are interested in psychological factors that contribute to the diagnosis, treatment, and prevention of physical dysfunction specialize in _____. (p. 294)

2. In DSM-IV, when a "general medical condition" is coded on Axis III, Axis I provides a major category called Psychological Factors Affecting Medical Condition. The suspected contributing factors are specified under six subcategories: (p. 295)
      a. mental disorder
      b.
      c.
      d.
      e.
      f. other/unspecified

3. The central features of AN are: a) intense fear of _____ coupled with refusal to maintain adequate _____, usually associated with an obviously erroneous complaint of being _____; b) loss of original body weight at least to a level ____% of that expected on the basis of height/weight norms; c) disturbance of _____ or undue influence of the latter in determining self-evaluation; d) absence of at least three consecutive menstrual periods. List several methods of preventing weight gain used by bulimics. What problems are typically associated with purging types of BN? (pp. 296-297; pp. 297-298)

4. The point prevalence of the full syndromes among adolescent and young adult U.S. women are estimated to be between _____% and ____% for anorexia nervosa, and between ____% and ___% for bulimia. (p. 300)

5. According to Garner (1997), how do changes in average body weight of American young women compare with changes in the average weight of cultural icons of attractiveness? (p. 302)

6. What is *set-point theory*, and how is it relevant to eating disorders? (p. 303)

7. Nearly all authorities agree that , like AN patients, a large proportion of BN patients show a long-standing pattern of _____ which appears to manifest itself in widespread _____, particularly if the person perceives herself as overweight. _____ may be another shared characteristic of both AN- and BN- disposed patients. (p. 305)

8. Fairburn et al.'s (1997) study indicated that bulimic women were statistically differentiated from the general psychiatric control group (and from the normal one on such risk factor items as: (p. 306)

a. high _____ _____

b. other family members _____

c. degree of critical comment from other family members about _____, _____, or _____.

9. Humphrey (1989) found that parents of anorexics communicated with their daughters in abnormally complicated ways, providing _____ that at once communicated both _____ and disregard of their daughter's attempts to express themselves. (p. 306)

10. Anorexics and bulimics have a common problem of being deeply but ambivalently involved with their parents in power struggles concerning their _____ and _____. (p. 307)

11. What are the treatments of choice for anorexia, bulimia, and binge eating disorder? Explain (pp. 307-308)

Health, attitudes, and coping resources

12. Why are some surgeons reluctant to operate unless the patient has a reasonably optimistic attitude about the outcome? (p. 308)

13. What difference might it make if a cancer patient, for example, believed in his or her doctor, had faith in the treatment, and had an overall positive mental outlook compared to a patient who had lost hope? (pp. 308-310)

Autonomic excess and tissue damage

14. Describe how the adaptivity of autonomic nervous system arousal, although adaptive among lower animals, has become obsolete to a degree among human beings. (p. 310)

Psychosocial factors and the immune system

15. The organism has been invaded by an antigen--that is, a substance recognized as foreign. Once this foreign substance has been detected, B- and T-cells become activated and _____, deploying the various forms of counterattack mediated by each type of cell. (p. 311; Figure 8.4, p. 312)

16. B-cells, which are formed in the _____, perform their defensive function by producing antibodies that circulate in the blood _____. B-cell functioning is involved chiefly with protection against the more common varieties of _____ infection. (p. 311; Figure 8.4, p. 312)

17. T-cells mediate immune reactions that, while slower, are far more _____ and _____ in character. These cells mainly generate an attack that is _____ to a given invading antigen. (p. 311; Figure 8.4, p. 312)

18. The three types of immune reactions mediated by T-cells are: (p. 311)

    a) _____ of certain types of antigens, especially nonbacterial ones.

    b) _____ and in certain instances _____ of the other antibody-based division of the defense system.

    c) _____ of the immune response when danger subsides.

19. Psychosocial factors were originally thought to play little or no role in the pervasive immune breakdown characteristic of AIDS (HIV-1). More recent research suggests that behavioral interventions, such as _____, had positive psychological and _____ effects among groups of uninfected high-risk and early-stage infected gay men. (p. 311)

20. More recently, Kemeny and colleagues presented evidence that a _____ mood was associated with enhanced HIV-1 activity among infected gay men, confirming in this group the more general point that psychological _____ compromises _____. (p. 311)

21. Many stressors such as sleep deprivation, marathon running, space flight, and death of a spouse have been shown to be associated with diminished _____ _____. Until recently, researchers were convinced that the _____ _____ axis was the pathway by which stress affected the immune response. However, recent research has turned up a number of competing paths. We now know that a number of other hormones, including growth hormone, _____, and _____, respond to stress and also affect immune competence. The same is true of a variety of neurochemicals, including _____. There may even be direct neural control of the secretion of immunologic agents, as suggested by the discovery of nerve endings in the _____, _____, and _____ _____. (pp. 312-313)

22. In a surprising result, it was found that immunosuppression can be _____ _____--that is, it can come to be elicited as an acquired response to previously neutral stimuli. (p. 313)

23. Often stress appears to speed up the _____ or increase the _____ of a disorder, and to interfere with the body's _____ _____ and other homeostatic repair functions. (pp. 313-314)

Lifestyle as a factor in health maintenance

24. Numerous aspects of the way we live significantly affect the risk of developing physical illnesses. These include: (p. 314)

   a. _____
   b. lack of _____
   c. _____
   d. excessive _____ and _____ use
   e. constantly facing high-stress situations
   f. ineffective ways of dealing with day-to-day problems

25. Even in cases when the evidence for causation is extremely strong, it is difficult for many people to change their life-styles to reduce their risk of disease--an incentive that may seem _____ for healthy people. (p. 314)

Essential hypertension

26. What changes in blood distribution take place when an individual is subjected to stress? (p. 315)

27. Blood pressure below 140/90 is considered _____; blood pressure above 160/100 is considered unambiguously high. The first number in a blood pressure reading is the _____ pressure (occurring when the heart contracts); the second is the _____ pressure (or between-beat pressure). (p. 315)

28. Hypertension is estimated to afflict more than _____ Americans, and it is a major predisposing factor for strokes and cardiovascular disease. The incidence among blacks is about _____ high as among whites. (p. 315)

29. Why are so many people unaware that they have hypertension? (p. 315)

30. The "suppressed rage" hypothesis of hypertension suggests that hypertensives often must keep their anger to themselves and outwardly appear submissive and controlled. McClelland has developed a variant of the suppressed rage hypothesis that attributes hypertension to the need to inhibit the expression of power motives. However, the text suggests the more general concept that the common factor is the _____ of strong _____ to perform acts poorly tolerated by society. (p. 316)

Coronary heart disease and the "Type A" behavior pattern

31. Coronary heart disease (CHD) is the nation's number one killer. It is a potentially lethal blockage of the arteries supplying blood to the heart muscle (called the myocardium). The clinical picture of CHD includes (1) _____, which is severe chest pain and signals that insufficient blood is getting to the heart muscle; (2) _____, which is complete blockage of a section of the blood supply to the heart and leads to death of heart muscle tissue; and (3) disturbance of the heart's _____ conduction consequent to arterial blockage, resulting in interruption or stoppage of pumping action and leading to sudden death. (p. 316)

32. The Type A behavior pattern as conceptualized by Friedman and Rosenman is characterized by excessive competitive drive, time urgency, and hostility manifested in accelerated speech and motor activity. Type B behavior is the absence of Type A characteristics. Respond true or false to the following questions about Type A and Type B behaviors. (pp. 316, 320-321)

    a. The alternative approaches to measuring Type A behavior produce consistent results, which suggests widespread agreement on the definition of this concept. True or False

    b. Not all components of Type A behavior are equally predictive of CHD. The intense anger arousal and aggressivity/hostility component of the pattern is most correlated with coronary artery deterioration. True or False

    c. The Western Collaborative Group Study (WCGS) typed people for A-B type and followed their health for over 8 years. The strong virtue of this study is that it was retrospective. True or False

    d. In the WCGS, Type A personalities were approximately twice as likely as Type B personalities to have developed CHD by the end of the study. True or False

    e. The Framingham Heart Study is a prospective study that began in 1948. It has demonstrated that the Type A-CHD correlation holds for women as well as for men. True or False

    f. Some aspect of the Type A behavior pattern, most likely general negative affect that remains unexpressed, contributes to the development of potentially lethal CHD. True or False

33. What is the primary difference between "workaholics" and Type A personalities? (p. 320)

34. What is the cause of atherosclerosis? (Highlight 8.2, p. 319)

35. List the warning signs of heart attack. (Highlight 8.2, p. 317)

    a.

    b.

    c.

    d.

Recurrent headaches

36. More than _____ million Americans suffer from tension or migraine headaches. Among college students, one study reported that _____ percent reported headaches at least once or twice a week. (Highlight 8.4, p. 322)

37. The typical migraine occurs in two phases. Complete the following description of the physiological changes associated with each stage of migraine headache. (Highlight 8.4, p. 322)
   a. First phase: alterations in the brain's electrical activity--may cause victims to experience a(n) _____.
   b. Second phase:

38. Do stressors play an important role in cluster headaches? (Highlight 8.4, p. 322)

39. Are the physiological changes that lead to tension headaches indisputably different from the changes that lead to migraine headaches? (Highlight 8.4, p. 322)

40. At what life period do tension and migraine headaches typically begin? (Highlight 8.4, p. 322)

41. According to the study by Andrasik and colleagues, are tension or migraine headaches more indicative of psychological problems? (Highlight 8.4, p. 322)

Psychogenic physical disease: Biological factors

42. The three general biological causal factors involved in all disease are genetic factors, differences in _____ reactivity and _____ weakness, and disruption of _____ equilibrium. (pp. 322-324)

43. In Liljefors and Rahe's twin study of the role of life stress in coronary heart disease, what was the critical difference between the twins in each pair? What are the implications of their findings? (p. 324)

44. Sometimes a particular organ is especially vulnerable because of heredity, _____, or prior _____. (p. 301)

45. In the autonomic reactivity/somatic weakness theory, presumably the _____ _____ in the chain of visceral organs will be the organ affected. Thus, for example, a person who has inhereited a weak stomach will be prone to _____ _____ during anger or anxiety. (p. 301)

Psychogenic physical disease: Psychosocial factors

46. What are the three major psychosocial factors that play a prominent role in causing many diseases? (p. 325)

47. How is the incidence of illness related to the following variables:
    a. Hardiness (Hafen et al.) (p. 325)
    b. Marital problems, divorce (Bloom et al.) (p. 326)
    c. Bereavement (Stroebe & Stroebe) (p. 326))

48. A group of seriously ill breast cancer patients who had been assigned to _____ _____ (and thus developed strong, mutually supportive ties) survived on average _____ as long as a comparable group of women given only standard medical treatment. (p. 326)

49. It is hypothesized that certain physical disorders may arise through _____ _____ of symptom and behavioral patterns. (p. 326)

50. Regardless of how a physical symptom may have developed, it may be elicited by suggestion and maintained by the reinforcement provided by secondary gains. The ability of suggestion to elicit a physical symptom was demonstrated by Bleeker (1968) among asthmatics. What did this experiment involve, and how were the results interpreted? (p. 326)

Psychogenic physical disease: Sociocultural factors

51. How common are psychophysiologic illnesses among nonindustrialized peoples? (p. 327)

52. Which psychogenic illness shows large effects on prevalence of both social classes and gender in our own society? Explain(p. 327)

53. The following are the biological treatments used for psychogenic illnesses. Briefly indicate what each treatment accomplishes. (pp. 327-328)
    a. Mild tranquilizers
    b. Antidepressant medication
    c. Other drugs (e.g., nicotine-delivering skin patch)

54. In the treatment of psychosocially medicated illness, one-to-one, verbally oriented psychotherapies have been relatively ineffective. On the other hand, _____ therapy has shown promising results. (p. 328)

55. Kelley, Lumley, & Leisin (1997) found that rheumatoid arthritis patients experienced an _____ in emotional distress during the active phase of treatment (_____), but then show _____ in their medical status over follow-up. (p. 328)

56. _____ treatment for psychogenic diseases had until recently generally failed to live up to the enthusiasm it generated when first introduced some 30 years ago. Its effects rarely exceeded those that could be obtained in simpler and cheaper ways, as by providing systematic _____ training. That situation may be changing, although it is still not entirely clear that _____ is anything more than an elaborate means to teach patients to _____. There have been increasingly favorable reports in recent years regarding efficacy for _____ in the control of musculoskeletal pain. (pp. 328-329)

57. On what assumption is behavior therapy for physical disorders based? (p. 329)

58. How successful are relaxation techniques in the treatment of simple tension headaches and hypertension? (p. 329)

59. Some cognitive behavior therapists have worked to modify maladaptive behaviors such as rushing, impatience, and hostility--characteristics of Type A personalities. Others such as Kobasa (1985) have been experimenting with methods to increase _____, which is defined as the ability to withstand stressful circumstances and remain healthy in the face of them. (p. 329)

60. Sociocultural treatment measures are targeted more toward preventive efforts and are typically applied to selected populations or subcultural groups. Within these groups, efforts are made to alter certain _____ to reduce the overall level of susceptibility to a disorder. (pp. 329-330)

◊ **CRITICAL THINKING ABOUT DIFFICULT TOPICS**

1. In contrast to the disorders discussed so far in your text, there has been a much larger emphasis on the role of society and the family in the development of the eating disorders. What is the rationale behind this? Why is the emphasis less on individual causal factors, as opposed to family and sociocultural variables? In discussing your answer, note that early age of onset does not sufficiently explain this, considering that other disorders, such as phobias, begin at an early age as well.

2. As with the anxiety disorders, the depressive disorders, the somatic disorders, and the dissociative disorders, neuroticism has once again been discussed as a key personality vulnerability factor for the eating disorders   What is it about this trait that creates a susceptibility to so many psychological disorders?   Do you believe that the factor is a cause or consequence of the disorder?   Are the pathways involved the same for each of the disorders?

3. As you have seen in previous chapters, unequivocal demonstrations of the contributions of stress to psychopathology are difficult to produce. In contrast, the present chapter offers undeniable evidence of the role of stress in physical illness. What accounts for this

difference? In thinking about your answer, consider that the immune system is known to be involved in the resistance to physical illnesses and that many components of the immune system response to stress can be measured (e.g., p. 313). That is, it is possible to measure the *immediate* effects of stress on an *underlying process* (the immune response), which allows a more definitive determination of causal relationships. Can you think of any similar underlying processes for anxiety disorders and depression that could unequivocally show the causal effects of stress?

4. The methodologies of family, twin, and (more rarely) adoption studies together provide clear evidence for a role of genetic factors in psychopathology and physical illnesses. This conclusion tells us nothing, however, about *what* is inherited--leaving unanswered many of the most interesting questions. Regarding genetic contributions to psychogenic diseases, for example, your text notes the difficulty of determining whether a genetic contribution acts through "an underlying physical vulnerability for acquiring the disease in question" or "the psychological makeup of the individual and his or her stress tolerance" (p. 323). In the first case, there might be an "organ weakness," in which, for example, the cardiovascular system is prone to development of atherosclerosis (see Highlight 8.2, p. 317). In the second case, the person may be anxiety-prone or unduly sensitive to stress, as a result of which the person responds with a stress response to many minor irritations, thereby working a hardship on the cardiovascular system. Can you apply this train of thought to psychopathology? Given that we have evidence for a strong genetic contribution to schizophrenia and to bipolar affective disorder and for a moderate genetic contribution to depression and anxiety disorders, what underlying processes might be inherited?

5. To pursue the previous question further, the processes mediating a genetic influence on global behavior and functioning might be very complex. Consider two examples. First, a person's physical attractiveness has an important effect on his or her social interactions--i.e., on the way the world responds to him or her. Imagine that research first showed an important genetic contribution to the personality trait of "sociability," but that as time passed it was determined that much of the genetic effect was on the person's physical attractiveness--i.e., those who inherited physical attractiveness became more sociable. Thus, the apparent causal pathway involved a genetic effect on the person's physical attractiveness, an effect of physical attractiveness on the social environment (positive reactions, greater popularity), and an effect of a positively responsive social environment on the personality trait of sociability. Would you consider this a genetic or an environmental influence? Second, there is a substantial (estimates vary, but probably about 50%) genetic influence on IQ, and low IQ carries with it a number of disadvantages: a person with low IQ is likely to experience school failure with

subsequent occupational and economic disadvantage and may even suffer in peer relations. These disadvantages may cumulate to make the world more stressful for a person with an IQ of 75 than for a person with an IQ of 125. In view of this, when considering evidence for an effect of genetic factors on any stress-related illness or form of psychopathology, is it possible that some of the genetic effect is mediated by inheritance of lower IQ?

6. In discussing the immune system, your text states that "while efforts to relate specific stressors to specific physical diseases have not generally been successful, stress is becoming a key underlying theme in our understanding of the development and course of virtually all organic illness" (p. 287). In discussing "the problem of specificity" (p. 322) your text discusses a model that elsewhere has been called the "organ weakness" hypothesis--the hypothesis that which organ system breaks down in response to stress will depend on which organ is the "weakest" link (p. 324). For example, a person born with a weak stomach may have problems with peptic ulcers, whereas a person born with a tendency to respond to stressors with increased vasoconstriction may develop problems in the cardiovascular system. Consider three different explanations for why a person develops essential hypertension. (a) The person is exposed to an environment that specifically induces reactivity of the cardiovascular system and, therefore, works a hardship on the mechanisms regulating blood pressure. (b) The person is a blood pressure responder--i.e., when stressed the person reacts most strongly with an increase in blood pressure but normal response in other organ systems. This excessive blood pressure reactivity works a hardship on the mechanisms regulating blood pressure. (c) The person has a weakness in the mechanisms regulating blood pressure, which break down under normal levels of stress. Evidence for option (a) is difficult to find, although not altogether absent. On the whole, options (b) and (c)--the organ weakness models--seem likely to be more important. In options (b) and (c) there is a psychological contribution in the sense that the stress response is activated by psychological stimuli, but do you see any component of personal maladjustment or emotional disturbance in those models? In those models, would the likelihood of illness be increased as a result of the person's being in a particularly stressful environment or by being strongly anxiety-prone? What if you think of quantitative individual differences in the organ weakness? Would some individuals require greater stress or anxiety-proneness to produce hypertension if there is only a modest degree of "organ weakness"? Can you think of ways to apply these models to psychopathology--e.g., bipolar affective disorder and schizophrenia?

7. The text states that some of the best established risk factors are not easy to alter, "even in cases where virtual proof of causation exists" (p. 314). Why is it so difficult to change human behavior? Note the implications for the efficacy of psychological interventions. It is not that psychological factors are not important in the etiology of psychopathology and physical illness, but rather that psychological interventions must deal with resistance to change that is so strong that individuals readily risk death rather than change their habits. Does this explain the great popularity of biological treatments?

◊ CHAPTER 8 QUIZ

Circle the best of the four answers provided and check them according to answers provided at the back of this study guide. Be sure you understand why each answer is correct.

1. Health psychology deals with the diagnosis, treatment and prevention of: (p. 294)
   a. anxiety disorders.
   c. stress disorders.
   b. physical disorders.
   d. psychogenic physical disorders.

2. Which of the following is not one of the six subcategories of Psychological Factors Affecting Physical Illness on Axis I of DSM-IV? (p. 295)
   a. repressed anger
   b. personality traits or coping style
   c. mental disorder
   d. stress-related physiological response

3. Which of the following would be the best diagnosis for a person who meets the criteria for anorexia but who also has binging and purging episodes? (pp. 297-298)
   a. eating disorder not otherwise specified
   b. anorexia nervosa, binge eating/purging subtype
   c. bulimia nervosa
   d. binging and purging disorder

4. In which of the following disorders do patients appear not to overvalue thinness? (p. 298)
   a. anorexia nervosa
   b. binge eating disorder
   c. bulimia nervosa
   d. eating disorder, not otherwise specified

5. Which, according to Strober (1997), is *not* a premorbid personality trait of anorexia: (p. 305)
   a. lack of conformity and oppositional style
   b. excessive rumination and perfectionism
   c. preference for routine, order, and predictable environments
   d. high emotional reserve and cognitive inhibition

6. Which of the following is *not* a feature of typical families of anorexic patients: (p. 306)
   a. poor skills in conflict resolution
   b. overencouragement of autonomous strivings
   c. emphasis on propriety
   d. limited tolerance of psychological tension

7. The immune function is divided into two branches, which are: (p. 311)
   a. blood-related and lymph-related.
   b. glandular and nervous.
   c. humoral and cellular.
   d. red cell-mediated and white cell-mediated.

8. B-cells produce antibodies which are involved chiefly with protection against the more common varieties of: (p. 311)
   a. bacterial infection.
   b. cancerous growth.
   c. cellular dysfunction.
   d. viral infection.

9. Psychosocial factors were originally thought to play little or no role in the pervasive immune breakdown characteristic of AIDS (HIV-1). More recent research suggests that behavioral interventions, such as _____, had positive psychological and immunocompetence effects among groups of uninfected high-risk and early-stage infected gay men. (p. 311)
   a. treatment of depression
   b. aerobic exercise
   c. relaxation training
   d. group therapy

10. The finding of nerve endings in the thymus suggests that: (p. 315)
    a. the thymus is centrally involved in the General Adaptation Syndrome.
    b. the HPA interpretation is correct.
    c. there is direct neural control of immunological agents.
    d. the placebo effect is mediated by the pons.

11. Which of the following is the *least* likely cause of hypertension? (p. 315)
    a. kidney dysfunction
    b. unremitting stress
    c. excessive sodium intake
    d. lack of metabolic retention of sodium

12. Severe chest pain resulting from too little oxygenated blood being delivered to the heart muscle is called: (Highlight 8.2, p. 317)
   a. angina pectoris.
   c. myocardial infarction.
   b. arrhythmia.
   d. tachycardia.

13. According to Friedman and Rosenman, all of the following indications are involved in the Type A behavior pattern *except*: (p. 316)
   a. excessive competitive drive with poorly defined goals.
   b. hostility.
   c. impatience or time urgency.
   d. decelerated speech and motor activity.

14. In the Framingham Heart Study, all of the following groups showed Type A associations *except*: (p. 320)
   a. blue collar men.
   c. white collar men.
   b. blue collar women.
   d. white collar women.

15. A variably experienced but painless disturbance having odd sensory (particularly visual), motor, and/or mood components is associated with: (Highlight 8.4, p. 322)
   a. tension headaches.
   c. migraine headaches.
   b. essential hypertension.
   d. asthma.

16. Sociocultural treatment of psychogenic diseases is targeted *most often* toward: (p. 330)
   a. encouraging diseased individuals to seek help.
   b. obtaining social support after treatment.
   c. preventing pathogenic life-style behaviors.
   d. raising money for research.

| Chapter 9
| *Personality Disorders*

◊ OVERVIEW

In this chapter several specific disorders of personality are discussed. With these disorders we encounter, for the first time, behavior that is not episodic and that, generally, is not exacerbated by stress. Rather, the personality disorders represent ingrained "lifestyles" or characteristic patterns that are maladaptive of meeting the individual's needs. Usually, these maladaptive approaches significantly impair at least some aspect of functioning. Often, the person with a personality disorder ends up imposing on other people's rights in order to obtain his or her goals. Chapter 9 includes descriptions of the various types of personality disorders (which vary considerably in form and severity), their causal patterns, and their treatment. Special treatment is given to one particular personality disorder--antisocial personality and psychopathy--because of the extensive research on this topic.

◊ CHAPTER OUTLINE

I. Clinical Features of Personality Disorders
    A. DSM-IV's Five Criteria
    B. Difficulties in Diagnosing Personality Disorders

II. Categories of Personality Disorders
    A. Paranoid Personality Disorder
    B. Schizoid Personality Disorder
    C. Schizotypal Personality Disorder
    D. Histrionic Personality Disorder
    E. Narcissistic Personality Disorder
    F. Antisocial Personality Disorder
    G. Borderline Personality Disorder
        1. Comorbidity with Other Axis I Disorders
        2. Comorbidity with Other Personality Disorders

H. Avoidant Personality Disorder
I. Dependent Personality Disorder
J. Obsessive-Compulsive Personality Disorder
K. Provisional Categories of Personality Disorder in DSM-IV
    1. Passive-Aggressive Personality Disorder
    2. Depressive Personality Disorder
L. Overview of Personality Disorders

III. Causal Factors in Personality Disorders
  A. Biological Causal Factors
  B. Psychological Causal Factors
    1. Early Learning Experiences
    2. The Psychodynamic View
  C. Sociocultural Causal Factors

IV. Treatments and Outcomes
  A. Adapting Therapeutic Techniques to Specific Personality Disorders
  B. Treating Borderline Personality Disorder
    1. Psychosocial Treatments
    2. Efficacy Studies
  C. Treating Other Personality Disorders
    1. Treating Other Cluster A and B Disorders
    2. Treating Cluster C Disorders

V. Antisocial Personality and Psychopathy
  A. Psychopathy and Antisocial Personality Disorder
    1. The Two Dimensions of Psychopathy
  B. The Clinical Picture in Antisocial Personality and Psychopathy
    1. Inadequate Conscience Development
    2. Irresponsible and Impulsive Behavior
    3. Rejection of Authority
    4. Ability to Impress and Exploit Others
    5. Inability to Maintain Good Relationships
    6. Patterns of Behavior
  C. Causal Factors in Psychopathy and Antisocial Personality
    1. Genetic Influences
    2. Deficient Aversive Emotional Arousal and Conditioning
    3. More General Emotional Deficits

◊ LEARNING OBJECTIVES

After studying this chapter, you should be able to:

1. List the clinical features of the personality disorders and problems associated with diagnosis. (pp. 333-336)

2. Compare and contrast the different types of personality disorders and identify the three clusters into which most personality disorders are grouped. (pp. 336-350)

3. Summarize what is known about the biological, psychological, and sociocultural causal factors of personality disorders. (pp. 350-352)

4. Discuss the difficulties of treating individuals with personality disorders and describe the approaches to treatment that have been tried. (pp. 353-356).

5. Compare and contrast the DSM-IV concept of antisocial personality and Cleckley's concept of psychopathy. (pp. 356-357)

6. List the clinical features of psychopathy and antisocial personality. (pp. 357-362)

7. Summarize the biological, psychosocial, and sociocultural causal factors in psychopathy and antisocial personality and the integrated developmental perspective. (pp. 362-366)

8. Explain why it is difficult to treat psychopathy and antisocial personality and describe the most promising of the as yet unproven approaches to treatment. (pp. 366-369)

personality (p. 333)

personality disorder or character disorder (p. 333)

temperament or characteristics (pp. 334)

paranoid personality disorder (pp. 336-337; Table 9.1, p. 337)

schizoid personality disorder (Table 9.1, p. 337; pp. 338-339)

schizotypal personality disorder (Table 9.1, p. 337; pp. 339-340)

histrionic personality disorder (Table 9.1, p. 337; p. 340)

narcissistic personality disorder (Table 9.1, p. 337; pp. 340-342)

antisocial personality disorder (Table 9.1, p. 337; pp. 342-343; 356-369)

borderline personality disorder (Table 9.1, p. 337; pp. 343-344)

avoidant personality disorder (Table 9.1, p. 337; pp. 344-346)

dependent personality disorder (Table 9.1, p. 337; pp. 346-347)

obsessive-compulsiv personality disorder (Table 9.1, p. 337; pp. 347-348)

passive-aggressive personality disorder (Table 9.1, p. 337; pp. 348-349)

depressive personality disorder (Table 9.1, p. 337; p. 349)

retrospective studies (p. 350)

schemas (p. 354)

psychopathy or sociopathy (p. 356)

Psychopathy Checklist (p. 357)

behavioral inhibition system (p. 362)

passive avoidance learning (p. 362)

behavioral activation system (p. 363)

oppositional defiant disorder (p. 364)

burned-out psychopath (p. 368)

◊ NAMES YOU SHOULD KNOW

Thomas Widiger

Lee Anna Clark

Otto Kernberg

Heinz Kohut

Theodore Millon

Hervey Cleckley

Robert Hare

David Lykken

Hans Eysenck

Lee Robins

◊ CONCEPTS TO MASTER

1. Define *personality disorder* and explain three broad reasons for the high frequency of misdiagnosis of the personality disorders. (pp. 333-336)

2. List and describe the general characteristics of three clusters of personality disorders, and note two additional disorders that appear in DSM-IV. (p. 336; Table 9.1, p. 337; pp. 348-349)

3. Describe and differentiate among the following personality disorders in Cluster I: paranoid, schizoid, and schizotypal. (Table 9.1, p. 337; pp. 336-340)

4. Describe and differentiate among the following personality disorders in Cluster II: histrionic, narcissistic, antisocial, and borderline. (Table 9.1, p. 337; pp. 340-344)

5. Describe and differentiate among the following personality disorders in Cluster III: avoidant, dependent, and obsessive-compulsive. (Table 9.1, p. 337; pp. 344-348)

6. Beck and Freeman argue that personality disorders can be characterized in terms of interpersonal strategies they use, patterns of behavior they have underdeveloped or overdeveloped, and their characteristic core dysfunctional beliefs. Use this scheme to compare the personality disorders. (pp. 349-350; Table 9.2, p. 350)

7. Explain why we know comparatively little about the causal factors in personality disorders, and summarize what we do know about the biological, psychological, and sociocultural factors that seem implicated. (pp. 350-352)

8. Zanarini et al. (1990) found that borderline personality disorder patients reported higher rates of emotional, verbal, physical, and sexual abuse, as well as higher rates of emotional withdrawal, as compared to patients with other personality disorders. Explain the shortcomings of this and many other studies that make the results only suggestive. (p. 351)

9. List several reasons why personality disorders are especially resistant to therapy, and describe treatment strategies for persons who are already too dependent or who are hypersensitive to any perceived criticism from the therapist. (pp. 353-354).

10. Describe three criteria, in addition to being 18 or older, that must be met before an individual is diagnosed as an antisocial personality, according to DSM-IV. (p. 335)

11. List personality traits that help to define psychopathy that are not included in the DSM-IV criteria for antisocial personality disorder. (p. 356)

12. Identify the two dimensions of psychopathy found in Hare's Psychopathy Checklist based on Cleckley's criteria and indicate how they relate to the DSM-IV concept of antisocial personality disorder. Which group of psychopaths is *not* detected by the DSM-IV diagnosis of antisocial personality disorder, even though the latter concept is broader than the former? (p. 357)

13. Summarize Fowles' application of Gray's theory to psychopathy, including the roles of the behavioral inhibition system, the behavioral activation system, and the fight/flight system. (pp. 362-363)

14. Describe the two independent factors during childhood that predict who will develop an adult diagnosis of psychopathy or antisocial personality. How do these findings relate to the current diagnoses of conduct disorder and oppositional defiant disorder? What other diagnosis is often a precursor to adult psychopathy or antisocial personality disorder? Explain. (pp. 364-365)

15. How, according to Moffitt and Lynam (1994) might neuropsychological risk predispose the development of antisocial disorders? (You may wish to refer to Chapter 14, in which this question is pursued in more detail.) (p. 365)

16. Discuss cross-cultural research on psychopathy. What is one of the primary variables in which cultural variations occur? (pp. 365-366)

17. Outline and discuss the major psychosocial and sociocultural variables identified by Capaldi and Patterson as contributing to poor and ineffective parenting. Given poor parenting, what is the causal pathway to an antisocial life-style? (p. 365; Figure 9.1, p. 366)

18. Explain why most individuals with antisocial personalities seldom come to the attention of mental hospitals and clinics, and evaluate the success of traditional psychotherapy in treating this disorder. (pp. 366-367)

19. According to Beck and Freeman, what self-serving dysfunctional beliefs do psychopaths tend to hold, and how does cognitive therapy aim to modify such cognitions? (pp. 367-368)

20. Discuss efforts at prevention of psychopathy and antisocial personality disorder. How effective do these interventions appear to be? (Highlight 9.2; p. 369)

21. Identify and explain two major problems that make Axis II diagnoses quite unreliable. (pp. 370-371)

22. What do the authors of the text suggest to resolve the difficulties with Axis II? (p. 351)

◊ STUDY QUESTIONS

Introduction

1. Successful adjustment throughout life is primarily a matter of flexibly adapting to _____ _____, _____, and _____ associated with each life stage. (p. 333)

2. Personality disorders typically do not stem from debilitating reactions to stress. Rather, they stem largely from the gradual development of _____ and _____ personality patterns, which result in persistently maladaptive ways of _____, _____, and relating to the world. (p. 333)

3. The actual prevalence of personality disorders is unknown, in part because many individuals never come in contact with mental health or legal agencies. However, estimates available from a very large epidemiological study (Robins et al.) suggest that the prevalence of antisocial personality is between _____ and _____ percent, which is consistent with more recent estimates (Weissman) of about ____ to ____ percent in the U.S. and Canada. (p. 333)

Clinical features of personality disorders

4. In the DSM-IV the personality disorders are coded on a separate axis, _____, because they are regarded as being different enough from the standard psychiatric syndromes to warrant separate classification. These reaction patterns are so deeply embedded in the personality structure that they are extremely resistant to _____. (p. 333)

Personality disorders

5. Respond true or false to the following statements about personality disorders. (p. 334)
   People with personality disorders:
   a. Cause as much difficulty for others as for themselves. True or False
   b. Almost always show bizarre behavior that is out of contact with reality. True or False
   c. Almost always experience a good deal of emotional suffering. True or False
   d. Experience difficulty with mutually respectful and satisfying relationships. True or False
   e. Show persistent behavioral deviations that are intrinsic to their personality. True or False
   f. Learn from their previous troubles. True or False

Types of personality disorders

6. List the personality disorders that belong to each cluster: (p. 336)
   a. Cluster I: odd or eccentric individuals
   b. Cluster II: dramatic, emotional, and erratic individuals
   c. Cluster III: anxious, fearful individuals

7. Fill in the clinical description in the following personality disorders:

Personality Disorder	Clinical Description
Paranoid (p. 336)	Suspicious, distrustful, hypersensitive, bearing grudges, blaming others for their own mistakes.
Schizoid (p. 338)	

Schizotypal (p. 339)   Socially isolated and withdrawn. Oddities of thought, perception, and speech: highly personalized and superstitious thinking, magical thinking, magical rituals, and ideas of reference.

Histrionic (p. 340)

Narcissistic (p. 340)   Exaggerated sense of self-importance (grandiosity), preoccupied with being admired, lacking in empathy, not uncommonly take advantage of others, often envious of others.

Borderline (p. 343)

Avoidant (p. 344)   Extreme social inhibition, hypersensitive to criticism, lonely and bored, experience acute distress, low self-esteem.

Dependent (p. 346)

Obsessive-compulsive (p. 347) Excessively concerned with maintaining order, perfectionistic, very careful in order to avoid making mistakes, preoccupied with trivial details, devoted to work to the exclusion of leisure activities, excessively conscientious and inflexible about moral issues, have difficulty delegating tasks to others, rigid and stubborn.

Passive-aggressive (p. 348)

Depressive (p. 349)

Causal factors in personality disorder

8. There is a current wealth of knowledge regarding antecedents for the personality disorders, including that of antisocial personality disorder. True or False. (p. 350)

9. Research on the causal factors of personality disorders is difficult. One major problem in studying the causes of personality disorders stems from the high level of _____. Widiger and Rogers found that ____ percent of patients with a diagnosis of personality disorder also qualified for at least one more diagnosis of personality disorder. Even in a nonpatient sample, Zimmerman and Coryell found that almost ____ percent showed _____. An additional problem is that many people with these disorders are never _____, with the consequence that only _____ study is possible. (p. 350)

10. Theories that link constitutional reaction tendencies to the development of personality disorders are not supported by evidence. True or False (pp. 350-351)

11. Suggestions that early learning contributes to personality disorders are speculative and inferential. True or False (pp. 351)

12. The incidence of personality disorders has varied over time. Some clinicians believe that personality disorders have increased in American society in recent years. True or False (p. 352)

Treatment and outcome

13. Under what circumstances do persons with personality disorders generally get involved with psychotherapy? (p. 353)

14. How do the difficulties personality disordered people have with personal relationships, acting out, and avoiding problems affect the course of psychotherapeutic treatments? (p. 354)

15. For personality disordered individuals who become identified with their therapy group, or who are sufficiently "hooked" into couples therapy that they do not flee the sessions when their behavior comes under scrutiny, the intense feedback from _____ or _____ often is more acceptable than confrontation by a _____ in individual treatment. (p. 354)

16. What are schemas and what is their relevance to Beck and Freeman's cognitive approach to treating the personality disorders? (p. 354)

17. For the pharmacological treatment of borderline personality disorder, low doses of _____ medication have modest but significant effects that are broad-based, _____ antidepressants are ineffective, but that antidepressant drugs from the same class as _____ are promising, as are _____ _____. (pp. 354-355)

18. Probably the most promising treatment for borderline personality disorder is the recently developed _____ behavior therapy. (p. 355)

19. Linehan's dialectical behavior therapy for borderline personality disorder involves a problem-focused treatment in which the hierarchy of goals includes: (p. 354)
    a.
    b. decreasing behaviors that interfere with therapy
    c.
    d.
    e. other goals the patient chooses

Antisocial personality and psychopathy

20. With its strong emphasis on behavioral criteria that reasonably can be measured objectively, DSM-III and IV have broken from the tradition of psychopathy researchers, in an attempt to increase the reliability of the diagnosis. However, much less attention has been paid to its _____--that is, whether it measures a _____ construct and whether that construct is the same as psychopathy. (pp. 356)

21. What is the single best predictor we have of violence? (p. 357)

22. Whichever diagnosis is used, individuals with antisocial personality disorder or psychopathy include a mixed group of individuals: (p. 357)
    a. unprincipled business professionals
    b.
    c. crooked politicians
    d.
    e.
    f. assorted criminals

23. The prevalence of antisocial personality in American men is approximately _____ percent according to several large epidemiological surveys. Among women, the prevalence is approximately _____ percent. (p. 357)

24. Describe Widom's (1977) approach to recruiting research participants and the type of people who volunteered. (Highlight 9.1, p. 358)

Clinical picture in antisocial personality and psychopathy

25. Fill in the missing information on the following chart that summarizes the personality characteristics of antisocial persons: (pp. 358-362)

Area of Functioning	**Behavior Typical of the Antisocial Person**
Conscience development	
Feelings of anxiety and guilt	Act out tension rather than worrying: apparent lack of anxiety and guilt combined with appearance of sincerity allows them to avoid suspicion
Impulse control	
Frustration tolerance	Seldom forego immediate pleasure for future gains; live in the present; unable to endure routine jobs or accept responsibility
Ability to accept authority	
Profit from experience	Despite difficulties they get into and the punishments they receive, they continue to behave as if they are immune from the consequences of their actions

Interpersonal and sexual relationships

Ability to manipulate others

Causal factors in psychopathy and antisocial personality: Biological factors

26. Results of twin and adoption studies show a modest heritability for antisocial or criminal behavior and probably for psychopathy. These effects are stronger for _____ criminality than for _____ criminality. Researchers also note that _____ _____ factors interact with genetic predispositions to determine which individuals become criminals or antisocial personalities. (p. 362)

27. Many investigators--e.g., Lykken, Eysenck, and Hare--have found that antisocial individuals seem to lack normal fear and anxiety reactions. What appears to happen in the development of antisocial persons as a result of their lack of anxiety and fear? (p. 362)

28. According to Fowles, deficient anxiety conditioning seems to stem from psychopaths having a deficient _____ _____ _____, which has been proposed by Gray to be the _____ _____ of anxiety. Further explain Fowles's conception of deficient anxiety conditioning. (p. 362)

29. What three features of psychopathy are accounted for by Fowles's hypothesis that psychopaths have a deficiency in behavioral inhibition and a normal (or possibly overactive) behavioral activation system? (p. 363)

    a.

    b.

    c.

30. Patrick and his colleagues found that psychopaths did not show a larger _____ _____ as a result of being in a fearful state, a finding that is in direct contrast to the nonpsychopaths who did show the larger response. (p. 363)

Causal factors in psychopathy and antisocial personality: Family relationships

31. Although the loss of a parent during childhood was more common among antisocial subjects than normal controls, the authors of the text conclude that this factor can only be a partial or interactive cause of antisocial personality. Why did Hare suggest that parental loss per se is not the factor of key significance? (pp. 363-364)

32. Children who had experienced substantiated _____ _____ and _____ were more likely to show symptoms of antisocial personality disorder than were children matched on: _____, _____, _____, and _____ _____. (p. 364)

Treatment and outcomes

33. In general, traditional psychotherapeutic approaches have not proven very effective in altering the personality problems of psychopaths. Among the factors inherent in the psychopathic individual's personality that make the prognosis for psychotherapy very poor are the inability to trust, to _____, to learn from _____, and to _____ _____. (p. 366)

34. Perhaps the most promising therapeutic approach is _____ therapy. (p. 367)

35. List several common targets of cognitive-behavioral interventions for individuals with antisocial personality. (p. 367)

36. What is meant by a "controlled situation," and how important is it to successful treatment of antisocial persons? Why? (p. 367)

37. Which is more difficult to treat: psychopathy or antisocial personality disorder? (p. 368)

38. Why do many antisocial persons seem to improve after age 40? (p. 368)

Unresolved issues

39. Some studies have found that patients were given an average of _____ personality disorder diagnoses. (p. 370)

40. Axis II diagnoses (the personality disorders) are more unreliable than diagnoses made for Axis I (mental disorders). The authors of the text suggest the following two reasons for the unreliability: (p. 370)
   a. DSM-IV assumes that we can make a clear distinction between _____ and _____ of a personality disorder when, in fact, the personality processes classified on Axis II are _____ in nature.
   b. There are enormous _____ in the kinds of symptoms that people can have who nevertheless obtain the same diagnosis. For example, for borderline personality, a person had to meet _____ out of eight possible symptom criteria, and this means that there are ___ different ways to meet the criteria for this diagnosis. Even more amazing, the comparable figures for the number of ways to meet DSM-III-R criteria for antisocial personality disorder were calculated to be nearly _____ different ways. The ultimate status of _____ in future editions of the DSM is uncertain.

◊ CRITICAL THINKING ABOUT DIFFICULT TOPICS

1. In the field of psychometrics, reliability sets the upper limit of validity. That is, if you are trying to assess constructs such as "intelligence" or "psychopathy," the meaningfulness (validity) of the construct is to be found in the nonrandom variation in test scores (reliability) and not in the random variation (error variance). Thus, an extremely unreliable assessment cannot be valid. Taking this principle to heart, DSM IV has emphasized reliable measurement. In the case of psychopathy, however, your text implicitly raises the possibility that validity may have been sacrificed: "much less attention has been paid to validity--that is, whether it measures a meaningful construct and whether

that construct is the same as psychopathy" (p. 356). Can you explain how validity might be sacrificed in emphasizing reliability? Think about concepts such as "social class" or "standard of living" and whether they might be reliably indexed by measuring a family's electric power consumption. Over a wide range of incomes, power consumption probably does show a positive correlation with both income and social class, and it can be measured quite reliably. However, these concepts usually refer to a broader set of variables that are not adequately indexed by power consumption. Can you think of other examples where inappropriate use of highly reliable measures may undermine validity?

2. In the case study of Donald S. (pp. 360-361), the following statements express Donald's view: "Although his behavior is self-defeating in the long run, he considers it to be practical and possessed of good sense. Periodic punishments do nothing to decrease his egotism and confidence in his own abilities"(p. 361). Thus, Donald thinks his behavior reflects a rational hedonism. Read his case history again and see whether you agree, or whether you can attribute some of his behavior to deficits. For example, is it rational to break out of prison with only one month left to serve, when recapture means automatic conviction (there is no difficulty in proving who escaped from prison)? Would a rational hedonism lead one to this degree of indifference to others, or does his behavior reflect a deficit in attachments?

3. Your text nicely states the problem of using a categorical approach to Axis II diagnoses when "the personality processes classified on Axis II are dimensional in nature" (pp. 370-371). At the same time, as you have seen in earlier chapters, it can be difficult to make categorical distinctions with Axis I disorders: they vary quantitatively in the degree of severity and do not show a "point of rarity" that would make it easy to distinguish between the presence and absence of the disorder. What possible difference between some Axis I disorders and Axis II disorders could make applying a categorical model even more problematic with personality disorders? In developing your answer, note that personality is usually assumed to be normally distributed in the population and that changing the cut-points (or threshold) for a diagnosis of a personality disorder "can have drastic effects in the apparent prevalence rates of a particular personality disorder diagnosis" (pp. 370-371). In contrast, we usually would not think that bipolar affective disorder or schizophrenia is normally distributed in the population--with the result that small changes in the cut-point for diagnosis would not have drastic effects on estimates of prevalence. Thus, there are two components to this issue: (a) whether the phenomenon in question is dimensional in the sense that there is a continuum of severity, and (b) whether it is normally distributed with huge numbers of the milder forms in the "normal" population (personality disorders) or whether it is relatively rare in the "normal" population with only a small number of milder forms (bipolar affective disorder). What do you think is the distribution of other Axis I disorders, such as anxiety disorders and unipolar depression?

◊ CHAPTER 9 QUIZ

Circle the best of the four answers provided and check them according to answers provided at the back of this study guide. Be sure you understand why each answer is correct.

1. Personality disorders are: (p. 333)
   a. reactions to stress.
   b. intrapsychic disturbances.
   c. episodic in nature.
   d. maladaptive ways of perceiving, thinking, and relating.

2. According to a very large epidemiological study (Robins et al.), the prevalence of antisocial personality disorder is about _____ percent of our population. (p. 333)
   a. 3   c. 23
   b. 13   d. 33

3. Personality disorders are coded on Axis _____ of DSM-IV. (p. 333)
   a. I   c. III
   b. II   d. IV

4. Which of the following is not one of the three reasons given for the high rate of misdiagnoses of personality disorders? (p. 335)
   a. the diagnostic criteria are often not very precise or easy to follow
   b. the diagnostic categories are not mutually exclusive
   c. the personality characteristics that define personalities are dimensional in nature
   d. clinicians often do not receive sufficient training in the diagnosis of personality disorders

5. Individuals with this personality disorder typically show oddities of thought, perception or speech: (Table 9.1, p. 337; p. 339)
   a. schizoid   c. histrionic
   b. schizotypal   d. antisocial

6. Which of the following personality disorders is characterized by loneliness and boredom? (p. 344)
   a. avoidant
   b. schizotypal
   c. schizoid
   d. paranoid

7. An individual is frequently late for work and meetings, misses appointments, forgets about assignments, refuses to follow instructions, and seems unmotivated. This is an example of _____ personality disorder. (p. 348)
   a. passive-aggressive
   b. avoidant
   c. narcissistic
   d. borderline

8. Establishing the causal factors of personality disorders hasn't progressed very far for all the following reasons except: (p. 350)
   a. there is a high level of co-morbidity.
   b. affected individuals do not seek professional help.
   c. only prospective studies have been possible so far.
   d. the personality disorders have only received consistent attention since 1980.

9. Patients with _____ personality disorder reported significantly higher rates of emotional, verbal, physical, and sexual abuse, than patients with other personality disorders. (p.351)
   a. antisocial
   b. obsessive
   c. borderline
   d. schizoid

10. Several large epidemiological studies found that the prevalence of antisocial personality disorder is: (p. 357)
    a. about equal for males and females.
    b. higher for females than for males.
    c. higher for males than for females.
    d. higher in prepubertal females than in prepubertal males.

11. Research evidence indicates that a primary reaction tendency typically found in psychopathic individuals is: (p. 362)
    a. deficient aversive emotional arousal.
    b. passive avoidance conditioning.
    c. oversensitivity to noxious stimuli.
    d. phlegmatic temperament.

12. According to Fowles' application of Gray's motivational theory, psychopaths are deficient in: (p. 362)
    a. reactivity of the fight\flight response.
    b. reactivity of the behavioral activation system.
    c. active avoidance learning.
    d. reactivity of the behavioral inhibition system.

13. While a number of early studies linked antisocial personality formation with losing a parent at an early age, Hare suggested that the key factor was the: (pp. 363-364)
    a. age at which the loss occurred.
    b. emotional family disturbance before the parent left.
    c. length of the marriage before the loss.
    d. sex of the parent who left.

14. In the Capaldi and Patterson model, the key factor that mediates the influence of other factors and increases the probability of antisocial behavior in the child is: (p. 365)
    a. parental antisocial behavior.
    b. divorce and other parental transitions.
    c. parental stress and depression.
    d. ineffective discipline and supervision.

15. Which of the following medications appear to be least effective in treating psychopathic and antisocial personalities? (pp. 366-367)
    a. antipsychotic drugs
    b. SSRIs
    c. lithium
    d. antianxiety drugs

| Chapter 10 |
| Substance-Related and Other Addictive Disorders |

◊ OVERVIEW

It has been estimated that many of America's health problems are due to self-injurious practices such as excessive drinking, smoking, and overeating. Such behaviors are considered addictive when these substances or activities, as well as others, are needed and used pathologically. Chapter 10 covers the major addictive disorders, focusing primarily on alcohol and drug abuse and dependence, as well as discussing the non-substance-related addictions of hyperobesity and pathological gambling. A great deal of background information is presented to help document the extent of the various addictive behaviors and their costs to society. Treatment approaches that have been developed for each specific addiction are then described.

◊ CHAPTER OUTLINE

I. Alcohol Abuse and Dependence
    A. The Prevalence, Comorbidity, and Demographics of Alcoholism
    B. The Clinical Picture of Alcohol Abuse and Dependence
        1. Alcohol's Effects on the Brain
        2. Development of Alcohol Dependence
        3. The Physical Effects of Chronic Alcohol Use
        4. Psychosocial Effects of Alcohol Abuse and Dependence
        5. Psychoses Associated with Alcoholism
    C. Biological Causal Factors in the Abuse and Dependence of Alcohol and Other Substances
        1. The Biochemistry of Addiction
        2. Craving and Genetic Vulnerability
        3. Genetic Influences and Learning
    D. Psychosocial Causal Factors in Alcohol Abuse and Dependence
        1. Failures in Parental Guidance
        2. Psychological Vulnerability

3. Stress, Tension Reduction, and Reinforcement
4. Expectations of Social Success
5. Marital and Other Intimate Relationships
E. Sociocultural Factors
F. Treatment of Alcoholism
   1. Use of Medications in Treating Alcoholics
      a) Medications to Block the Desire to Drink
      b) Medications to Lower the Side Effects of Acute Withdrawal
      c) Medications to Treat Co-Ocurring Disorders
   2. Psychological Treatment Approaches
      a) Group Therapy
      b) Environmental Intervention
      c) Behavior Therapy
      d) Controlled Drinking Versus Abstinence
         (1) Alcoholics Anonymous
   3. Outcome Studies and Issues in Treatment
      a) Programs in the Workplace
      b) Inpatient or Outpatient Treatment
      c) The Value of Professional Treatment
      d) Relapse Prevention

II. Drug Abuse and Dependence
  A. Opium and its Derivatives (Narcotics)
    1. Effects of Morphine and Heroin
    2. Causal Factors in Opiate Abuse and Dependence
       a) Neural Bases for Physiological Bases
       b) Addiction Associated with Psychopathology
       c) Addiction Associated with Sociocultural Factors
    3. Treatments and Outcomes
  B. Cocaine and Amphetamines (Stimulants)
    1. Cocaine
    2. Amphetamines
       a) Causes and Effects of Amphetamine Abuse
       b) Treatments and Outcomes
  C. Barbiturates
    1. Effects of Barbiturates
    2. Causal Factors in Barbiturate Abuse and Dependence
    3. Treatments and Outcomes

D. LSD and Related Drugs (Hallucinogens)
   1. LSD
   2. Mescaline and Psilocybin
E. Marijuana
   1. Effects of Marijuana

III. Other Addictive Disorders: Hyperobesity and Pathological Gambling
A. Extreme Obesity
   1. Causes of Persistent Overeating
      a) Biological Factors
      b) Psychosocial Factors
      c) Sociocultural Factors
   2. Treatment of Extreme Obesity
      a) Impact of Failed Weight Loss Treatment Programs
B. Pathological Gambling
   1. Clinical Picture in Pathological Gambling
   2. Causal Factors in Pathological Gambling
   3. Treatments and Outcomes

IV. Unresolved Issues: The Genetics of Alcoholism

V. Summary

◊ LEARNING OBJECTIVES

After studying this chapter, you should be able to:

1. Outline the major divisions of psychoactive substance-related disorders, define alcohol abuse and alcohol dependence, summarize the many negative consequences of alcohol for both the individual and society, and indicate the prevalence and gender ratio of excessive drinking. (pp. 374-377)

2. Describe the clinical picture of alcohol abuse, including the biological and psychological effects of chronic consumption of alcohol. (pp. 377-383)

3. Review the biological, psychosocial, and sociocultural contributors to alcohol abuse and dependence. (pp. 383-390)

4. Summarize the research findings on the results of treatment and relapse prevention for alcohol-dependent persons. (pp. 390-397)

5. List the specific drugs and their effects, summarize theories of causal factors, and review treatments for the following drugs of abuse: Opium and its derivatives (pp. 400-403), cocaine and amphetamines (pp. 403-406), barbiturates (p. 406), LSD and other hallucinogens (pp. 406-408), marijuana (pp. 408-409), and caffeine and nicotine (pp. 398-399).

6. Characterize the behavioral manifestations, etiologies, and resistance to treatments of hyperobesity and pathological gambling. Compare and contrast these disorders with the substance-abuse and dependence disorders. (pp. 409-416)

◊ TERMS YOU SHOULD KNOW

---

addictive behavior (p. 374)

psychoactive drugs (p. 374)

organic impairment (p. 374)

toxicity (p. 374)

psychoactive substance abuse (p. 374)

psychoactive substance dependence (p. 374)

tolerance (p. 374)

withdrawal symptoms (p. 374)

alcoholism (p. 376)

binge drinkers (p. 376; Highlight 10.1, pp. 388-389)

blackouts (p. 379)

hangover (p. 379)

alcohol dependence syndrome (p. 379)

alcoholic psychoses (pp. 381-382)

alcohol withdrawal delirium (p. 382)

alcohol amnestic disorder (formerly Korsakoff's syndrome) (p. 382)

mesocorticolimbic dopamine pathway (MCLP) (p. 383; Figure 10.1; p. 384)

ventral tegmental area (p. 383; Figure 10.1, p. 384)

nucleus accumbens (Figure 10.1, p. 384)

brain reward pathway (p. 383; Figure 10.1, p. 384)

alcohol-risk personality (p. 384)

alcohol flush reaction (pp. 384-385)

tension reduction (p. 387)

reciprocal influence model (p. 387)

detoxification (p. 391)

Disulfiram (Antabuse) (p. 391)

Naltrexone (p. 391)

aversive conditioning (p. 392)

emetine hydrochloride (p. 392)

controlled drinking versus *abstinence* (p. 393)

Alcoholics Anonymous, Al-Anon, and Ala-Teen (pp. 393-394)

Project MATCH (p. 395)

relapse prevention (pp. 396-397)

abstinence violation effect (p. 396)

caffeinism (Highlight10.3, p. 398)

nicotine withdrawal (Highlight10.3, pp. 398-399)

nicotine replacement therapy (NRT) (Highlight10.3, p. 399)

opium (p. 400)

alkaloids (p. 400)

morphine (p. 400)

soldier's illness (p. 400)

analgesic (p. 400)

heroin (p. 400)

codeine (p. 400)

snorting (p. 400)

skin popping (p. 400)

mainlining (p. 400)

rush (p. 400)

withdrawal symptoms (p. 401)

endorphins (p. 402)

methadone hydrochloride (pp. 402-403)

buprenorphine (p. 403)

cocaine (p. 403)

crack (p. 403)

amphetamines (p. 405)

Benzedrine (amphetamine sulfate) (p. 405)

Dexedrine (dextroamphetamine) (p. 405)

Methedrine (methamphetamine hydrochloride) (p. 405)

narcolepsy (p. 405)

barbiturates (p. 406)

Pentobarbitol (p. 406)

silent abusers (p. 406)

potentiates (p. 406)

hallucinogens (pp. 406-407)

model psychoses (p. 407)

LSD (lysergic acid diethylamide) (p. 407)

bad trip (p. 407)

◊ NAMES YOU SHOULD KNOW

G. Alan Marlatt

Kelly Brownell

1. Psychoactive substance-induced organic mental disorders and psychoactive substance-abuse and dependence disorders are the two major divisions of "addictive or psychoactive substance-related disorders." Define what it means to be included in each of these two divisions. (p. 374)

    a. Psychoactive substance-induced organic mental disorders

    b. Psychoactive substance-abuse and -dependence disorders

2. Describe three major physiological effects of alcohol. (pp. 377-379)

3. Describe some physical ailments that can result from chronic alcohol use, and explain how these may lead to interpersonal and occupational problems. (pp. 379-381)

4. Alcohol withdrawal delirium is a form of psychosis that may occur following a long drinking spree when the person is in a state of withdrawal. List the symptoms and indicate how long they last and how dangerous they are. (p. 382)

5. Describe the memory deficit that occurs in alcoholic amnestic disorder. (p. 382)

6. Describe the mesocorticolimbic dopamine pathway, and indicate what it has to do with addiction to psychoactive drugs. (p. 383; Figure 10.1; p. 384)

7. How do the physiological patterns of prealcoholics differ from that of low-risk, non-alcoholics? (pp. 384-385)

8. List and describe five major psychosocial factors that may be partially responsible for the development of alcohol dependence. (pp. 385-390)

9. What are the rates of alcoholism among Muslims, Mormons, and Orthodox Jews? How much of the world's consumption of alcohol takes place in Europe and European-influenced countries? What do these facts tell us about the power of sociocultural factors on drinking? (p. 390).

10. List the strengths and limitations of Disulfiram (Antabuse) treatment. (p. 391)

11. Describe three psychosocial interventions - excluding AA - that have been used to treat alcohol-dependent persons. (pp. 391-393)

12. Discuss the controversy over controlled-drinking treatment programs and review the empirical findings regarding controlled-drinking outcomes. (p. 393)

13. Briefly describe how AA, Al-Anon, and Al-Ateen family groups operate. Discuss the reported success of this treatment, as well as why one should be skeptical about its effectiveness. (pp. 393-394)

14. Summarize the history of the use of opium and its derivatives over the last 5000 years. (p. 400)

15. Describe the major physical and psychosocial effects of morphine and heroin use. (pp. 400-401)

16. List and explain three major causal factors in the development of opiate dependence. (p. 402)

17. Describe some psychosocial and biological treatments that have been used as therapy for opiate dependent individuals. (pp. 402-403)

18. Evaluate the success of using methadone hydrochloride--with and without psychotherapy or psychosocial support. Compare the benefits of methadone treatment with that of buprenorphine treatment. (pp. 402-403)

19. Describe some physical and psychological effects of cocaine use and some symptoms that are experienced in withdrawal. (pp. 403-404)

20. List current uses of the amphetamines, and describe the causes and effects of amphetamine abuse. Note some physical and psychological effects of withdrawal. (pp. 405-406)

21. Describe some of the effects of barbiturate abuse, list some of its causes, and summarize the dangers of withdrawal from this class of drugs. (p. 406)

22. Describe the physical and psychological effects of using LSD, and note the treatment used for the acute psychoses induced by its use. (p. 407)

23. List the effects of using mescaline and psilocybin, and compare these effects with those of LSD. (pp. 407-408)

24. List several variables that influence the effects of marijuana, and discuss marijuana's short-term and long-term effects. (pp. 408-409)

25. Define hyperobesity, and list some biological, psychosocial, and sociocultural factors that may underlie its development. (pp. 409-411)

26. Describe and evaluate several biological and psychosocial interventions that have been used to treat hyperobesity. (pp. 411-413)

27. Define pathological gambling and describe its symptoms. (pp. 413-414)

28. Summarize what is known about the causes of and treatments for pathological gambling. (pp. 414-416)

29. Summarize the evidence both for and against a strong genetic link in alcoholism. (pp. 416-417)

Alcohol abuse and dependence: Definition, prevalence, significance

1. The World Health Organization prefers the term _____ syndrome to the term alcoholism. It defines this syndrome as ". . . a state, _____ and usually also physical, resulting from taking alcohol, characterized by behavioral and other responses that always include a _____ to take alcohol on a continuous or periodic basis in order to experience its _____ effects, and sometimes to avoid the discomfort of its _____; _____ may or may not be present. (p. 375).

2. A large NIMH epidemiological study reported that the lifetime prevalence of alcoholism is _____ percent. (p. 376)

3. Complete the following lists of some of the ways in which alcoholism harms the individual and is a drain on society: (p. 376)

Individual harm
a. Leads to a _____ shorter life span
b. Is the _____ major cause of death--after coronary heart disease and cancer
c. _____ impairment, including _____ shrinkage, occurs in a high proportion
d. About ___ percent commit suicide

Harm to others:
a. Related to ___ percent of all deaths
b. Related to _____ of deaths and major injuries in auto accidents
c. Related to ___ percent of all murders
d. Related to ___ percent of all assaults
e. Related to ___ percent or more of all rapes
f. Related to one out of every _____ arrests

4. What is the ratio of male alcoholics to female alcoholics? (p. 376)

Clinical picture of alcohol abuse and dependence

5. Alcohol is a depressant. Indicate how alcohol: (p. 377)

   1. affects higher brain centers

   2. affects behavior

6. If the percent of alcohol in the blood reaches _____ percent, the person is intoxicated. When the blood alcohol reaches _____ percent the individual passes out, and concentrations of blood alcohol above 0.55% usually cause death. (pp. 377-378)

7. Does alcohol help a person sleep more soundly? Explain. (Table 10.1, p. 378)

8. Does alcohol produce a true addiction in the same sense that heroin does? Explain. (Table 10.1, p. 378)

9. The legal level of intoxication, 0.1% blood alcohol level, would be reached after a 150-pound man had drunk _____ bottles of beer in one hour. It would require _____ hours for the alcohol to leave the body before it was safe to drive. (Table 10.2, p. 379)

10. List and define five early warning signs of drinking problems. (Table 10.3, p. 380)
    a.
    b.
    c.
    d.
    e.

11. How commonly are birth defects related to alcohol abuse? (Highlight 10.2, p. 381)

12. The liver works on assimilating alcohol into the system. How is it affected by large amounts of alcohol? (p. 380)

13. How can excessive intake of alcohol lead to malnutrition? (p. 380)

14. According to Lishman, evidence is beginning to show that an alcoholic's brain could be accumulating _____ even when no extreme organic symptoms are evident. (p. 381)

15. Alcoholic amnestic disorder is considered to be caused by _____ deficiency and other dietary inadequacies associated with chronic alcohol consumption. (p. 383)

Causes of alcohol abuse and dependence

16. Cotton completed a review of 39 studies of families of alcoholics and nonalcoholics. He found that almost _____ of alcoholics had at least one parent with an alcohol problem. (p. 383)

17. Cloninger et al. found strong evidence for the inheritance of alcoholism. They found the following rates of alcoholism: _____ percent among women with no alcoholic parents, _____ percent among women with one alcoholic parent, and _____ percent among women whose parents were both alcoholics. (pp. 383-384)

18. Finn (1990), studying persons at risk for alcoholism, has described an "alcohol risk personality." Some characteristics are: someone who is impulsive, prefers taking _____, is emotionally _____, has difficulty planning and _____ _____, finds that alcohol is helpful dealing with _____, and does not experience hangovers. (p. 384)

19. Fenna et al. (1971) and Wolff (1972) suggested that a hypersensitive reaction to alcohol occurs among Asian and Eskimo persons. This reaction includes _____ of the skin, a drop in _____, heart palpitations, and _____ following the ingestion of alcohol. This results from a _____ _____ that fails to break down alcohol molecules during the metabolic process. It is found in roughly _____ of all Asians. (pp. 384-385)

20. What do the authors of the text mean by the expression "alcoholic personality?" (p. 386)

21. About 75-80% of the studies of alcoholic personalities have shown an association between addictive disorders and _____ personality. (p. 386)

22. What is the only characteristic common to the backgrounds of most problem drinkers? How well does this characteristic predict alcoholism? Is it a cause or an effect? (p. 386)

23. In Cox and Klinger's motivational model of alcohol use, alcohol is consumed to bring about _____ changes, such as _____ effects, and even indirect effects, such as peer approval. In short, alcohol is consumed because it is _____ for the individual. (p. 387)

24. Many treatment programs try to identify personality or life-style factors in a relationship that serve to _____, _____, or to _____ drinking behavior. (p. 388)

25. How important is alcoholism as a cause of marital discord? (pp. 388-389)

26. Europe and six countries that have been influenced by European culture make up less than 20 percent of the world's population yet consume 80 percent of the alcohol. Thus, it appears that religious sanctions and social customs can determine whether alcoholism is one of the _____ commonly used in a given group or society. What country has the highest rate of alcoholism? (p. 390)

Treatment and outcomes

27. A _____ approach to the treatment of drinking problems appears to be most effective. The objectives of treatment programs include detoxification, _____, control over _____ behavior, and development of an individual's realization that he or she can _____ and lead a much more rewarding life without alcohol. (p. 391)

28. Why are drugs such as Valium (a minor tranquilizer) used during the detoxification process? (p. 391)

29. Antabuse (disulfiram) is not considered a complete treatment for alcoholism. When might Antabuse be used? (p. 391)

30. Sometimes spouses and children of alcoholics are included in group therapy. Complete each item in the list of reasons why this is done. (p. 392)

   a. The alcoholic is part of a disturbed family in which . . .

   b. Because family members are frequently the most victimized by the alcoholic's addiction, they often tend to be . . .

   c. Members of the family may unwittingly . . .

31. Relapses and continued deterioration are generally associated with a lack of _____ _____ or with living in a stressful environment. (p. 392)

32. There are several behavioral approaches to treating alcoholism. One involves injecting an emetic (i.e., a drug that causes the person to become extremely nauseated and to vomit). How does this treatment work and what is the purpose of repeating this procedure over several days? (p. 392)

33. One of the promising procedures for treating alcoholics is the cognitive-behavioral approach recommended by Marlatt (1985). Often referred to as a skills-training procedure, the program is aimed at younger problem drinkers who are considered to be at risk for developing more severe drinking problems on the basis of their family history of alcoholism or their current heavy consumption. The procedure has four components. Complete the following list: (pp. 392-393)
   1. Teaching facts about alcohol
   2. Developing coping skills in situations associated with increased risk of alcohol use
   3.
   4.

34. Brandsma, et al. (1980) found that AA had a high dropout rate. What, according to Chappel, were some explanations for this finding? (p. 394)

35. Polich et al. (1981) studied the course of alcoholism after treatment. Fill in the percentages they reported among treated alcoholics with serious drinking problems: (pp. 394-395)

_____ percent abstained for four years.

_____ percent showed alcohol-related problems.

_____ percent maintained alcohol dependency.

_____ percent had alcohol-related adverse consequences.

36 Under what conditions is treatment for alcoholism likely to be most effective? (p. 395)

37. On what ten characteristics did Project MATCH researchers match their patients? (p. 395)

38. Define the following components of a cognitive-behavioral approach to relapse prevention. (pp. 396-397)

a. Indulgent behaviors

b. Mini-decisions

c. Abstinence violation effect

Caffeine and nicotine

39. Respond with true or false to the following statements regarding caffeine and nicotine: (Highlight 10.3, pp. 398-399)
   a. They both are considered health problems today. True or False
   b. It is easy to stop using them. True or False
   c. "Caffeinism" is included in DSM IV. True or False

Drug abuse and dependence

40. The psychoactive drugs most commonly associated with abuse and dependence in our society are: narcotics, _____, _____, antianxiety drugs, and hallucinogens. (p. 397)

41. Drug abuse and dependence may occur at any age but are most common during _____ and _____ and vary according to metropolitan area, race, and _____, _____ status, and other demographic characteristics. (p. 398).

42. In a study of applicants for employment at a large teaching hospital in Maryland, Lange et al. found that _____ percent had detectable amounts of illicit drugs in their tests. Marijuana was detected among _____ percent of those who tested positively, followed by cocaine (_____ percent) and opiates (_____ percent). (p. 399)

43. Complete the following table that summarizes psychoactive drug abuse: (Table 10.4, p. 397)

Classification	Sample drug	Effect
Sedatives	Alcohol	Reduce tension, facilitate social interaction, blot out feelings
Sedatives	Nembutal	
Stimulants		
	Heroin	Alleviate physical pain, induce relaxation and reverie, alleviate anxiety and tension
Psychedelics		Induce changes in mood, mind expansion
Antianxiety		

264

Opium and its derivatives (narcotics)

44. What happened to the rate of heroin addiction during the 1960s, and what has happened since 1975? (p. 400)

45. What happens if a person takes heroin repeatedly for 30 days? (p. 400)

46. What is likely to happen if this person now stops taking the heroin abruptly? (pp. 400-401)

47. Is withdrawal from heroin dangerous and painful? What are the typical symptoms of heroin withdrawal? (p. 401)

48. What are the effects of heroin use during pregnancy? (p. 401)

Causal factors in opiate abuse and dependence

49. What is the single most common cause for heroin use given by addicts? (p. 402)

50. The human body produces its own opium-like substances, called _____, in the brain and pituitary gland. These substances are believed to play a role in an organism's reaction to _____. (p. 402)

51. What were the distinguishing features found among a large number of addicts studied by Gilbert and Lombardi? (p. 402)

52. What changes are seen in the young addict who has joined the drug subculture? (p. 402)

Opiate abuse: Treatment and outcomes

53 Has psychotherapy been found to add significant benefit to that achieved through the use of methadone alone according to Woody et al.? (p. 403)

54. How is buprenorphine similar to and different from methadone treatment? (p. 403)

Cocaine and amphetamines (stimulants)

55. What are the effects of taking cocaine? (p. 403)

56. Does tolerance to cocaine develop? (p. 404)

57. What factors are associated with poorer outcomes in treatment for cocaine dependency? (p. 405)

58. What are two problems encountered in treatment for cocaine dependency? (p. 405)

59. What are the legitimate medical uses of amphetamines? (p. 405)

60. Why has there been a light decrease in metamphetamine-related visits to the emergency room during the mid-1990s? (p. 405)

61. Are amphetamines addicting? (p. 405)

62. Does one build up tolerance to amphetamines? (p. 405)

63. What are the major physiological effects of excessive amphetamine use? (p. 405)

64. When does amphetamine psychosis occur? (pp. 405-406)

65. What happens when an established user of amphetamines abruptly stops taking the drug? (p. 406)

Barbiturates (sedatives)

66 How can barbiturates cause death? (p. 406)

67. What are the side effects of chronic use of barbiturates? (p. 406)

68. Describe the typical symptoms of barbiturate withdrawal. (p. 406)

69. What age group is most often found to be addicted to barbiturates? Why? (p. 406)

70. How can symptoms of barbiturate withdrawal be minimized? (p. 406)

LSD and related drugs (hallucinogens)

71. Name four hallucinogenic drugs: (p. 407)
    a.
    b.
    c.
    d.

72. What effects does LSD have on sensory perception? (p. 407)

73. Is there evidence that LSD enhances creativity? (p. 407)

74. What are the therapy goals for treating LSD dependence? (p. 407)

Marijuana

75. What is the difference between marijuana and hashish? (p. 408)

76. During the early 1970s, what proportion of teenagers and young adults experimented with marijuana? (p. 408)

77. Describe the following effects of marijuana: (p. 408)

    a. Psychological effects:

    b. Short-range physiological effects:

78. Does marijuana lead to physiological dependence? (p. 409)

79. Does marijuana lead to psychological dependence? (p. 409)

Hyperobesity

80. Weiss defined hyperobesity as 20 percent in excess of desirable weight. According to Kuczmarski, what percent of men and women are obese? (p. 409)

81. The text defines hyperobesity as _____ pounds or more above ideal body weight. (p. 409)

82. How does obesity put a person at greater risk for death? (p. 409)

83. What similarity between obesity and personality disorders makes it reasonable to consider obesity in the context of addictive disorders? (p. 410)

84. Obesity in adults is related to the number and size of the adipose cells (fat cells) in the body. People who are obese have markedly more adipose cells than people of normal weight. What happens when weight is lost? (p. 410)

85. How might overfeeding a child predispose him or her to obesity in adulthood? (p. 410)

86. What is the cognitive-behavioral explanation for obesity? (pp. 410-411)

87. Is weight related to social class? (p. 411)

88. What do the authors of the text conclude about the effectiveness of the following methods of losing weight? (pp. 411-412)

a. Overeaters Anonymous and Weight Watchers

b. Fasting or starvation diets

c. Diet drugs

d. Behavioral management methods

Pathological gambling

89. In what ways can gambling be considered an addictive disorder? (p. 413)

90. An estimated ___ to ___ million Americans get hooked on gambling. (p. 413)

91. How can compulsive gambling be explained by the principle of intermittent reinforcement? (p. 414)

92. How did Rosten (1961) characterize the compulsive gambler? (p. 414)

93. Work by Aronoff has pinpointed Laotian refugees as very high risk group for compulsive gambling. What four factors are thought to account for the problem of gambling in this group of people? (p. 415)

   a.
   b.
   c.
   d.

94. If a gambler joins a Gambler's Anonymous group, how likely is it that he/she will overcome the addiction to gambling? (p. 415)

95. List the treatment approaches used to assist compulsive gamblers at the Brecksville, Ohio, Veteran's Administration Medical Center. (pp. 415-416)

◊ CRITICAL THINKING ABOUT DIFFICULT TOPICS

1. The World Health Organization defines alcohol dependence syndrome as ". . . a state, psychic and *usually* also physical, resulting from taking alcohol, characterized by *behavioral* and other responses that *always* include a compulsion to take alcohol on a continuous or periodic basis in order to experience its *psychic* effects, and sometimes to avoid the discomfort of its absence; tolerance *may or may not* be present. (p. 375). Point out the instances of an emphasis on psychological rather than biological aspects in this definition.

2. Your text discusses activation of the "pleasure pathway" and "the brain reward system" (pp. 383; Figure 10.1, p. 384) by addictive drugs. Can you explain the difference between these two sources of reinforcement? (Compare termination of punishment versus consumption of food when hungry.)

3. Alcoholics Anonymous tries to "lift the burden of personal responsibility" by helping alcoholics to "see themselves as not as weak-willed or lacking in moral strength, but rather simply as having an affliction" (p. 394). Can you see in these comments the issue concerning free will versus determinism raised in the "Critical Thinking About Difficult Issues" section in Chapter 2?

4. The primary purely biological theory of substance abuse assumes that "addiction" derives from a state of physiological dependency that causes addicts to consume the drug in order to avoid the horrors of withdrawal. Consider the following statements from the text:

   - "Central to the neurochemical process underlying addiction is the role the drug plays in activating the 'pleasure pathway' . . . . Drugs that activate the brain reward system obtain reinforcing action and, thereby, promote further use" (p. 383).

   - "Among the immediate effects of mainlined or snorted heroin is a euphoric spasm (the rush) lasting 60 seconds or so, which many addicts compare to a sexual orgasm" (p. 400).

   - ". . . withdrawal from heroin is not always dangerous or even very painful" (p. 401).

   - "The ill health and general personality deterioration often found in opium addiction do not result directly from the pharmacological effects of the drug, but are usually products of the sacrifice of money, proper diet, social position, and self-respect as an addict becomes more desperate to procure the required daily dosage" (p. 401).

- ". . . the three most frequently cited reasons for beginning to use heroin were pleasure, curiosity, and peer pressure. Pleasure was the single most widespread reason--given by 81 percent of addicts" (p. 402).

- ". . . addicts on methadone [an opioid similar to heroin] can function normally and hold jobs . . ." (p. 403).

After reading these statements can you see why the purely biological theory of substance abuse does not fit the facts well? Can you articulate a psychobiological theory consistent with the view held by many that substance abuse is "abuse of a reinforcer"?

CHAPTER 10 QUIZ

Circle the best of the four answers provided and check them according to answers provided at the back of this study guide. Be sure you understand why each answer is correct.

1. A person who shows tolerance for a drug or withdrawal symptoms when it is unavailable illustrates: (p. 374)
   a. psychoactive substance abuse.
   b. psychoactive substance dependence.
   c. psychoactive substance toxicity.
   d. psychoactive substance-induced organic mental disorders and syndromes.

2. The life of the average alcoholic is about _____ years shorter than that of the average citizen. (p. 376)
   a. 3   c. 12
   b. 6   d. 18

3. A person is considered intoxicated when the alcohol content of the bloodstream reaches _____ percent. (p. 377)
   a. 0.1
   b. 0.5
   c. 1.0
   d. 1.5

4. Mr. H. is 75 and has been an alcoholic for 15 years. He has a lot of trouble remembering things that just happened. In order to avoid embarrassment, he often makes up things so others won't know he forgot. Mr. H.'s disorder is probably: (p. 382)
   a. alcohol amnestic disorder.
   b. alcohol idiosyncratic intoxication.
   c. alcohol withdrawal delirium.
   d. chronic alcoholic hallucinosis.

5. The only personality characteristic that appears common to the backgrounds of most problem drinkers is: (p. 386)
   a. general depression.
   b. emotional immaturity.
   c. inadequate sexual adjustment.
   d. personal maladjustment.

6. A cultural attitude of approbation and permissiveness toward drinking, such as exists in France, generally: (p. 390)
   a. is correlated with a low rate of alcoholism and problem drinking.
   b. is a sign that alcoholism has been accepted as a normal behavior pattern.
   c. is associated with the common use of alcohol as a means of coping with stress.
   d. has no significant effect on either alcoholism or drinking behavior.

7. Extinction of drinking behavior by associating it with nausea is a procedure called: (p. 392)
   a. Antabuse.
   b. systematic desensitization.
   c. covert sensitization.
   d. aversive conditioning.

8. In their four-year follow-up of a large group of treated alcoholics, Polich et al. (1981) found that _____ percent continued to show alcohol-related problems. (pp. 394-395)
   a. 7
   b. 18
   c. 36
   d. 54

9. In an extensive comparative study of several different treatments for alcoholism, Brandsma found that the Alcoholics Anonymous treatment was: (p. 396)
   a. better than some treatments and worse than others.
   b. equally as effective as all others.
   c. less effective than all others.
   d. more effective than all others.

10. According to Marlatt's cognitive-behavioral view, alcoholic relapse is typically based upon: (p. 396)
   a. accidental "falling off the wagon."
   b. an overpowering psychological craving.
   c. small, apparently irrelevant decisions.
   d. sudden increases in stressor strength.

11. The human body produces its own opium-like substances called _____ in the brain and pituitary gland. (p. 402)
   a. antibodies
   b. dopamines
   c. endorphins
   d. phagocytes

12. Which of the following personality disorders has the *highest* incidence among heroin addicts? (p. 402)
   a. antisocial
   b. avoidant
   c. compulsive
   d. dependent

13. Cocaine is classified as a(an): (p. 403)
   a. hallucinogen.
   b. narcotic.
   c. sedative.
   d. stimulant.

14. The drug that once was thought to be useful for inducing "model psychoses" is: (p. 407)
   a. cocaine.
   b. LSD.
   c. heroin.
   d. marijuana.

15. Apparently, adipose cells (fat cells): (p. 410)
   a. increase in number and size when an adult gains weight.
   b. have no relation to obesity.
   c. decrease in size, but not number, when an adult loses weight.
   d. change chemical structure in obese adults.

16. Goodwin and his colleagues concluded that which of the following situations put a son at *greatest* risk of becoming alcoholic? (p. 415)
   a. being born to an alcoholic parent
   b. being born to nonalcoholic parents
   c. being raised by an alcoholic parent
   d. being raised by nonalcoholic parents

| **Chapter 11** |
| *Sexual Variants, Abuse, and Dysfunctions* |

◊ OVERVIEW

Chapter 11 opens with an introduction discussing the enormous variability within and between cultures in sexual practices and attitudes - particularly homosexuality, which is not viewed in DSM-IV as a mental disorder. The chapter then covers three separate sections that are related to sexual behavior: sexual variants, sexual abuse, and sexual dysfunctions. The first of the three sections on sexual behavior discusses paraphilias, in which unusual objects, rituals, or situations have become centrally important to the person's full sexual satisfaction. It also discusses gender identity disorders, in which the person strongly rejects his or her biological sex and wishes to be of the opposite sex. Some of these behaviors are considered minor criminal offenses--e.g., exhibitionism or voyeurism--as well as being included as mental disorders in DSM-IV. The next section treats the major crimes of sexual abuse: childhood sexual abuse, pedophilia, incest, and rape. Only one of these (pedophilia) is listed as a mental disorder in DSM-IV, though the victims of the crimes are, of course, at increased risk for mental disorders. The last section concerns the sexual dysfunctions. These are problems that may interfere with an individual's full enjoyment of sexual relations. The sexual dysfunctions are not mental disorders but are simply problems that interfere with full sexual enjoyment and are readily treated.

◊ CHAPTER OUTLINE

I.   Sociocultural Influences on Sexual Practices and Standards
     A. Case I: Degeneracy and Abstinence Theory
     B. Case II: Ritualized Homosexuality in Melanesia
     C. Case III: Homosexuality and American Psychiatry
         1. Homosexuality as Sickness
         2. Homosexuality as Nonpathological Variation

II. Sexual and Gender Variants
    A. The Paraphilias
        1. Fetishism
        2. Transvestic Fetishism
        3. Voyeurism
        4. Exhibitionism
        5. Sadism
        6. Masochism
    B. Causal Factors and Treatments for Paraphilias
        1. Treatments for Paraphilias
    C. Gender Identity Disorders
        1. Gender Identity Disorder of Childhood
        2. Transsexualism
        3. Treatment

III. Sexual Abuse
    A. Childhood Sexual Abuse
        1. Prevalence of Childhood Sexual Abuse
        2. Consequences of Childhood Sexual Abuse
        3. Controversies Concerning Childhood Sexual Abuse
        4. Children's Testimony
        5. Recovered Memories of Sexual Abuse
    B. Pedophilia
    C. Incest
    D. Rape
        1. Prevalence
        2. Is Rape Motivated by Sex or Aggression
        3. Rape and Its Aftermath
        4. Rapists
    E. Treatment and Recidivism of Sex Offenders
        1. Goals of Treatment
        2. Effectiveness of Psychosocial Treatments
        3. Biological and Surgical Treatments

IV. Sexual Dysfunctions
    A. Dysfunctions of Sexual Desire
    B. Dysfunctions of Sexual Arousal
        1. Male Erectile Disorder

     2. Female Sexual Arousal Disorder
  C. Orgasmic Disorders
     1. Premature Ejaculation
     2. Male Orgasmic Disorder
     3. Female Orgasmic Disorder
  D. Disorders Involving Sexual Pain
     1. Vaginismus
     2. Dyspareunia

V. Unresolved Issues: Long-Term Consequences of Childhood Sexual Abuse

VI. Summary

◊ LEARNING OBJECTIVES

After studying this chapter, you should be able to:

1. Provide a number of examples of sociocultural influences in sexual practices and cultural standards and values. (pp. 421-424; Highlight 11.1, pp. 426-427)

2. Define, give examples of, and describe the clinical features of the following paraphilias: fetishism, transvestic fetishism, voyeurism, exhibitionism, sadism, and masochism. (pp. 425-434)

3. Discuss the most effective treatments for paraphilias, and summarize causal factors implicated in their etiology. (pp. 433-434)

4. Define and describe the clinical features and treatment of the gender identity disorders (gender identity disorder of childhood, transsexualism). (pp. 434-438)

5. Review what is known about the frequency and nature of childhood sexual abuse. Discuss the controversies surrounding both childhood testimony regarding sexual abuse and adult "recovered memories" of childhood sexual abuse. (pp. 438-442)

6. Define pedophilia and summarize what is known about pedophiles. (pp. 442-443)

7. Review what is known about the frequency and nature of incest. (pp. 443-444)

8. Summarize what is known about rape and rapists, and discuss the issues regarding the frequency of rape and the motivation of rapists. Describe attempts to treat sex offenders. (pp. 445-452)

9. Define the sexual dysfunctions, describe their general features, review etiological theories, and summarize the major approaches to treatment. (pp. 452-458)

10. Knowledgeably discuss the difficulty of deciding whether childhood sexual abuse causes borderline personality disorder. (pp. 458-459)

◊ TERMS YOU SHOULD KNOW

---

sexual variants (pp. 420; 425-438)

sexual abuse (p. 420; 438-448)

sexual dysfunctions (pp. 420; 452-458)

degeneracy theory and *abstinence theory* (pp. 421-422)

homosexuality (pp. 422-424; Highlight 1.1, pp. 426-427)

paraphilia (pp. 425, 428-434)

fetishism (pp. 425, 428)

transvestic fetishism (pp. 428-430)

voyeurism (p. 430)

exhibitionism (pp. 430-431)

sadism (pp. 431-432)

masochism (pp. 432-433)

autoerotic asphyxia (p. 432)

erotic target location (p. 433)

aversion therapy (p. 434)

covert sensitization (simple versus *assisted)* (p. 434)

gender identity disorder (pp. 434-435)

cross-gender identification (pp. 434-435)

gender dysphoria (p. 435)

transsexualism (pp. 435-437)

autogynephilia (p. 437)

"recovered" memories (p. 439)

pedophilia (pp. 442-443)

penile plethysmograph (p. 443)

incest (pp. 443-444)

rape (pp. 445-448)

statutory rape (p. 445)

"victim-precipitated" rape (p. 446)

chemical castration (p. 449)

Depo-Provera (medroxyprogesterone acetate) (p. 449)

sexual desire disorders (pp. 453-454)

hypoactive sexual desire disorder (p. 453)

sexual aversion disorder (p. 453)

male erectile disorder (formerly *impotence*) (pp. 454-455)

priapism (p. 455)

female sexual arousal disorder (formerly *frigidity*) (pp. 455-456)

premature ejaculation (pp. 456-457)

male orgasmic disorder (p. 457)

female orgasmic disorder (pp. 457-458)

vaginismus (p. 458)

dyspareunia (p. 458)

◊ NAMES YOU SHOULD KNOW

John Money

Ray Blanchard

Kurt Freund

Richard Green

David Finkelhor

Stephen Ceci

Raymond Knight

William Masters and Virginia Johnson

1. Explain how the case histories of (a) homosexuality in Melanesia and (b) homosexuality and American Psychiatry illustrate that opinions about acceptable and normal sexual behavior vary over time and across cultures. (pp. 422-424)

2. What is the role of androgen in the most influential etiological model of sexual orientation? (Highlight 11.1, p. 427)

3. Discuss evidence from Bailey et al.'s twin studies (1991, 1993) regarding the influence of genetic and environmental factors in human sexual orientation. (Highlight 1.1, p. 427)

4. Define *paraphilias* and list eight examples recognized in DSM-IV. (p. 425)

5. Define *fetishism*, summarize the clinical picture, and give several examples. (p. 425, 428)

6. Define *transvestic fetishism*, and summarize what is known about the clinical picture and personalities of transvestites. (pp. 428-430)

7. Define *voyeurism*, list two other terms that are synonyms, and describe its clinical features. (p. 430)

8. Define *exhibitionism*, describe its clinical features, and indicate how its frequency varies with culture. (pp. 430-431)

9. Define sexual *sadism* and describe its varied manifestations, including that inflicted by serial killers. (pp. 431-432)

10. Define sexual *masochism* and describe its varied manifestations, including autoerotic asphyxia. (pp. 432-433)

11. Describe Money's attempt to account for the fact that almost all paraphilics are male. (p. 433)

12. What do Freund and Blanchard mean by "erotic target location"? How does this concept help to account for the fact that people with paraphilias often have more than one paraphilia? (pp. 433-434)

13. Describe cognitive-behavioral treatments for paraphilias, including the effectiveness of these treatments as found in Maletzky's (1998) study. (p. 434)

14. What are the arguments in favor of and against labeling children with gender identity disorder as "disordered"? (p. 435)

15. Distinguish the two types of male to female transsexuals, and discuss their developmental course. (pp. 436-437)

16. List the short-term consequences of childhood sexual abuse and explain why knowledge about the long-term consequences is more uncertain. (pp. 438-439)

17. Critically evaluate the validity of children's testimony regarding sexual abuse. (p. 439; Highlight 11.2, pp. 440-441)

18. Describe the methods and results of the "Sam Stone Study," and explain the implications for preschool children's testimony. (Highlight 11.2, pp. 440-441)

19. Summarize the issues surrounding "recovered" memories of sexual abuse. (pp. 439, 442)

20. Define pedophilia and describe its clinical features, including the results of studies investigating the sexual responsesof pedophiles. (pp. 442-443)

21. What do we know about the incidence and prevalence patterns of incest and rape? Why are these rates difficult to estimate, and what factors contribute to the variation between estimates? (pp. 444, 445)

22. On what basis do the authors reject the hypothesis that sexual desire is not involved at all in rape? (pp. 445-446)

23. What is the evidence in support of the hypothesis that rape might be considered a category of paraphilia? (pp. 447-448)

24. List the three goals of therapies for sex offenders and describe the approaches taken to achieve these goals. (pp. 448-451)

25. Compare and contrast dysfunctions of sexual arousal with orgasmic disorders in men and women. (pp. 454-458)

26. Summarize research on the role of anxiety and other potential causal factors in male erectile disorder. (pp. 454-455)

27. List several treatments for male erectile disorder and female sexual arousal disorder. (pp. 455-456)

28. Summarize the treatments for and the etiological theories of the orgasmic disorders (i.e., premature ejaculation, male orgasmic disorder, and female orgasmic disorder). (pp. 456-458)

29. Why is it understandable that dyspareunia is often associated with vaginismus in women? (p. 458)

30. Discuss the complexities (in terms of methodological issues) of attempting to determine whether childhood sexual abuse causes borderline personality disorder. (pp. 458-459)

◊ STUDY QUESTIONS

Introduction

1. Few people are always happy with their sex lives, but a significant minority have psychological problems that make sexual fulfillment especially difficult. The three general sets of difficulties considered in the chapter are problematic sexual _____, sexual _____, and sexual _____. (p. 420)

Sociocultural influences on sexual practices and standards

2. Although some aspects of sexuality and mating are cross-culturally universal, others are quite variable. For example, all known cultures have taboos against sex between _____, but attitudes toward _____ vary considerably. (p. 421)

3. Recent large, carefully selected samples from the United States, France, and England suggest that the rate of adult homosexual behavior is between ____ and ____ percent, with the rate of exclusively male homosexuality between ____ and ____ percent. The analogous rates for female homosexuality are approximately _____ those for males. (Highlight 11.1, p. 426)

4. What explanation is offered for the high number of sexual partners reported by gay men? (Highlight 11.1, p. 427)

The paraphilias

5. These are a group of persistent sexual behavior patterns in which unusual objects, _____, or _____ are required for sexual satisfaction to occur. (p. 425)

Fetishism

6. In fetishism, sexual interest typically centers on some body part or an inanimate object. Describe how fetishists get their desired objects and what they do with them once obtained. (p. 425)

7. How does the illegal act itself (that is, illegally obtaining the desired object) typically affect the fetishist? (p. 428)

8. How can fetishes be developed through conditioning? (p. 428)

Transvestic fetishism

9. What, according to Blanchard (1989, 1992) is the psychological motivation behind transvestic fetishism? (p. 428)

10. Are most transvestites homosexuals or heterosexuals? (p. 428)

Voyeurism

11. Voyeurism, also known as scotophilia and inspectionalism, refers to obtaining sexual pleasure through looking at other people undressing or having sex. What age group commits the majority of voyeuristic acts? (p. 430)

12. Many men enjoy looking at women. Under what conditions does this normal behavior become voyeurism? (p. 430)

13. What factors serve to reinforce voyeuristic behavior? (p. 430)

14. If a voyeur is married, how well adjusted would he be expected to be in his sexual relationships with his wife? (p. 430)

15. How viable is pornography as an alternative source of gratification for voyeurs? (p. 430)

Exhibitionism

16. What is the typical clinical picture and pattern of an exhibitionist? (pp. 430-431)

17. How variable are the locations in which exposure typically occurs? Who is the typical victim of a male exhibitionist? (p. 430)

Sadism

18. On what does the arousal of sadistic individuals depend? (p. 431)

19. Sometimes sadistic activities are associated with objects other than human beings such as _____. (p. 431)

20. According to Warren, Dietz, and Hazelwood, what is the typical clinical picture of sexually sadistic serial killers? (pp. 431-432)

Masochism

21. Which appears to be more common: masochism or sadism? (p. 432)

22. How is the clinical picture of masochism related to that of sadism? (p. 432)

Causal factors for paraphilias

23. Two facts about paraphilia are likely to be etiologically important: (p. 433)
    a. Almost all paraphilics are _____.
    b. People with paraphilias often _____.

24. According to Money (1986), male vulnerability to paraphilias is closely linked to their greater dependence on what? (p. 433)

Treatments for paraphilias

25. Much of cognitive therapy involves restructuring cognitive distortions. List three examples of cognitive distortions that may maintain paraphilic behavior. (p. 434)

Gender identity disorders

26. Gender identity disorder is characterized by two components: (pp. 434-435)
    a.
    b.

27. Although mere tomboys frequently have many or most of the traits of (a) preferring boys' clothing and hair styles and (b) engaging in activities seen in girls with gender identity disorders, tomboys differ in that they do not desire to _____, or to grow up _____. (p. 435)

28. What is the most common outcome of boys with gender identity disorder? (p. 435)

29. How do autogynephilic transsexuals differ from homosexual transsexuals? (pp. 436-437)

30. Has psychotherapy been successful in altering gender identity in transsexuals? (p. 437)

31. Describe what procedures are involved in the following surgical changes of sex: (p. 437)

    1. Male-to-female

    2. Female-to-male

32. What do follow-up studies reviewed by Green and Fleming reveal about the satisfaction of persons who have had sex-change surgery? (p. 437)

Sexual abuse

33. List three reasons for the marked increase in research of childhood sexual abuse. (p. 438)

34. After a retrial and five years in jail, the jury acquitted Raymond. Buckey because of the jury's concern that the interviewers had _____ the children into telling stories of abuse using _____ or _____ methods of _____. (p. 439)

35. In children's testimony regarding sexual abuse, the use of sexually anatomically correct dolls _____ improve the accuracy of the reports of where (or even if) they were touched. (p. 439)

36. Stephen Ceci found that preschoolers are not deficient at distinguishing between whether they performed an act or whether someone else performed the act, but they do have a deficit in distinguishing between _____ versus _____ acts when both were done by themselves. (Highlight 11.3, pp. 440-441)

Pedophilia

37. Most pedophiles are men. About 2/3 of their victims are _____, typically between the ages of _____ and _____. (p. 442)

38. In pedophilia, the preferred sexual partner is a _____, and the sexual contact frequently involves _____. (pp. 442-443)

39. Respond to the following questions: (p. 443)
    a. Do most pedophiles use force?
    b. Do most pedophiles show sexual arousal only to children?
    c. Is the most common type of pedophile drawn to children because he feels in control with them?

40. There has been a rash of pedophilia among the Catholic clergy: at least _____ priests were charged with sexual abuse during the 1980s. (p. 443)

Incest

41. Culturally prohibited sexual relations between family members, such as a brother and sister or a parent and child, are known as incest. Describe the consequences of inbreeding. (pp. 443-444)

42. Incest is thought to be grossly underreported to authorities, but Williams and Finkelhor found almost _____ cases of "intrafamilial sexual abuse" in 1985. In two studies, _____-_____ incest was five times more common than _____-_____ incest. (p. 444)

43. How common is mother-son incest compared to father-daughter? (p. 444)

44. Incestuous fathers tend to be of lower _____ than other fathers, but they do not typically evidence serious _____. Indeed, they are often _____, _____ and claim devotion to their families. Most incestuous fathers are not _____. (p. 444)

45. The wives of men who commit incest were often _____ themselves as children, and in more than _____ of such cases the wife often _____ even if she knows about the incest. (p. 444)

Rape

46. What happened to the incidence of reported rape from 1979 to 1990 according to the National Crime Survey data? (p. 445)

47. Using data from the National Crime Survey, which draws on a probability sample of 59,000 households, the authors estimate that the lifetime risk of total (reported and unreported) rapes or attempted rapes is _____ to _____ percent. (p. 445)

48. Respond to the following questions: (p. 446)
    a. Is rape a repetitive activity?
    b. Are most rapes planned?
    c. Do a third of rapes involve more than one offender?
    d. Does a close relationship between victim and offender mean the victim is more likely to be brutally beaten?

49. Far from being a seductress, the woman repeatedly victimized by rape is often quite _____ and _____. (p. 447)

50. How old is the typical rapist? (p. 447)

51. Unfortunately, most sexual assaults are not reported and, of those that are, less than _____ percent result in conviction. Convictions often bring _____. (p. 448)

Treatment and recidivism of sex offenders

52. What are the two concerns about the practical effectiveness of therapies that attempt to modify sexual arousal patterns via aversion therapy? (p. 449)

53. What is Lupron, how effective is it, and how does it compare to Depo-Provera? (p.449)

54. What is the recidivism rate of castrated sex offenders as compared to that of uncastrated sex offenders? (pp. 449-450)

Sexual dysfunctions

55. The term *sexual dysfunction* refers to impairment either in the desire for sexual gratification or in the ability to achieve it. Sexual dysfunctions are caused by _____ _____ _____ and _____, as well as _____ factors. (p. 452)

56. What is the most common female sexual dysfunction, and why has it inspired less research than male sexual dysfunctions? (p. 454)

57. Explain the distinction between lifelong and situational erectile disorder. (p. 454)

58. According to Barlow et al., preoccupation with _____ _____ about _____ rather than anxiety per se, appears to be responsible for inhibiting sexual arousal. (p. 454)

59. Circle the correct term. Prolonged or permanent erectile insufficiency before the age of 60 is relatively: Common or Rare (p. 454)

60. What is priapism, and what are three things that may cause it? (p. 455)

61. Can insufficiency due to organic causes be differentiated from psychogenic insufficiency by the presence of nocturnal erections? (p. 455)

62. LoPicolo's (1978) rule for determining when a male is a premature ejaculator is an inability to tolerate as much as _____ minutes of stimulation without ejaculation. Younger men are notorious for their "quick trigger," and longer periods of abstinence increase the likelihood of premature ejaculation. (p. 456)

63. How is premature ejaculation treated, and what is the success rate for the treatments? (p. 457)

64. Which is more difficult to treat: lifelong or situational female orgasmic disorder? Why, according to Beck? (p. 458)

65. Vaginismus is an involuntary spasm of the muscles at the entrance to the vagina that prevents penetration and intercourse. In some cases, women who suffer from vaginismus also have sexual arousal disorder, possibly the result of conditioned fears associated with _____. (p. 458)

66. The medical term for painful coitus (sexual intercourse) is _____. It can occur in men but is far more common in women. (p. 458)

◊ **CRITICAL THINKING ABOUT DIFFICULT TOPICS**

1. Freund and Blanchard's concept of erotic target location assumes that men are not born with a heterosexual orientation, but rather they "must learn which stimuli together constitute a female sex partner, who is their target stimulus" (p. 434). Evidence from the biological model of human sexual orientation appears to conflict with this model. How? Cite evidence to support your answer.

Freund and Blanchard's model suggests that our biological motivations are quite diffuse and can be channeled in many different directions. Can you think of other examples? Consider cultural variations in dress, hairstyles, and personal ornamentation. More basically, consider the large cultural variations in food preferences. The need for food is biologically determined, but the precise foods that satisfy this biological motivation appear to be strongly influenced by learning. Can you explain how such an inherited motivational process can be so shaped by learning?

2. Your text notes that, although sexual advances to prepubertal children are viewed as a psychiatric disorder and diagnosed as pedophilia in DSM-IV, rape and incest (including advances directed at postpubertal children) are not. Your text interprets this difference as reflecting "the seriousness with which society views these offenses and its preference for treating coercive sex offenders as criminals rather than patients" (p. 438). On what basis would you decide whether sexual advances directed at postpubertal children should be seen as reflecting psychopathology or as simple criminal behavior? Would you make the same attribution for a biological father and a step-father? If not, why not? More generally, what are the defining features of any psychiatric disorder?

◊ **CHAPTER 11 QUIZ**

Circle the best of the four answers provided and check them according to answers provided at the back of this study guide. Be sure you understand why each answer is correct.

1. A form of paraphilia in which there usually is not a "victim" is: (p. 428)
   a. voyeurism.   c. sadism.
   b. exhibitionism.   d. transvestism.

2. Which of the following persons is most likely to engage in voyeurism? (p. 430)
   a. a married woman who is unhappy with her sexual relations
   b. a homosexual man who is "in between" lovers
   c. an adolescent male who is shy and feels inadequate in relations with women
   d. an elderly man who lives by himself

3. Most exhibitionists: (p. 431)
   a. are young adult males.
   b. are middle-aged married males.
   c. are also aggressive and assaultive.
   d. try to have sexual relations with their victims.

4. In Maletzky's (1998) treatment outcome study of nearly 1500 paraphilic offenders, the *lowest* rates of success were found for: (p. 434)
   a. exhibitionism.
   b. nontransvestic fetishism
   c. voyeurism.
   d. transvestic fetishism.

5. The most common adult outcome of boys with gender identity disorder appears to be: (p. 435)
   a. homosexuality.
   b. heterosexuality.
   c. homosexual transsexualism.
   d. heterosexual transsexualism.

6. Most transsexuals who are sexually attracted to men and who recall being extremely feminine in childhood are: (p. 436)
   a. female to male transsexuals
   b. homosexual transsexuals
   c. autogynephilic transsexuals
   d. nonhomosexual transsexuals

7. Raymond Buckey, who helped run McMartin Preschool, was accused in 1983 of child sexual abuse. After five years in jail and a retrial, he was acquitted due to concerns about: (p. 439)
   a. the bizzareness of the charges.
   b. the extreme rarity of preschool sexual abuse charges.
   c. falsification of evidence by parents.
   d. the manner in which interviewers elicited children's testimony.

8. In the "Sam Stone Study," Ceci found that ____ percent of children given a prior stereotype and asked leading questions during the initial interviews continued to give inaccurate testimony even when gently challenged, compared with only ____ percent among control children. (Highlight 11.2, pp. 440-441)
   a. 5, 1
   b. 14, 4.5
   c. 23, 8
   d. 44, 2.5

9. Incest is almost certainly more common than is known because many victims: (p. 444)
   a. do not consider themselves victimized.
   b. have no desire to stop.
   c. are not educated.
   d. are unable to break from the familial pressure.

10. In Williams and Finkelhor's study, incestuous fathers tended to be _____ _____ than other fathers. (p. 444)
    a. more impulsive
    b. of lower intelligence
    c. more psychopathic
    d. less religious

11. Which of the following best distinguishes incarcerated rapists from date rapists? (p. 447)
    a. hostile masculinity
    b. impulsive, antisocial behavior
    c. emotionally detached, predatory personalities
    d. promiscuity

12. Impairment of either the desire for sexual gratification or of the ability to achieve it is termed sexual: (p. 452)
    a. dysfunction.
    b. incompetence.
    c. perversion.
    d. variation.

13. Which of the following is the most common male sexual dysfunction? (p. 456)
    a. lack of sexual interest
    b. anxiety about sexual performance
    c. retarded ejaculation
    d. climaxing too early

14. According to the findings of Diokno, Brown, and Herzog (1990), more than _____ of married men over age 70 had some erectile difficulties. (p. 454)
    a. one-fourth
    b. one-half
    c. two-thirds
    d. three-fourths

15. Which of the following is likely to be the *least* effective treatment for premature ejaculation? (p. 457)
    a. yohimbine
    b. pause-and-squeeze technique
    c. clomipramine
    d. prozac

| Chapter 12 |
| The Schizophrenias |

◊ OVERVIEW

The schizophrenias include some of the most extreme deviations of psychopathology possible. For this reason, this condition fascinates many people, including psychologists. Because schizophrenia involves disorders in thought, perception, affect, motor behavior, and social relationships, researchers have hoped that the study of schizophrenia--where the processes have broken down—might in turn lead to better understanding of unimpaired psychological functioning.

Several different types of schizophrenia are described in Chapter 12, and then the biopsychosocial causal factors of the whole group are discussed. Evidence for biological causal factors, in particular, are emphasized in the section. Overall, the causes of schizophrenia have been more thoroughly researched than many of the other conditions studied so far. Finally, the treatment of schizophrenia--with antipsychotic drugs and psychosocial approaches--is described and evaluated. The chapter concludes with a short discussion of the clinical picture and etiology of delusional disorders.

◊ CHAPTER OUTLINE

I. The Schizophrenias
    A. Origins of the Schizophrenia Concept
    B. Prevalence and Onset

II. The Clinical Picture in Schizophrenia
    A. Disturbance of Associative Linking
    B. Disturbance of Thought Content
    C. Disruption of Perception
    D. Emotional Dysfunction
    E. Confused Sense of Self
    F. Disrupted Volition

G. Retreat to an Inner World
H. Disturbed Motor Behavior
I. Continuing Problems in Defining Schizophrenia

III. The Classic Subtypes of Schizophrenia
  A. Undifferentiated Type
  B. Catatonic Type
  C. Disorganized Type
  D. Paranoid Type
  E. Other Schizophrenic Patterns

IV. Causal Factors in Schizophrenia
  A. Biological Factors in Schizophrenia
    1. Genetic Influences
    2. Twin Studies
    3. Adoption Studies
    4. Studies of High Risk Children
    5. Biochemical Factors
    6. Neurophysiological Factors
    7. Neuroanatomical Factors
       a) Brain Mass Anomalies
       b) Deficit Localization
    8. Neurodevelopmental Issues
    9. Interpreting the Biological Evidence: Diathesis/Stress
  B. Psychosocial Factors in Schizophrenia
    1. Damaging Parent-Child and Family Interactions
       a) Destructive Parental Interactions
       b) Faulty Communications
    2. The Role of Excessive Life Stress and Expressed Emotion
  C. Sociocultural Factors in Schizophrenia

V. Treatments and Outcomes
  A. The Effects of Antipsychotic Medication
  B. Psychosocial Approaches in Treating Schizophrenia
    1. Family Therapy
    2. Individual Psychotherapy
    3. Social-Skills Training and Community Treatment

◊ LEARNING OBJECTIVES

After studying this chapter, you should be able to:

1. Review the history of the concept of schizophrenia and identify its major clinical features. (pp. 464-465, 465-469)

2. Discuss the prevalence and onset of schizophrenia, including sex, age, and sociocultural differences. (pp. 464-465)

3. List the DSM-IV criteria for the diagnosis of schizophrenia. (Table 12.2, p. 468)

4. Compare and contrast the subtypes of schizophrenia. (pp. 470-476; Table 12.3, p. 470)

5. Summarize the biological, psychosocial, and sociocultural causal influences in schizophrenia. (pp. 476-492)

6. Evaluate the various biological and psychosocial treatments for schizophrenia. (pp. 493-496)

7. Describe the clinical features and subtypes of delusional disorders. (pp. 496-498; Highlight 12.2, p. 498)

8. Summarize what is known about the causal factors in and treatments for delusional disorders. (pp. 498-500)

9. Discuss current issues in treating schizophrenia, including limitations of antipsychotics, and the need for expanded psychosocial intervention. (pp. 500-501)

◊ TERMS YOU SHOULD KNOW

schizophrenia (p. 463)

psychosis (p. 463)

delusional disorder (p. 463)

dementia praecox (p. 464)

positive syndrome schizophrenia and *Type I schizophrenia* (p. 465)

negative syndrome schizophrenia and *Type II schizophrenia* (p. 465)

disorganized schizophrenia (p. 466)

*formal thought disorder (*or *derailment* or *loosening of associations)* (p. 466)

cognitive slippage (p. 467)

word salad (p. 467)

delusions (p. 467)

breakdown of perceptual selectivity (p. 468)

hallucinations (p. 468)

anhedonia (p. 468)

blunting (of affect) (pp. 468-469)

cosmic or oceanic feelings (p. 469)

provisional construct (p. 469)

undifferentiated type (of schizophrenia) (p. 470-471; Table 12.3, p. 470)

catatonic type (of schizophrenia) (p. 471-473; Table 12.3, p. 470)

catatonic stupor (p. 472)

echopraxia (p. 472)

echolalia (p. 472)

disorganized type (of schizophrenia) (p. 473-474; Table 12.3, p. 470)

paranoid type (of schizophrenia) (p. 474-476; Table 12.3, p. 470)

residual type (of schizophrenia) (p. 476; Table 12.3, p. 470)

schizoaffective disorder (p. 476)

schizophreniform disorder (p. 476)

index (in a genetic risk study) (p. 476)

polygenic (p. 477)

twin studies (pp. 477, 480-481)

concordance (pp. 477, 480)

monochorionic (p. 480)

hypofrontality (p. 481, 487)

age-correlated schizophrenia index rate (p. 481)

adoption strategy (p. 481)

studies of high-risk children (pp. 482-483)

chemical imbalance (p. 483)

dopamine hypothesis (p. 483)

Clozaril (p. 483)

Zyprexa (p. 483)

Risperdal (p. 483)

"cognitive dysmetria" (p. 484)

smooth pursuit eye movement (SPEM) (p. 484)

computerized axial tomography (CAT) (p. 485)

magnetic resonance imaging (MRI) (p. 485)

sulci (p. 486)

neurodegenerative and neurodevelopmental processes (p. 486)

basal ganglia (pp. 486-487)

season of birth effect (pp. 487-488)

double bind communication (pp. 490-491)

amorphous style (of thinking) (p. 491)

fragmented style (of thinking) (p. 491)

communication deviance (p. 491)

expressed emotion (EE) (pp. 491-492)

major tranquilizers (p. 493)

social recovery (p. 494)

assertive community treatment (ACT) *or intensive case management* (ICM) (p. 496)

paranoia (p. 496)

delusional disorder (p. 496)

shared psychotic disorder (folie à deux) (p. 496)

brief psychotic disorder (p. 496)

persecutory type (of delusional disorder) (p. 497)

jealous type (of delusional disorder) (p. 497)

erotomanic type (of delusional disorder) (p. 497)

somatic type (of delusional disorder) (p. 497)

grandiose type (of delusional disorder) (p. 497)

ideas of persecution (p. 497)

delusions of grandeur (p. 497)

paranoid illumination (Highlight 12.2, p. 498; p. 500)

paranoid pseudo-community (Highlight 12.2, p. 498; p. 500)

Emil Kraepelin

Eugen Bleuler

Nancy Andreasen

Timothy Crow

Irving Gottesman

Kenneth Kendler

Paul Meehl

◊ **CONCEPTS TO MASTER**

---

1. The original term for the schizophrenias was *dementia praecox*. In light of our current views, the term *dementia praecox* is misleading because there is no convincing evidence that schizophrenia leads to permanent mental deterioration. Later, Bleuler introduced the term *schizophrenia*, which means split mind. He did not mean "split personality" by this term. What did he mean? (p. 464)

2. Distinguish between positive-syndrome and negative syndrome schizophrenia, list some near-synonyms for each, and discuss whether they are meant to be dichotomous or continuous variables. Describe other classifications of general symptom patterns of schizophrenia. (pp. 465-466)

3. List and describe eight symptom domains that are relevant to the construct of schizophrenia. (pp. 466-469)

4. List the DSM-IV criteria for the diagnosis of schizophrenia. (Table 12.3, p. 470)

5. Describe four major subtypes of schizophrenia that have been identified, and review three additional schizophrenic patterns that appear in DSM-IV. (pp. 470-476)

6. Compare and contrast the onset, course, and prognosis for each of the four identified subtypes of schizophrenia, as well as the three additional schizophrenic patterns. (pp. 470-476)

7. Review the evidence from twin studies in support of a genetic contribution to schizophrenia and describe the confounding factors that make it more difficult to draw genetic etiologic conclusions from the classical twin study method. (pp. 480-481)

8. List the findings for 27 pairs of discordant MZ twins in the study by Torrey and colleagues (1994) and explain the implications of these findings. (p. 481)

9. What were the major findings of the following studies (p. 482):
   a) the follow-up study of 47 adoptees born to schizophrenic mothers in state hospitals

   b) the Danish adoption study

   c) Tienari et al.'s adoption study

10. What is the "dopamine hypothesis?" Explain the basis for the following statement in your text: "In recent years, however, the dopamine hypothesis has proved oversimplistic and inadequate as a general formulation of etiology." (p. 483)

11. Describe the deficiencies in smooth pursuit eye movement that have been observed in schizophrenics and in some of their close relatives and discuss the implications of these findings. (p. 484)

12. In addition to smooth pursuit eye movement deficiencies, what other abnormal *neurophysiological processes* have been found to be associated with increased risk for schizophrenia? (p. 484)

13. What *neuroanatomical anomalies* differentiate schizophrenic patients from controls? (pp. 485-486)

14. Describe the debate over whether these anomalies are neurodegenerative, neurodevelopmental, or both. (p. 486)

15. To what extent are long-term antipsychotics responsible for these brain anomalies? (p. 486)

16. Explain what is meant by *hypofrontality*, summarize the evidence in support of this concept, and note the authors' cautionary statement about these findings. Also, discuss how temporolimbic structures are thought to be involved in schizophrenia. (p. 487)

17. Describe Walker's methodology and summarize her findings regarding early childhood deficits in emotional and facial expressions, motor skills, and neuromotor functioning among individuals who later developed schizophrenia. How do the authors of the text later explain how such deficits might increase the risk of developing schizophrenia? (pp. 489-490)

18. Discuss other evidence for the association between early developmental deviation and schizophrenic risk. (pp. 487-488)

19. Describe theories of pathogenic parent-child and family interactions, as well as some caveats regarding this type of research. (pp. 490-491)

20. What is expressed emotion (EE)? Describe the findings for a genuinely causal role of EE in precipitating relapse of psychotic episodes. (pp. 491-492)

21. Summarize the results of research concerning the possibility that some general sociocultural factors may contribute to the development of schizophrenia. (pp. 492-493)

22. What were the results of the Hegarty et al. (1994) review of treatments and outcomes in schizophrenia over the last century? To what did he attribute the recent decline in improvement rates? (p. 494)

23. List and describe the major pharmacological and psychosocial approaches to treating schizophrenia. (pp. 494-496)

24. List and describe six types of delusional (paranoid) disorders that appear in DSM-IV, and explain why formal diagnosis of delusional disorder is difficult. (pp. 496-497)

25. Describe the clinical symptoms that characterize delusional (paranoid) disorders, and explain the causal factors that contribute to its development. (pp. 497-500)

26. What is "paranoid illumination," and how does it lead to the establishment of a paranoid "pseudo-community"? (Highlight 12.2, p. 498; p. 500)

27. Explain why the picture of treatments for delusional disorders is so bleak. (p. 500)

28. Discuss the assertion for expanded psychosocial intervention for schizophrenia. What factors impede such expansion of treatment? (pp. 500-501)

◊ STUDY QUESTIONS

Introduction

1. The "final common pathway" in the schizophrenias is a significant loss of _____ with _____, often referred to as _____. (p. 463)

2. The hallmark of schizophrenia is a more or less sharp _____ _____. The component processes underlying this detachment from reality include peculiarities in _____, _____, perception, feeling, sense of self, and manner of _____. (p. 463)

3. Currently, are delusional disorders considered manifestations of schizophrenia or as distinct from schizophrenia? (p. 463)

The schizophrenias

4. The term _____ was adopted by the German psychiatrist Emile Kraepelin to refer to a group of conditions that all seemed to have the feature of mental deterioration beginning early in life. (p. 464)

5. Schizophrenia appears to be more common in "traditional small-scale" societies than in more "modern well-developed" societies. True or False (p. 464)

6. During any given year, approximately _____ % of adult U.S. citizens - over _____ million people - meet diagnositc criteria for schizophrenia (p. 464)

7. About _____ percent of all admissions to state and county mental hospitals are diagnosed as schizophrenic. Because schizophrenic individuals often require prolonged or repeated hospitalization, they have historically occupied about _____ of all available mental hospital beds in this country. (pp. 464-465)

8. The median age (i.e., the age that has exactly half the cases below it and half the cases above it) of initial onset for schizophrenic disorders is _____. (p. 465)

9. Complete the following list of reasons why schizophrenia is considered the most serious of all psychotic disorders. (p. 465)
   a. The schizophrenic disorders are complex.
   b. The schizophrenic disorders have a high rate of _____ (especially at the beginning of adult life).
   c. The schizophrenic disorders have a tendency to . . .

Clinical picture in schizophrenia

10. Explain how positive syndrome schizophrenia differs from negative syndrome schizophrenia. Compare this differentiation with that of the Type I versus Type II patterns. (p. 465-466)

11. Dolphus et al. (1996) suggested that there are at least four discriminable patterns of schizophrenia signs: _____, _____, _____, and _____. However, since most patients display a _____ picture, it is not clear that this proposal adds much to our understanding. (p. 466)

12. The DSM-IV diagnostic criteria for schizophrenia are very behaviorally specific regarding the symptoms that must be present; the decrements of life functioning that must occur; the absence of symptoms of affective disorder, organic disorder, autistic disorder; and the duration of symptoms for at least six months. Complete the following list of the symptoms at least two of which must be present to qualify for a diagnosis of schizophrenia: (Table 12.2, p. 468)
    a. Delusions
    b. Prominent hallucinations
    c.
    d.
    e.

13. The text describes eight domains of disturbed behavior that are relevant to the construct of schizophrenia. These characteristics are listed in the following chart. Fill in the empty spaces by writing a short description of the characteristic or providing a clinical example chosen from the text to illustrate the characteristic as appropriate. (pp. 466-469)

Characteristics of Schizophrenia		
Characteristic	**Brief Description**	**Example**
Disturbance of associative linking		Patient says "I cannot be a nincompoop in a physical sense (unless Society would feed me chemicals for my picture in the nincompoop book)."
Disturbance of thought content	Many types of delusions may be seen	

Disruption of perception	Breakdown in perceptual selectivity occurs; hallucinations may be seen	
Emotional dysfunction	a)

b) | a) Patient can't find pleasure in almost any life events.

b) Patient may laugh wildly at news of a parent's death. |
Confused sense of self		Patient feels tied up to universal powers.
Disrupted volition	A disruption of goal-directed activity occurs	
Retreat to an inner world		Young person develops fantasy world talking with imaginary people.
Disturbed motor behavior		Patient is in a stupor with rigid posture or shows ritualistic mannerisms with bizarre grimace."

Problems in defining schizophrenic behavior

14. It must be kept in mind that the schizophrenias remain a _____ construct one whose definition has evolved and changed over time, with substantial effects on _____ / _____ relative to other disorders, and even on observed clinical outcomes for persons assigned the diagnosis. (p. 469)

Subtypes of schizophrenia

15. Match the following types of schizophrenia with the appropriate definition: (pp. 470-476; Table 12.3, p. 470)

a. Undifferentiated	__	Those persons who are in remission following a schizophrenic episode and show only mild signs of schizophrenia.
b. Paranoid type	__	A form of schizophrenia that occurs at an early age and includes blunting, inappropriate mannerisms, and bizarre behavior.
c. Catatonic type	__	A person in whom symptoms of schizophrenia have existed for six months or less.
d. Disorganized type	__	A person who shows absurd, illogical, changeable delusions and frequent hallucinations.
e. Residual type	__	A form of schizophrenia in which all the primary indications of schizophrenia are seen in a rapidly changing pattern.
f. Schizoaffective disorder	__	A person who shows some schizophrenic signs as well as obvious depression or elation.
g. Schizophreniform disorder	__	A type of schizophrenia characterized by alternating periods of extreme excitement and extreme withdrawal.

16. What are *echolalia* and *echopraxia*? (p. 472)

17. Catatonic patients may pass suddenly from states of extreme stupor to great excitement, and they may become violent. True or False. (p. 472)

18. What has happened to the relative frequency of paranoid schizophrenia and undifferentiated schizophrenia in recent years, and what reasons are given for these changes? (p. 474)

19. Under what circumstances might a paranoid schizophrenic become violent? (p. 474)

20. At the present time, all new cases of schizophrenia would first receive a diagnosis of _____ until the symptoms have been established for six months. After six months, if symptoms persist, a formal schizophrenic diagnosis can be applied. (p. 476)

Causal factors in schizophrenia: Biological influences

21. According to Torrey et al. (1994), the overall pairwise concordance rates for schizophrenia are _____ % in MZ twins and _____ % in DZ twins. Thus, a reduction in shared genes from 100% to 50%, reduces the risk of schizophrenia nearly _____%. Also, _____ % gene-sharing with a schizophrenic proband is associated with a lifetime risk of _____ %. In absolute terms, though this is low, it is still markedly higher than that of the general population. (p. 480)

22. If schizophrenia were *exclusively* a genetic disorder, what concordance rate for identical twins would be found? (p. 480)

23. Torrey et al.'s (1994) study of 27 pairs of MZ twins who were discordant for schizophrenia stongly implicates _____ _____ as often playing a role in the causal patterns of schizophrenia. What specific findings led to this conclusion? (p. 481)

24. The Danish adoption study found a preponderance of schizophrenia in _____ relatives - as compared to _____ relatives - of schizophrenic adoptees. (p. 482)

25. The Danish adoption study, however, did not include independent assessments of the _____-_____ _____ of the _____ _____ into which index (those who became schizophrenic) and control (those who did not) youngsters had been placed. (p. 482)

26. There appears to be an interaction between _____
_____ and an unfavorable _____ in the
causal pathway leading to schizophrenia. (p. 482)

27. How well have studies of high-risk children paid off? (p. 482)

28. Summarize the authors' overall conclusion regarding a genetic basis for schizophrenia based
on evidence from high-risk research, family studies, twin studies, and adoption methods. (p.
483)

29. The most attractive biochemical approach to schizophrenia has been the dopamine
hypothesis, based on the observation that all of the
_____ had the common property of
_____. (p. 483)

30. According to the dopamine hypothesis, schizophrenia is the product of _____
_____ at certain synaptic sites. Variants of this view include hypotheses that a
schizophrenic person has too many _____ or
that these _____ have for some reason become _____. (p.
483)

31. Numerous findings indicate that persons who are merely at increased risk for schizophrenia
often experience difficulties in _____, in _____, and in certain
other indicators of cognitive functioning prior to any schizophrenic breakdown. (p. 484)

32. Research literature going back many decades documents an enormous variety of ways in
which attentional and cognitive processes - seemingly dependent on intact neurophysiological
functioning - are disrupted among schizophrenic persons. The disjointed array of findings
reported remains baffling; as yet, there is no wholly satisfactory _____
_____ within which the pieces of the schizophrenia puzzle can be put
together. (p. 484)

33. In a minority of cases of schizophrenia, particularly among those of chronic, negative
symptom course, there is an abnormal enlargement of the brain's _____, as well as
enlarged sulci. Both findings imply a loss of _____--possibly
some type of _____ or degeneration. In a review of such findings, Bogerts concludes
that the findings are not generally consistent with the notion of _____

_____, and favors the hypothesis of some type of anomaly in _____ brain development. (p. 486)

34. In a review of neuroimaging studies, Gur and Pearlson conclude that the evidence implicates primarily three brain structures. These are the _____, the _____, and the _____. It is agreed, however, that few of these findings are _____ for schizophrenia. (pp. 486-487)

35. What is meant by the neurodevelopmental "wiring" deficiencies, which are thought to cause schizophrenia? (p. 487)

36. The observation that people who become schizophrenic are more likely than people in general to have been born in the winter and early spring months is known as the "_____ ____ _____ _____." Bradbury and Miller (1985) hypothesized that this influence was some type of _____ process or _____ complications (or both). (p. 487-488)

Causal factors in schizophrenia: Psychosocial influences

37. Much of the available psychosocially oriented research in schizophrenia is seriously _____. Much of it is also of _____ quality. Why, according to your text?. (p. 490)

38. What have several researchers (e.g., Mishler & Waxler; Liem) noted about the impact of schizophrenic children's behavior on their parents? (p. 490)

39. In a group of 14 families with schizophrenic offspring, Lidz and colleagues (1965) failed to find a single family that functioned in an effective and reasonably well-integrated manner. Eight of the 14 couples lived in a state of _____ _____ _____, in which the continuation of the marriage was constantly threatened. In the other six couples, a maladaptive state of _____ had been reached in which some family members entered into a collusion to allow another member to behave abnormally. (p. 490)

40. Bateson (1959, 1960) coined the term _____ _____
_____ to describe the conflicting and confusing nature of
communications among members of schizophrenic families. Give an example of this. (p.
490-491)

41. Singer and Wynne (1963, 1965) have described two deficient communication patterns in
schizophrenic families. In their later research, they used the term *communication deviance* or
_____ _____ _____ to refer to these deficiencies. Name
and describe each of these patterns. (p. 491)

42. Were Goldstein and colleagues (1978) able to confirm a link between communication
deviance and schizophrenia in their longitudinal study employing a variant of a high-risk
strategy? (p. 491)

43. Relapse into schizophrenia following remission is often associated with a certain negative
communication called expressed emotion (EE). What two components appear critical in the
pathogenic effects of EE? (p. 491)
   a.
   b.

Schizophrenia: Treatment and outcomes

44. How did introduction of phenothiazine treatment for schizophrenia in the mid-1950s
transform the environment of mental hospitals practically "overnight"? (p. 493)

45. The chance that a schizophrenic patient admitted to a modern mental hospital and given
pharmacotherapy will be discharged in a matter of weeks is ____ to _____ percent.
However, the chance a patient will be readmitted during the first year after release is high. (p.
493)

46. After attending a meeting of Schizophrenics Anonymous, Roger Brown concluded that there is something about schizophrenia that the antipsychotic drugs _____ or even always _____ on a long-term basis. These members had not shown what mental health professionals call _____ _____; that is, the ability to manage independently as an effective economic and interpersonally connected unit within one's society. (p. 494)

47. Hogarty et al. (1997) reported on a controlled three-year trial of "_____ therapy," which involves a staged, nonpsychodynamic approach, oriented to the learning of _____ skills for managing emotion and stressful events. (p. 495)

48. What is involved in assertive community treatment (ACT) and intensive case management (ICM)? (pp.495-496)

Delusional (paranoid) disorder

49. What is *folie à deux*? (p. 496)

50. DSM-IV requires that diagnoses of delusional disorder be specified by type on the basis of the predominant theme of the delusions. Complete the following list of the types of delusions that may be seen. (p. 497)

Type of Delusion	Description
a. Persecutory type	a. The belief that one is being subjected to bad treatment. Often leads to lawsuits to seek redress.
b.	b.
c.	c. The belief that a famous person is in love with you or desires a sexual relationship with you.
d. Somatic type	d.
e.	e.

51. Place the following stages in the development of paranoid thinking in their proper order: hostility, protective thinking, paranoid illumination, delusions, suspiciousness. (Highlight 12.2, p. 498)

a. _____

b. _____

c. _____

d. _____

e. _____

Unresolved issues

52. The authors believe that the difficulties in expanding psychosocial intervention are two-fold. What are these difficulties? (p. 500)

a)

b)

53. Despite such difficulties, what economic losses would society incur, according to the authors, if treatment is limited to pharmacotherapy alone? (p. 501)

◊ CRITICAL THINKING ABOUT DIFFICULT TOPICS

1. In the polygenic model proposed by Gottesman (cited in your text on page 477, but covered very briefly), there are three sources of liability for schizophrenia that combine *additively* to produce the total liability: specific genetic, nonspecific genetic, and nonspecific environmental. Specific genetic liability means that the increased risk is specific to schizophrenia. Nonspecific genetic liability means liability that could also apply to other disorders, but which increases the risk of schizophrenia (presumably in individuals with specific genetic liability). Similarly, nonspecific environmental liability means liability that increases the risk for many disorders, including schizophrenia. A stressful environment is an example of a nonspecific environmental source of liability, because stress increases the risk of anxiety, depression, ulcers, hypertension, etc., as well as of schizophrenia. Can you think of possible candidates for nonspecific genetic liability? Refer back to Question 3 of this section in Chapter 8 for a suggestion that inheritance of low IQ may make the world more stressful. What about inheritance of an anxiety-prone personality?

2. In one follow-up adoption study (Heston, 1966), it was found that the adopted-away children of schizophrenic mothers were more likely (than controls) to be diagnosed as schizophrenic, but also as mentally retarded, neurotic (anxiety disorders), and psychopathic. Your text concludes that these findings suggest that "the genetic liability to schizophrenia is not specific to schizophrenia but also includes a liability for other forms of psychopathology" (p. 482). While it is true that what is inherited is broader than the DSM-IV diagnosis of schizophrenia, to try to include mental retardation, anxiety disorders, and psychopathy in the schizophrenia spectrum makes little sense. Can you think of other explanations? Consider two. First, it has been suggested that the fathers may have contributed genes increasing the risk of psychopathy. Second, as suggested in the preceding question, nonspecific genetic liability might involve low intelligence and anxiety-proneness. If you accept this argument, note how difficult it is to identify the forms of psychopathology that are *specifically* related to schizophrenia, because other genetic influences will affect the pathology seen among the relatives of schizophrenic index cases.

3. In Chapter 10 you learned that the mesocorticolimbic *dopamine* pathway is strongly involved in the brain reward system, also called the "pleasure pathway." In the present chapter, you have read that the vast majority of antipsychotic drugs may exert their effect by essentially completely blocking dopaminergic activity (p. 483). Can you offer any explanation for why blocking reward/pleasure pathways would be therapeutic for a disorder characterized by anhedonia and disruption of (rewarded) goal-directed activity? If you have trouble doing so, you are in good company. This apparent contradiction is difficult to explain. Undoubtedly, you will have noticed that this perspective underscores the complexity of schizophrenia, since it is difficult to explain why blocking dopamine activity is beneficial in some respects but not others.

Circle the best of the four answers provided and check them according to answers provided at the back of this study guide. Be sure you understand why each answer is correct.

1. In the United States, the estimated incidence of schizophrenia is as high as _____ percent of the population. (p. 464)
   a. .2
   b. .5
   c. .6
   d. .9

2. The median age of onset for schizophrenia is: (p. 465)
   a. below 15.
   b. around 35.
   c. over 45.
   d. older in females than males.

3. A schizophrenic's statement that he is "growing his father's hair" is an example of: (p. 466)
   a. anhedonia.
   b. autism.
   c. echolalia.
   d. cognitive slippage.

4. A schizophrenic who has feelings of being intimately tied up with universal powers (often associated with ideas of external control) is said to be experiencing: (p. 469)
   a. disrupted volition.
   b. confused sense of self.
   c. disruption of perception.
   d. retreat to an inner world.

5. Most instances of acute, reactive schizophrenic breakdown occurring for the first time appear _____ in type (p. 470):
   a. undifferentiated
   b. paranoid
   c. catatonic
   d. disorganized

6. The central feature of _____ schizophrenia is pronounced motor symptoms. (p. 471-472)
   a. undifferentiated
   b. catatonic
   c. disorganized
   d. paranoid

7. A person in whom symptoms of schizophrenia have existed for six months or less would be diagnosed as: (p. 476)
   a. undifferentiated type.
   b. catatonic type.
   c. disorganized type.
   d. schizophreniform disorder.

8. The results of twin studies of hereditary factors in the development of schizophrenia show: (p. 480)
   a. equal concordance rates for identical and fraternal twins.
   b. higher concordance rates for fraternal twins.
   c. higher concordance rates for identical twins.
   d. higher incidence of schizophrenia among twins than among others.

9. If schizophrenia were exclusively genetic, the concordance rate for identical twins would be _____ percent. (p. 480)
   a. 1   c. 50
   b. 25   d. 100

10. Monitoring over time children born to schizophrenic mothers is the research strategy known as: (p. 482)
    a. high-risk studies.   c. family studies.
    b. adoption studies.   d. twin studies.

11. Which of the following findings did *not* contribute to the demise of the dopamine hypothesis as the cause of schizophrenia? (pp. 483-484)
    a. Dopamine-blocking drugs also reduce psychotic symptoms for other disorders.
    b. The receptor-blocking effect is accomplished too quickly.
    c. Dopamine-blocking drugs are an antidote for drug-induced "bad trips."
    d. Dopamine-stimulating drugs cause hallucinations.

12. Because the brain normally occupies the skull fully, the enlarged ventricles of some schizophrenics imply a(an): (p. 486)
    a. decreased pressure on the brain.
    b. a loss of brain tissue mass.
    c. increased amount of spinal fluid.
    d. predisposition to hydrocephaly.

13. Which of the following was not a deficit found by Walker in her videotape study of preschizophrenic children? (p. 489)
    a. less positive emotion   c. cognitive slippage
    b. poor motor skills   d. neuromotor abnormalities

14. What proportion of schizophrenics continue to be resistant to drug (or any other) treatment and undergo an irreversible negative syndrome and/or disorganized deterioration? (p. 493)
    a. 10 percent
    b. 25 percent
    c. 50 percent
    d. 60 percent.

◊ OVERVIEW

The first half of this chapter covers neuropsychological brain disorders. These disorders are more or less the direct product of the physical interruption of established neural pathways in the brain. The chapter begins with a description of the types of symptoms appearing to result from brain damage, as well as the interaction of brain hardware and software. Next, the focus turns to the general clinical features of neuropsychological disorders and major neuropsychological syndromes. The devastating organic syndrome caused by the HIV-1 virus, and the causal processes and effects of Alzheimer's disease are covered in depth. Finally, neuropsychological problems secondary to head injury are reviewed.

The second half of the chapter covers mental retardation, including behaviors that are characteristic of the different levels or degrees of mental retardation. Causal factors and treatments for mental retardation are then reviewed. The last part of Chapter 13 discusses the clinical picture, causal factors, and treatments for the learning disorders (such as dyslexia). There is an emphasis on the lack of awareness and options available to the children suffering from them. Finally, issues regarding environmental influences on IQ test performance and the question of "culture-free" IQ tests are discussed.

◊ CHAPTER OUTLINE

I. Brain Impairment and Adult Disorder
    A. Neuropsychological Disorders and Brain Damage
        1. The Neuropsychology/Psychopathology Interaction
        2. Hardware and Software (A Useful, Though Crude Analogy)
        3. General Clinical Features of Neuropsychological Disorders
        4. Diagnostic Issues in Neuropsychological Disorders

B. Neuropsychological Symptom Syndrome
    1. Delirium
    2. Dementia
    3. The Amnestic Syndrome
    4. Neuropsychological Delusional Syndrome
    5. Neuropsychological Mood Syndrome
    6. Neuropsychological Personality Syndromes
C. Neuropsychological Disorder with HIV-1 Infection
    1. Prominent Features
    2. Prevalence Studies
D. Dementia of the Alzheimer's Type (DAT)
    1. The Clinical Picture in DAT
    2. Prevalence of DAT
    3. Causal Factors in DAT
        a) Neuopathology
        b) Gene-Environment Interaction in DAT
    4. Treatments and Outcomes in DAT
    5. Treating Caregivers
E. Vascular Dementia
F. Disorders Involving Head Injury
    1. The Clinical Picture Head Injury Disorders
    2. Treatments and Outcomes

II. Mental Retardation
    A. Levels of Mental Retardation
        1. Mild Mental Retardation
        2. Moderate Mental Retardation
        3. Severe Mental Retardation
        4. Profound Mental Retardation
    B. Brain Defects in Mental Retardation
        1. Genetic-Chromosomal Factors
        2. Infections and Toxic Agents
        3. Prematurity and Trauma (Physical Injury)
        4. Ionizing Radiation
        5. Malnutrition and Other Biological Factors
    C. Organic Retardation Syndromes
        1. Down Syndrome
        2. Phenylketonuria (PKU)

◊ LEARNING OBJECTIVES

After studying this chapter, you should be able to:

1. Describe the general features and symptomatic consequences of neuropsychological mental disorders. (pp. 504-508)

2. List and characterize the major neuropsychological syndromes. (pp. 508-511)

3. Explain the relationship between AIDS and the neuropsychological problems in the form of AIDS dementia complex. (pp. 511-512)

4. Define Dementia of the Alzheimer's Type (DAT), describe its clinical features, and summarize what is known about its etiology and treatment. (pp. 512-519)

5. Compare and contrast Vascular Dementia (VAD) and DAT. (pp. 519-520)

6. Outline the consequences of traumatic brain injury for neuropsychological functioning, as well as the factors affecting its prognosis. (pp. 520-523)

7. List the four levels of mental retardation and describe the functioning associated with each level. (pp. 524-526)

8. Summarize the biological factors contributing to mental retardation and describe the subtypes of mental retardation based on specific biological etiologies. (pp. 526-531)

9. Explain what is meant by cultural-familial retardation and review attempts at explaining its etiology. (pp. 531-533)

10. Describe problems of assessment of mental retardation and review various approaches to treatment and prevention of mental retardation. (pp. 533-535)

11. Describe clinical features of specific learning disorders, and review attempts to explain the etiology of and to develop treatments for learning disorders. (pp. 535-539)

◊ TERMS YOU SHOULD KNOW

organic mental disorders (p. 504)

neuropsychological (p. 504)

diffuse brain damage (p. 504)

focal brain lesions (p. 504)

stroke (pp. 504, 519)

brain reserve capacity (p. 505)

dementia (p. 505)

gestalt processing (p. 506)

syndromes (p. 508)

delirium (p. 509)

dementia (p. 508)

amnestic syndrome (pp. 509-510)

neuropsychological delusional syndrome (p. 510)

neuropsychological mood syndrome (p. 510)

pseudodementia (p. 510)

neuropsychological personality syndrome (pp. 510-511)

AIDS dementia complex (ADC) (pp. 511-512)

AIDS-related complex (ARC) (p. 511)

Dementia of the Alzheimer's Type (DAT) (p. 512)

Alzheimer's disease (pp. 512-519)

senile dementia (p. 512)

presenile dementia (p. 512)

Pick's disease (p. 513)

Huntington's disease (p. 513)

senile plaques (p. 516)

neurofibrils (p. 516)

neurofibrillary tangles (p. 516)

granulovacuoles (p. 516)

acetylcholine (p. 516)

beta amyloid (p. 517)

apolpoprotein-E (Apo-E*)* (p. 517)

acetylcholinesterase (p. 518)

vascular dementia (VAD) (p. 519)

infarcts (p. 519)

closed head injury (CHI) (p. 520)

penetrating head injury (PHI) (p. 520)

retrograde amnesia (p. 520)

anterograde amnesia (p. 520)

intracranial hemorrhage (pp. 520-521)

subdural hematoma (p. 521)

petechial hemorrhages (p. 521)

cerebral edema (p. 521)

encephalopathy (p. 521)

punch drunk (p. 521)

mental retardation (pp. 523-535)

mild mental retardation (educable) (pp. 524, 525)

cultural-familial retardation (pp. 531-533)

mainstreaming (p. 534)

learning disorders (pp. 535-539

dyslexia (p. 536)

Integrative Strategy Instruction (ISI) (p. 538)

◊ CONCEPTS TO MASTER

1. Define neuropsychological mental disorders, and describe nine symptomatic consequences of these disorders that have mainly focal origins but commonly appear in the context of progressively diffuse damage. (pp. 504-505)

2. Compare and contrast the concepts of "hardware" and "software" as the authors apply them to the brain and mental processes. (pp. 505-506)

3. Describe the general functions attributed to the right and left hemispheres of the brain. (pp. 506-507)

4. Define *neuropsychological syndrome*. List and describe six types of syndromes that are typical of persons with organic brain pathology. (pp. 508-511)

5. What is meant by the concept of dementia and what processes are most seriously disturbed? (p. 509)

6. Describe the neuropsychological features of AIDS and the neuropathology of the AIDS dementia complex. (pp. 511-512)

7. Differentiate between senile and presenile dementias and describe two presenile types. (p. 512; Highlight 13.1, p. 513)

8. What is the typical neuropsychological and neuropathological course of Alzheimer's disease? (pp. 512-515)

9. What is the acetylcholine depletion theory of DAT etiology? (pp. 516-517)

10. Describe the connection between Down syndrome and DAT, and summarize the etiological theory involving apolipoprotein-E (ApoE). (pp. 517-518)

11. Describe the differences and similarities between DAT and vascular dementia (VAD). (pp. 519-520)

12. Review the physiological and neuropsychological aftereffects of severe cerebral injury. What are the typical stages from impact to recovery? (pp. 520-521)

13. Describe the controversy regarding whether the large numbers of relatively mild closed-head brain concussions and contusions produce significant long-standing symptoms or impairments of various abilities. (p. 521)

14. Define mental retardation and describe its classification by DSM-IV. (pp. 523-524)

15. List and describe the behavior of four levels of mental retardation Compare and contrast the prognosis for later mastery of academic and occupational skills, as well as for social adjustment and self-care across each of the four levels. (pp. 524-526)

16. List five biological conditions that may lead to mental retardation, and describe the various ways in which these factors cause mental retardation. (pp. 526-528)

17. Describe some of the physical characteristics of children born with Down syndrome. (pp. 528-530)

18. Discuss potential causes for the trisomy of chromosome 21, focusing on evidence investigating the effect of parental age at conception. (p. 530)

19. Describe the cause, diagnosis, and preventive treatment of phenylketonuria (PKU). (pp. 530-531)

20. List three types of cranial anomalies, and describe the clinical picture of each, as well as any diagnoses and/or treatments mentioned. (p. 531)

21. How does the concept of cultural-familial mental retardation support a contribution of environmental factors to the etiology of mental retardation? (pp. 531-533)

22. Describe some of the forms of care for the mentally retarded that are alternatives to institutionalization according to Tyor and Bell. (p. 534)

23. Discuss the pros and cons of the "mainstreaming" approach to the education of retarded children. What is a reasonable conclusion about mainstreaming at this point? (pp. 534-535)

24. Describe the Head Start program and discuss the strengths, weaknesses, frustrations, and potential benefits of this approach to preventing mental retardation. (p. 535)

25. What was implied by the term "minimal brain dysfunction" and why has this hypothesis fallen into disfavor? (p. 537)

26. As proposed by Worden (1986), list four comparisons of approaches used by "good learners" versus those with learning disorders. (p. 538)

◊ STUDY QUESTIONS

Brain disorders

1. When structural defects in the brain occur before birth or at an early age, _____ may result. Its severity depends largely on the severity of the defect. Other people who sustain prenatal or perinatal brain damage may experience normal mental development in most aspects of behavior, but suffer from specific cognitive or motor deficits, such as _____ disorders or _____. (p. 504)

2. Does it matter whether the brain damage occurs in early life before life skills have been developed or in adulthood after life skills have been mastered? (p. 504)

Brain impairment and adult disorder

3. The destruction of brain tissue may involve only limited behavioral deficits or a wide range of psychological impairments, depending on four variables. Complete the following list: (p. 504)
   a.
   b.
   c. The individual's total life situation
   d.

Neuropsychological disorders and brain damage

4. Loss of the ability to process anything but the simplest of information is often described as _____ _____. (p. 505)

5. Impairment in the initiation of behavior is sometimes referred to as _____ ____
_____ _____. (p. 505)

6. Respond true or false to the following statements:
   a. Most neurologically impaired individuals develop psychiatric symptoms. True or False (p. 505)
   b. A person can have a breakdown in the brain's hardware without effects on the processing of software, or past and present experience. True or False (p. 506)
   c. Cell bodies and neural pathways in the brain have the power of regeneration but it is slow. True or False (p. 506)
   d. The amount of tissue damage to the brain does not predict impairment of function. True or False (p. 506)
   e. The location of damage may be of significance in predicting the impact of an injury because the parts of the human brain are specialized in their function. True or False (pp. 506-507)

7. It is possible to make certain generalizations about the likely effects of damage to particular parts of the brain. Complete the following chart that summarize these. (p. 507)

Area of the Brain Damaged	Probable Clinical Picture
Frontal areas	either passivity and apathy or impulsiveness and distractibility
Right parietal area	
Left parietal area	
Temporal area	
Occipital area	

8. Psychiatric and personality disorders are classified on Axes I and II of DSM-IV. Where are the neuropsychological mental disorders classified? What about neuropsychological mental disorders that result in dementia? (pp. 507-508)

Neuropsychological symptom syndromes

Symptoms based on brain damage listed in the DSM-IV are grouped by the authors into six clusters: (1) delirium, (2) dementia, (3) amnestic syndrome; (4) neuropsychological delusional syndrome, (5) neuropsychological mood syndrome, and (6) neuropsychological personality syndromes. Respond to each of the following questions about these symptom clusters:

9. Match the following: (p. 509)

a. Delirium	___ Caused by degenerative processes of old age, repeated strokes, infections, tumors, injuries, and dietary deficiencies.
b. Dementia	___ Caused by head injury, toxic or metabolic disturbances, insufficient blood to brain, withdrawal from alcohol or other drugs, and lack of oxygen to the brain.

10. Which of the following would a person with amnestic syndrome have the most problem remembering? (p. 509)
    a. The name of the doctor who just introduced him- or herself one second before.
    b. What he or she had for breakfast.
    c. Details of his or her childhood from 50 years ago.

11. Is overall cognitive functioning impaired in the amnestic syndrome as it is in dementia? (p. 509)

12. Are the most common forms of amnestic syndrome, those due to alcohol or barbiturate addiction, considered reversible? (pp. 509-510)

13. Fill in the following chart which summarizes the most common causes of the following neuropsychological syndromes: (pp. 509-511)

Organic Syndrome	Common Etiological Factors
Delirium	head injury, toxic or metabolic disturbances, insufficient blood to brain, withdrawal from alcohol or other drugs, and lack of oxygen to the brain.
Dementia	
Amnestic syndrome	
Neuropsychological delusional syndrome	
Neuropsychological mood syndrome	
Neuropsychological personality syndrome	

Neuropsychological disorder with HIV-1 infection

14. Contrary to initial assumptions, the organic brain effects associated with AIDS patients was not due to secondary infections, but due to the presence of the _____ itself. (p. 511)

15. AIDS dementia complex (ADC) damage appears to be concentrated in _____ regions notably the _____ _____ _____, the tissue surrounding the _____, and deeper gray matter structures such as the _____ _____ and _____. (p. 511)

351

16. The clinical features of AIDS dementia complex (ADC) include psychomotor slowing, _____, _____, and perhaps _____. ADC progresses rapidly and the later phases include behavioral regression, _____, _____, _____, and marked _____. (p. 512)

17. Presently, the question of treatment for ADC is intimately tied to that involving _____ or _____ of the HIV-1 infection itself. Unfortunately, experience with AZT therapy in the more general AIDS context suggests that its initially hopeful effects may prove temporary. It remains true, therefore, that _____ is the only certain defensive strategy. Why are AZT's effects probably temporary? (p. 512)

Dementia of the Alzheimer's type (DAT)

18. Why is diagnosis of Alzheimer's disease often difficult and uncertain? (p. 513)

19. Name four factors which influence the variability of the clinical picture of DAT. (p. 513)

20. Describe the onset of Alzheimer's disease. (pp. 513-514)

21. Approximately _____ of all DAT patients show a course of simple deterioration, that is, they gradually lose mental capacities. Symptoms of psychopathology are brief and inconsistent over time. It is less frequent but not uncommon for Alzheimer's disease patients to develop a decidedly paranoid orientation, becoming markedly suspicious and developing jealousy delusions. (pp. 514-515)

22. How common is Dementia of the Alzheimer's type: (p. 515)
    a. among persons over 65 years old?
    b. among persons over 85 years old?
    c. among nursing home residents?

23. The neurological degeneration that occurs in Alzheimer's disease includes degenerative changes in neurons (senile plaques and neurofibrillary tangles) and an abnormal appearance of small holes in neuronal tissues, called granulovacuoles, as a result of cell degeneration. While there is widespread destruction of neurons in DAT, among the earliest and most severely affected are a cluster of cell bodies located in the _____ and involved in the release of _____. This observation has given rise to the _____ depletion theory of DAT etiology. (p. 515)

24. Studies of the composition of the senile plaques in DAT reveal that their cores consist of a sticky protein substance, called _____, that also occurs in abnormal abundance in other parts of DAT patients' brains. In fact, _____ has recently been shown to be in itself neurotoxic, causing cell death. As yet, however, the source and specific role of this protein in DAT brains remain unclear. (p. 516)

25. What evidence is there that DAT is not determined solely by genetics? (pp. 516-517)

26. There have been attempts to control at least some of the more troublesome behaviors associated with DAT such as _____, _____, inappropriate _____, and inadequate _____ skills using _____ approaches, such as systematic _____ _____. (p. 518)

27. Some DAT patients respond to _____ or _____ medication to help with modulating their emotions and impulses. (p. 518)

28. Why has so much attention been given to the caregivers of those with DAT? (pp. 518-519)

29. Why is the reluctance to hospitalize a DAT patient justifiable? On the other hand, why is hospitalization reasonable with the emergence of confusion, gross and argumentative demeanor, stuporous depression, inappropriate sexual behavior, etc.? (p. 519)

Vascular dementia (VAD)

30. A sudden interruption of the blood supply to parts of the brain is a _____.
    (p. 519)

31. When a series of small strokes occur, the condition is known as _____ dementia, the underlying cause of 10% of all dementia. (p. 519)

32. The characteristics between VAD and DAT are similar, but the decline in VAD is less smooth because of: (a) the discrete character of _____; (b) variations over time in the volume of blood delivered by a _____; and (c) a tendency for VAD to be associated with more severe _____. (p. 519)

Disorders involving head injury

33. Few persons with traumatic brain injury (TBI) find their way into mental institutions because: (p. 520)

34. What are the three types of TBI distinguished by clinicians? (p. 520)

35. What causes people to experience retrograde amnesia after accidents? (p. 520)

36. Why is boxing potentially dangerous? (p. 521)

37. Common aftereffects of moderate brain injury are chronic headaches, anxiety, irritability, dizziness, easy fatigability, and impaired memory and concentration. How common is epilepsy after a head injury? (p. 522)

38. What four factors inflluence the likelihood that children with TBI will be adversely affected? (p. 523)

39. List six factors in the following short example suggesting that the patient has an unfavorable prognosis. (p. 523)

"An 18-year-old male who had several run-ins with the law during high school received a serious head injury in a motorcycle accident. He was in a coma for almost a month. The patient is currently suffering some paralysis and is very angry and depressed. He refuses to cooperate with his physical therapist. His parents, who live in a remote rural area where no rehabilitation facilities are available, will take him back home but are rather unenthusiastic about the prospect."

a.

b.

c.

d.

e.

f.

Mental retardation

40. The DSM-IV defines mental retardation as "significantly subaverage general intellectual functioning . . . that is accompanied by significant limitations in adaptive functioning in certain skill areas . . ." and manifested before age 18. The IQ cutoff for mental retardation used by DSM-IV is _____ . (pp. 523-524)

41. Is mental retardation associated with an increased risk of other disorders? Which ones? (p. 524)

42. Explain why the incidence of initial diagnoses of mental retardation increases markedly between ages 5 to 6, peaks at 15, and drops off sharply after that. (p. 524)

Levels of mental retardation

43. For most IQ tests the mean is _____ and the standard deviation is about _____ points. Thus, approximately _____ of the population score between IQ 85 and IQ 115. (p. 524)

44. Assuming that IQ scores are normally distributed, if IQ 70 is used as the cutoff for mental retardation, about _____ percent of the population would fall in the mental retardation range (i.e., below 70). (p. 524)

45. When we speak of varying levels of mental retardation, we are to a great extent speaking of levels of ability to succeed at _____. (p. 524)

46. Although an IQ test score lower than 70 tends to be the dominant consideration in the diagnosis of mental retardation, additional evidence is required. What additional evidence is required to make a diagnosis of mental retardation? (p. 524)

47. Fill in the following chart that summarizes the educational potential, level of care required, and the degree of physical deformities characteristic of each level of retardation: (pp. 524-526)

Level of Retardation	Description
Mild	Persons in this group are considered "educable." They can master simple academic and occupational skills and become self-supporting. Physically, these individuals are normal.
Moderate	Persons in this group are considered _____. Most can achieve partial independence in daily _____, acceptable behavior, and work within the family or other sheltered environment. Physically, these individuals usually appear _____ and ungainly.
Severe	Persons in this group are called "dependent retarded." They can develop limited levels of _____ and _____ skills. Physical handicaps are common.
Profound	Persons in this group are considered _____ retarded. They are capable of only the simplest tasks, and speech usually does not develop. They must remain in custodial care their whole lives. Serious physical deformities are common.

48. Of the mild, moderate, severe, and profound retardation levels, in which level do by far the greatest number of mentally retarded individuals fall? (p. 525)

49. Which levels of retardation can be diagnosed readily in infancy? (p. 526)

50. In 1992 the AAMR (American Association on Mental Retardation) adopted IQ _____ as the cutoff point for the diagnosis of mental retardation. (p. 526)

Brain defects in mental retardation

51. Mental retardation is associated with known organic pathology in _____ percent of the cases. In cases with organic pathology, retardation is virtually always moderate and is often severe. Profound retardation is rare and never occurs in the absence of obvious organic damage. (p. 526)

52. The authors of the text list five biological conditions that may lead to mental retardation. They are presented below. Complete the requested information. (pp. 526-527)

    a. *Genetic-chromosomal factors*
    Mental retardation tends to run in families, but _____ and _____ also run in families. Exposure to social disadvantage may lead to retardation even in children who have inherited average intellectual potential. In some relatively infrequent types of mental retardation such as _____, genetic factors play a clear role.

    b. *Infections and toxic agents*
    Illnesses in a pregnant woman that can cause mental retardation of the offspring include _____, _____, and German measles. After birth, viral _____ in the newborn child may lead to mental retardation. Environmental toxins that may cause mental retardation in children are _____ and lead. Similarly, an excess of _____ taken by a pregnant woman may lead to congenital malformations.

    c. *Prematurity and birth trauma*
    Brain damage leading to mental retardation occurs in 1 birth out of _____.

    d. *Ionizing radiation*
    The list of sources of harmful radiation includes diagnostic x-rays, leakages at _____ _____, and nuclear weapons testing.

    e. *Malnutrition*
    The negative impact of malnutrition on mental development may, at least in some cases, be viewed as a special case of _____ deprivation.

53. Complete the following list of seven disorders that are sometimes associated with mental retardation. (Table 13.3, p. 528)
    a. No. 18 trisomy syndrome
    b.
    c.
    d.
    e. Bilirubin encephalopathy
    f.

54. Down Syndrome is the best-known of the clinical conditions associated with _____ to _____ mental retardation. It occurs in 1 in every _____ babies born in the United States. (p. 528)

55. How has the life expectancy for individuals with Down syndrome changed over the past half century? (p. 529)

56. Are these children unusually placid and affectionate? (p. 529)

57. Is the intellectual defect in Down syndrome consistent across abilities? (p. 529)

58. Down syndrome is caused by an extra chromosome, number 21. (Normal children have 23 pairs of chromosomes--a total of 46. Down syndrome children have 23 pairs also, but "pair" 21 has three chromosomes instead of the normal two--a total of 47.) Where does the extra chromosome come from? (p. 530)

59. The risk of having a child with Down's syndrome is high if the mother is age _____ or older or the father is age _____ or older. (p. 530)

60. In phenylketonuria (PKU), a baby lacks a liver enzyme needed to break down _____, an amino acid found in many foods. (p. 530)

61. A child with phenylketonuria (PKU) appears normal until _____ to _____ months of age. (p. 530)

62. PKU can be identified by a simple test of the infant. What is this test, and, once found, what procedure can be used to prevent the disorder? (p. 530)

63. For a baby to inherit PKU, it appears that both parents must carry the _____ genes. (p. 530)

64. How severely retarded are microcephalic children? (p. 531)

65. What are the causes of microcephaly? (p. 531)

66. What is the outcome for hydrocephalic children today? (p. 531)

Cultural-familial mental retardation

67. Most mental retardation is of the _____ type. (p. 532)

68. Children whose retardation is cultural-familial in origin are usually _____ retarded. (p. 532)

The problem of assessing mental retardation

69. Complete the following list of the three factors that usually account for errors in measuring an individual's IQ: (p. 533)
   a. Errors were made in administering the test
   b.
   c.
   d. Limitations exist within the tests themselves

70. In the elaborated version of adaptive skills assessment recently proposed by the AAMR, many of the skills included _____ measured with existing techniques. (p. 533)

Treatment, outcomes, and prevention of mental retardation

71. Few retarded children are institutionalized today. Those likely to be institutionalized include two types. What are they? (pp. 516-517)

   a.

   b.

72. Are services for the mentally retarded adequate, and are all affected individuals being reached by specialized services? (p. 534)

73. List several alternate forms of care for the mentally retarded that began in the 1970s. (p. 534)

74. Typically, educational and training procedures involve mapping out target areas of improvement such as personal grooming, social behavior, basic academic skills, and _____ _____ for retarded adults. Within each area, the skills the individual needs to learn are broken down to their simplest components, and each component is taught separately. (p. 534)

Specific learning disorders

75. Learning disorders are identified by the discrepancy between the _____ academic achievement and their _____ performance in one or more traditional school subjects. (p. 536)

76. Typically, these children have full-scale IQs that are consistent with at least _____ achievement at school. (p. 536)

77. The academic problems associated with learning disabilities cannot be attributed to the following common, alternative explanations for poor academic performance. Complete the list. (p. 536)
   a. obvious crippling emotional problems
   b. lack of _____
   c. lack of cooperativeness
   d. lack of _____ to please teachers and parents

78. Respond to the following statements: (pp. 537-538)

   a. There is mounting evidence that LD is due to a specific central nervous system dysfunction. True or False
   b. Individuals with LD may experience deficient phonological processes. True or False
   c. The idea that LD is genetically transmitted has been virtually abandoned. True or False
   c. Cognitive and psychosocial perspectives on causation exist, but much of this line of research has been riddled with methodological flaws. True or False

79. Worden (1986) suggests we look at how people learn well and compare those strategies to the LD child. Complete the list of aspects of learning he suggests we look at: (p. 538)
   a. Memory strategies
   b.
   c.
   d.

80. There are several reasons for a bleak outlook in treatment for learning disorders: (p. 538)
   a. We still do not have a firm grasp of what is wrong with LD children.
   b.
   c. Few positive results have been reported even for the most researched learning disorders such as reading disorders.
   d.

81. Recently, Ellis has offered a comprehensive intervention model to facilitate learning in LD, called _____ (ISI). Although the model appears not to have been _____, its knowledge-based and systematic character is a welcome addition to the analysis of the educational problems presented by LD children. (p. 538)

◊ **CRITICAL THINKING ABOUT DIFFICULT TOPICS**

1. The topic of mental retardation provides perhaps the clearest illustration of phenomena that do--and do not--fit the categorical approach to conceptualizing the phenomena of this course. Can you indicate which forms of mental retardation fit a categorical model and which do not? Down syndrome and PKU (pp. 528-531) largely are either present or absent and thus meet the demands for a categorical approach. With respect to the phenomena of interest, children with Down syndrome have more in common with each other than with those who do not have Down syndrome. In contrast, cultural-familial retardation (pp. 531-533) applies to those who simply fall at the low end of the normal curve distribution of IQ (p. 524). When a cutoff of IQ 70 is applied to this continuous distribution, it is arbitrary to adopt a categorical view that someone with an IQ of 69 is retarded but that someone with an IQ of 71 is not. The person with IQ 69 has much more in common with someone whose IQ is 71 than with another "retarded" person with an IQ of 45. Similarly, the "normal" person with IQ 71 has more in common with the "retarded" person whose IQ is 69 than with another "normal" person whose

IQ is 110. Thus, a categorical approach is completely inappropriate for cultural-familial mental retardation. Having examined this question, how well do you think the topics of the preceding chapters fit a categorical approach?

2. Your text states that "the original IQ tests were devised for the explicit purpose of predicting academic achievement among schoolchildren. Thus, when we speak of varying levels of mental retardation, we are to a great extent speaking of levels of ability to succeed at schoolwork" (p. 524). How narrowly would you interpret the last part of that statement? Is a person with low IQ only at a disadvantage in the classroom, or is the disadvantage broader than that? Note that in diagnosing mental retardation, a dual criterion is applied: in addition to IQ below 70, the person must show "significant limitations in adaptive functioning" (pp. 523, 524). Does this requirement imply that low IQ has consequences outside the classroom? Your text says that "a person with an IQ of 50 or below will inevitably exhibit gross deficiencies in overall adaptive behavior as well" (p. 525). What do these statements indicate about the relationship between IQ and adaptive functioning?

3. IQ tests assess many different types of intellectual abilities, yet we use the overall score as the index of intelligence. Can you justify this failure to attend to the profile of individual mental abilities for each person? How do you conceptualize IQ? Is it a unitary phenomenon--a single variable capturing the essence of one's intellectual abilities? Alternatively, could it be a collection of more or less unrelated abilities whose aggregate score is useful because they are to some extent interchangeable--i.e., we can use whatever abilities we have to achieve educational and social goals? For example, one person may perform well because of an excellent memory, whereas another person may achieve good performance as a result of good conceptual ability in spite of a poor memory.

4. Some people oppose the study of genetic influences on behavior and psychopathology because they are threatened by their perception that there is nothing that can be done about "genetic disorders." There is hardly a better example of a genetic disorder than PKU (pp. 530-531), which is inherited as a simple Mendelian recessive disorder (i.e., the person receives a recessive gene for PKU from both parents) and it results in mental retardation in almost all affected individuals who consume a normal diet (i.e., the gene is highly penetrant). Does the PKU example support their fear that nothing can be done about genetic disorders? The treatment involves special diets that do not contain the amino acid phenylalanine. Under those dietary conditions, "intellectual functioning may range from borderline to normal" in spite of damage done by exposure to phenylalanine in utero and postnatally before diagnosis-- i.e., the gene is no longer highly penetrant. This example illustrates that a disorder that may be highly genetic under one set of environmental conditions may not develop under another set of environmental conditions. What does it mean, then, to say that something is a genetic disorder?

5. A fair number of experts in assessment would subscribe to the following description of IQ tests and test scores. IQ tests were developed in an educational context to evaluate academic abilities. Intelligence as measured by these tests is permissive of good school performance, but many factors (e.g., lack of motivation, emotional disturbance) can interfere with that performance in individuals with good intelligence. One of the major applications is to determine whether poor academic performance is attributable to poor intellectual ability or to other factors. Intelligence has demonstrated construct validity and cannot be reduced to school grades. Thus, IQ tests do measure something we can call "intelligence" and intelligence probably predicts, at least to a significant degree, adaptive functioning outside of the classroom. However, there probably are aspects of intellectual functioning and control of adaptive behavior that are not assessed by IQ tests, which limits their predictive utility. "Intelligence" absolutely should *not* be viewed as directly reflecting "the quality of brain tissue" (p. 539) or genetic factors. Measured intelligence, like all behavior, reflects the complex outcome of many genetic and environmental factors. Intelligence tests *attempt* to test material to which almost all individuals in the culture have been exposed and, therefore, have had an opportunity to learn. If this assumption is met, then differences in performance on the test will largely reflect differences in the intellectual abilities the person has developed as a result of the combination of nature and nurture, and IQ scores will predict (albeit imperfectly) academic performance and some adaptive behaviors outside the classroom. When an individual's score is lowered due to environmental factors, there are two possible reasons with very different implications. In one case, specific information is required to which the person has not been exposed, but failure to learn this material has not affected the person's general academic or intellectual abilities. An example would be questions about different breeds of cattle, to which urban-reared individuals may not have been exposed. If there were many instances of this type of "culture bias," the IQ score is truly biased in the sense that it would underpredict--i.e., the person would function better in most contexts than predicted by the IQ score, because the test did not accurately assess intellectual abilities. In the second case, the person's intellectual ability itself has been affected adversely by the environment. The best example is cultural-familial retardation, in which a child "suffers from an inferior quality of interaction with the cultural environment and with other people" (p. 531). To the extent that this environmental disadvantage has truly adversely affected intellectual ability, the IQ score will as validly predict academic performance and adaptive behaviors as for other individuals. If such adverse environmental factors are correlated with socioeconomic status, urban-rural backgrounds, or ethnicity, IQ scores will reflect these differences. The test is "culture-free" and unbiased in the sense that it accurately assesses current intellectual functioning and predicts equally well for all concerned, but it is not "culture-free" in the sense that there may be systematic differences in tested IQ as a function of sociocultural variables. How different is this view of IQ testing from that expressed by your text in the section on Unresolved Issues? Have the authors said the same thing in different words, or is their view different?

◊ CHAPTER 13 QUIZ

Circle the best of the four answers provided and check them according to answers provided at the back of this study guide. Be sure you understand why each answer is correct.

1. When structural defects in the brain occur before birth or at a very early age, the typical result is: (p. 504)
   a. mental retardation.
   b. delirium.
   c. dementia.
   d. amnesia.

2. In contrast to diffuse damage which results in dementia, focal lesions are _____ areas of abnormal change in brain structure. (p. 504)
   a. deep
   b. circumscribed
   c. large
   d. progressive

3. Computer hardware may be compared to the _____, while software may be compared to psychosocial experience. (p. 505)
   a. inner psyche
   b. genetic codes
   c. mental experience
   d. human brain

4. Some functions may be relearned after brain damage; however, there is usually _____ over a wide range of abilities. (p. 506)
   a. little damage
   b. unnoticed change
   c. loss of function
   d. increased metabolism

5. In DSM-IV, physical or medical disorders are coded on Axis: (p. 508)
   a. I.
   b. II.
   c. III.
   d. IV.

6. A rapid and widespread disorganization of complex mental processes caused by a generalized disturbance in brain metabolism is called: (p. 509)
   a. amnestic syndrome.
   b. hallucinosis.
   c. dementia.
   d. delirium.

7. Almost _____ percent of AIDS patients met DSM-IV criteria for dementia. (p. 511)
   a. 10
   b. 20
   c. 40
   d. 60

8. Outcome is particularly bleak for those with ADC because right now the only certain strategy is the _____ of the disease. (p. 511)
   a. prevention
   b. spread
   c. mutation
   d. destruction

9. Which of the following is the most common behavioral manifestation of Alzheimer's disease? (p. 514)
   a. simple deterioration
   b. jealousy delusions
   c. paranoid delusions
   d. psychopathological symptoms

10. One in _____ persons over age 65 in America are considered clinically demented. (p. 515)
    a. 1
    b. 2
    c. 6
    d. 10

11. DAT has been linked to _____, which is due to a trisomy involving chromosome 21. (p. 517)
    a. Huntington's chorea
    b. Down syndrome
    c. VAD
    d. Tay-Sach's disease

12. Vascular dementia involves a(an): (p. 519)
    a. appearance of senile plaques.
    b. continuing recurrence of small strokes.
    c. increase in neurofibrillary tangles.
    d. loss of neurons in the basal forebrain.

13. If a head injury is sufficiently severe to result in unconsciousness, the person may experience retrograde amnesia or inability to recall: (p. 520)
    a. events immediately following the injury.
    b. events immediately preceding and following the injury.
    c. events immediately preceding the injury.
    d. names or faces of friends.

14. Any functional equivalent of mental retardation that has its onset after age 17 must be considered a _____ rather than retardation. (p. 523)
  a. pervasive developmental disorder   c. learning disorder
  b. dementia   d. organic syndrome

15. When we speak of levels of mental retardation we largely are referring to levels of: (p. 524)
  a. neuronal activity.   c. development.
  b. ability to succeed at schoolwork.   d. structural damage to the brain.

16. Which of the following degrees of retardation is by far the most common? (p. 525)
  a. Profound   c. Severe
  b. Moderate   d. Mild

17. About _____ percent of the cases of mental retardation occur with known brain pathology. (p. 526)
  a. 5   c. 25
  b. 15   d. 35

18. Ionizing radiation may harm a child by acting directly on the _____ or may damage the sex chromosomes of either parent. (p. 527)
  a. fertilized egg   c. brain tissue
  b. womb   d. unfertilized egg

19. Newer research points not only to organic causes of retardation but also to a lack of _____ (pp. 531-532)
  a. specific enzymes.   c. normal environmental stimulation.
  b. education.   d. normal affection.

20. One reason the authors state that "mainstreaming" has not worked is: (pp. 534-535)
  a. lack of funding.   c. no classroom space.
  b. overall classroom climate.   d. classes that are too large.

21. Typically, a child with a learning disorder does not show overall poor performance but _____ difficulties. (pp. 535-536)
  a. emotional   c. physical
  b. specific   d. family

◊ OVERVIEW

Many of the mental disorders described in previous chapters do not develop until early or middle adulthood. There are some problems, however, that develop in childhood and adolescence. Some of these are unique to childhood, such as hyperactivity, and other problems, such as withdrawal, may be forerunners of serious adult psychopathology like depression or schizoid behavior. Thus, it is ill-advised to assume that children are simply "mini-adults." This chapter discusses the types of problems seen in children and adolescents, including attention-deficit hyperactivity disorder, oppositional defiant disorder, conduct disorder, anxiety disorders, childhood depression, enuresis, encopresis, sleepwalking, and tics, as well as delinquency. In each instance, there is an attempt to indicate the long-range outcome for the problem. It is important to place emphasis on the treatment of children and adolescents, because it is hoped that successful treatment at these stages may prevent the occurrence of more serious pathology.

◊ CHAPTER OUTLINE

I.   Maladaptive Behavior in Different Life Periods
    A. Varying Clinical Pictures
    B. Special Vulnerabilities of Young Children

II. The Classification of Childhood and Adolescent Disorders
    A. The Categorical Strategy
    B. The Dimensional Strategy
    C. Contrasting the Categorical and Dimensional Strategies

III. Disorders of Childhood
    A. Attention-Deficit Hyperactivity Disorder
        1. The Clinical Picture in Attention-Deficit Hyperactivity Disorder
        2. Causal Factors in Attention-Deficit Hyperactivity Disorder

3. Treatments and Outcomes
4. ADHD: Beyond Adolescence
B. Conduct Disorder and Oppositional Defiant Disorder
   1. The Clinical Picture in Oppositional Defiant Disorder
   2. The Clinical Picture in Conduct Disorders
   3. Causal Factors in Conduct Disorders
      a) A Self-Perpetuating Cycle
      b) Age of Onset and Links to Antisocial Personality Disorder
      c) Environmental Factors
   4. Treatments and Outcomes
      a) The Cohesive Family Model
      b) Behavioral Techniques
C. Anxiety Disorders of Childhood and Adolescence
   1. Separation Anxiety Disorder
   2. Selective Mutism
   3. Causal Factors in Anxiety Disorders
   4. Treatments and Outcomes
D. Childhood Depression
   1. The Clinical Picture in Childhood Depression
   2. Causal Factors in Childhood Depression
      a) Biological Factors
      b) Learning Factors
   3. Treatments and Outcomes
E. Symptom Disorders: Enuresis, Encopresis, Sleepwalking, and Tics
   1. Functional Enuresis
   2. Functional Encopresis
   3. Sleepwalking (Somnambulism)
   4. Tics
F. Pervasive Developmental Disorder: Autism
   1. The Clinical Picture in Autistic Disorder
      a) A Social Deficit
      b) An Absence of Speech
      c) Self-Stimulation
      d) Intellectual Ability
      e) Maintaining Sameness
   2. Causal Factors in Autism
   3. Treatments and Outcomes
      a) Medical Treatment

     b) Behavioral Treatment

     c) The Effectiveness of Treatment

IV. Planning Better Programs to Help Children and Adolescents

   A. Special Factors Associated with Treatment for Children and Adolescents

      1. Child's Inability to Seek Assistance

      2. Vulnerabilities Placing Children at Risk for Developing Emotional Problems

      3. Parents as Well as Child Needing Treatment

      4. Possibilities of Using Parents as Change Agents

      5. Problem of Placing the Child Outside the Family

      6. Value of Intervening Before Problems Become Acute

   B. Child Abuse

      1. Sexual Abuse

      2. Causal Factors in Child Abuse

      3. The Prevention of Child Abuse

   C. Child Advocacy Programs

V. Unresolved Issues: Can Society Deal with Delinquent Behavior?

   A. Personal Pathology as a Cause of Delinquency

      1. Genetic Determinants

      2. Brain Damage and Learning Disability

      3. Psychological Disorders

      4. Antisocial Traits

      5. Drug Abuse

   B. Pathogenic Family Patterns as a Cause of Delinquency

      1. Parental Absence or Family Conflict

      2. Parental Rejection and Faulty Discipline

      3. Relationship Outside the Family

   C. Undesirable Peer Relationships

   D. Dealing With Delinquency

VI. Summary

After studying this chapter, you should be able to:

1. List special features of childhood disorders that make them different from adult disorders, and describe how young children are especially vulnerable to develop psychological problems. (pp. 543-544).

2. Discuss general issues in the classification of childhood and adolescent disorders. (pp. 544-547)

3. Describe the clinical features, list several of the multiple causes, and summarize approaches to treatment of attention-deficit hyperactivity disorder. (pp. 547-551)

4. Describe the clinical features, causal factors, and treatment of conduct disorder and oppositional defiant disorder. (pp. 551-557)

5. Describe the clinical features, causal factors, and treatment of the anxiety disorders of childhood. (pp. 557-559)

6. Describe the clinical features, causal factors, and treatment of childhood depression. (pp. 559-562)

7. Summarize what is known about the symptom disorders of functional enuresis, functional encopresis, sleepwalking, and tics as they occur in children and adolescents. (pp. 562-565)

8. Describe the clinical features, causal factors, and treatment of autism. (pp. 565-570)

9. List and explain six special factors that must be considered in relation to treatment for children. (pp. 570-574)

10. Outline the findings regarding the prevalence of child abuse, list the deficits seen among abused children, discuss potential causal factors in child abuse, and summarize efforts to prevent child abuse. (pp. 574-577)

11. Describe the need for mental health services for children, and review the dificulties with recent efforts to increase the available resources. (pp. 577-578)

12. Discuss delinquency as a major societal problem, summarize the many causal factors involved in delinquency, and describe different ways that society deals with delinquency. (pp. 578-581)

◊ TERMS YOU SHOULD KNOW

developmental psychopathology (p. 543)

categorical strategy (of classification) (p. 546)

dimensional strategy (of classification) (p. 546)

presenting symptoms (p. 546)

Child Behavior Checklist (CBCL) (p. 546)

attention-deficit hyperactivity disorder (or hyperactivity) (p. 547)

Ritalin (p. 549)

Pemoline (p. 549)

conduct disorder (p. 551)

oppositional defiant disorder (p. 551)

juvenile delinquency (pp. 551, 578-581)

early-onset conduct disorder (p. 555)

adolescent-onset conduct disorder (p. 555)

deviant peer groups (p. 555)

cohesive family model (p. 556)

separation anxiety disorder (p. 557)

mature minors (p. 571)

emancipated minors (p. 571)

play therapy (p. 573)

mental health child advocacy (p. 577)

Children's Defense Fund (p. 577)

status offenses (p. 578)

continuous delinquents (p. 578)

adolescence-limited delinquency (p. 578)

recidivism rate (p. 581)

◊ NAMES YOU SHOULD KNOW

Dante Cicchetti (pp. 543, 574, 575, 576)

Stephen Hinshaw (pp. 548, 551, 555)

Jan Loney (p. 548)

William Pelham (p. 549)

Russell Barkley (Highlight 14.2, p. 550)

Benjamin Lahey (p. 551)

Terrie Moffitt (pp. 552, 554, 555)

Gerald Patterson (pp. 553, 555, 556

John Coie (p. 555)

Michael Rutter (pp. 555, 556, 568, 569)

◊ CONCEPTS TO MASTER

1. List and explain several special vulnerabilities of childhood. (p. 544)

2. Describe children's responses in the aftermath of a disaster, indicate both characteristics of the disaster and characteristics of children that make the situation more upsetting, and outline Vogel and Venberg's four-phase model for managing children's adjustment difficulties in a disaster. (Highlight 14.1, p. 545)

3. Explain three reasons why early childhood diagnostic systems were inadequate, and compare and contrast two kinds of systems that have been used. (pp. 544-547)

4. Define *hyperactivity*, and describe its clinical picture. (p. 547)

5. Although studies have failed to conclusively establish what causes ADHD, several potential causes have been suggested. Summarize the research on causal factors and ADHD, and describe which ones have been supported, and which ones have been discredited. (p. 548)

6. Compare and contrast the short-term effects of pharmacological and behavioral treatments of ADHD. (p. 549)

7. Summarize the long-term outcomes of individuals diagnosed as ADHD in childhood. (pp. 549, 551)

8. Summarize and discuss the controversy surrounding the use of drug therapy for ADHD. (Highlight 14.2, p. 550)

9. Define conduct disorder and oppositional defiant disorder, describe their clinical picture, and indicate the relationships among oppositional defiant disorder, early-onset conduct disorder, and adolescent-onset conduct disorder. (pp. 551, 554-555)

10. Discuss the contributions of social rejection (peer, teacher, parent) and deviant peer associations to the development of antisocial behavior. (p. 555)

11. Describe the family patterns that contribute to childhood conduct disorders and pathways by which they do this. (p. 555)

12. Summarize the assumptions and major features of Patterson's cohesive family model treatment strategy. (p. 556)

13. List several general characteristics of anxiety disorders in childhood and adolescence, and describe two subclassifications noted by DSM-IV. (pp. 557-558)

14. Explain six causal factors that have been emphasized in explanations of childhood anxiety disorders, and summarize what is known about their treatment. (pp. 558-559)

15. Discuss the symptoms associated with childhood depression and their relationship to adult depression. (p. 559-560)

16. Summarize the biological and learning factors that appear to contribute to the development of childhood depression. (pp. 560-561)

17. Define functional enuresis, summarize its clinical features, and discuss etiological factors. (pp. 562-563)

18. Conditioning procedures have proven successful in the treatment of enuresis. Describe how this treatment is conducted. (p. 563)

19. Describe the clinical picture, etiology, and treatment of Tourette's syndrome, as well as tics in general. (pp. 564-565)

20. Explain why autistic disorder is classified as a pervasive developmental disorder, and describe its clinical picture. (pp. 565, 566-568)

21. Summarize what is known about the causes and treatments of autistic disorders, giving special attention to educational and behavioral therapy. (pp. 569-570)

22. List and explain six special factors that must be considered in relation to treatment for children. (pp. 571-572, 574)

23. Explain why therapeutic intervention with children is a more complicated process than providing psychotherapy for adults, and discuss the procedures employed in family therapy and play therapy. (Highlight 14.4, p. 572, Highlight 14.5, p.573)

24. Describe the study by Wolfe and colleagues of families at high-risk for child abuse. What has been learned so far? (pp. 576-577)

25. Define *advocacy,* and evaluate the success of several governmental agencies and private groups that have tried to provide this function for children. (pp. 577-578)

26. Define *juvenile delinquency*, describe the seriousness of crimes committed by delinquents, and indicate how gender affects the probability of different types of crime. (p. 578)

27. Compare the causal roles of personal pathology, pathogenic famly patterns, and undesirable peer relationships in juvenile delinquency. (pp. 578-580)

28. Describe and evaluate several systems that have been used to deal with delinquency. (pp. 580-581)

◊ STUDY QUESTIONS

Introduction

1. Multisite studies in several countries have provided estimates of childhood disorder that range from ____ to ____ percent. In most studies, maladjustment is _____ among boys than among girls. (p. 543)

Maladaptive behavior in different life periods

2. Some of the emotional disturbances of childhood may be relatively _____-_____, and _____ than those occurring in adulthood. (p. 544)

3. Young children do not have as complex and realistic a view of themselves and their _____. As a result, they often have more difficulty coping with stress. They have a limited perspective and explain events with unrealistic concepts. On the other hand, although their _____ and lack of _____-_____ make them easily upset by problems that seem minor to the average adult, children typically _____ more _____ from their hurts. (p. 544)

Classification of childhood and adolescent disorders

4. Kraepelin's (1883) classic text on classification did not include childhood disorders. In 1952, a classification system for childhood was made available but it was inadequate. The authors list several reasons for the inadequacy of early childhood diagnostic systems. Complete the following list of these reasons: (pp. 544-546)

   a. In the past, the same categories used to classify adults were used for children.
   b. Children's symptoms are highly influenced by the family's _____ or _____ of the behavior.
   c. Symptoms were not considered with respect to a child's _____.

5. The general goals and methods employed by categorical and dimensional approaches are very different. It is therefore unlikely that there will ever be complete agreement between the two approaches with respect to the classification of children, although there will be overlap. On the following chart, place a "C" next to the choices that characterize the categorical approach to classification of childhood disorders. Place a "D" next to the choices that characterize the dimensional approach to the classification of childhood disorders. (p. 546)

a. Follows the disease model of psychopathology clinical study
b. Tends to have a smaller number of general classes covering numerous related behaviors
c. Based on the idea that behaviors are continuous and are found even among normals
d. Uses classes or types as the basis for classification
e. Can require the presence of relatively few symptoms to arrive at a diagnosis
f. Involves the application of sophisticated statistical methods, such as factor analysis

Attention-deficit hyperactivity disorder

6. Attention-deficit hyperactivity disorder, often called hyperactivity, is characterized by difficulties that interfere with effective task-oriented behavior in children – particularly _____, excessive _____ _____, and difficulties in sustaining _____. (p. 547)

7. Hyperactivity is the most frequent reason children are referred to mental health and pediatric facilities. It is estimated that between ____ and ____ percent of elementary school-aged children manifest the symptoms of hyperactivity. The disorder is 6 to 9 times more common in boys than girls. It occurs with greatest frequency before age _____, although some residual effects may persist into adolescence or adulthood. (p. 547)

8. Describe the clinical picture in hyperactivity in the following areas: (p. 547)

a. Muscular activity
b. Attention
c. Impulse control
d. Intelligence
e. Social maturity
f. Parental relationships

9. Complete the following summary of current thinking regarding the possible causes of hyperactivity: (p. 548)

  a. Biological basis: likely, but genetic basis has not been established.
  b. Diet:
  c. Parental personality problems: There are no clearly established psychological causes, but some evidence points to parental personality problems, particularly diagnoses of personality disorder or hysteria.

10. Cerebral stimulants, such as amphetamines, have a _____ effect on hyperactive children--just the opposite of what one might expect of a stimulant drug. (p. 549)

11. Some authorities consider stimulants the first drug of choice for treating ADHD. Although the drugs do not _____ hyperactivity, they have reduced the behavioral symptoms in about _____ to _____ of the cases in which medication appears warranted. For example, it has been found that medication reduced the problems of _____ but not the impulsivity in hyperactive children. (p. 549)

12. Carson and Bunner reported that studies of achievement over long periods of time _____ _____ that medication has beneficial effects. _____ has been expressed about the effects of the drugs, particularly when used in heavy dosages over time. (p. 549)

13. Behavior therapy is another effective approach to treating hyperactive children. What behavioral techniques are featured in treating ADHD? Give an example. (p. 549)

14. The use of behavioral treatment methods for hyperactivity has reportedly been _____ _____, at least for _____ gains. (p. 549)

15. Pelham and colleagues (1993) found that both behavior modification and medication therapy significantly reduced ADHD. _____, however, appeared to be the more effective element in the treatment. (p. 549)

16. Hyperactive behavior tends to diminish by the time some of the children reach their middle teens, although some of the research suggests that a small percentage of adolescents do retain their problems into later life   True or False (pp. 549,551)

384

17. What criticism has been made about the way children are selected to receive drugs? (Highlight 14.2, p. 550)

18. What criticism has been made about the purposes for which drugs are used in children? (Highlight 14.2, p. 550)

19. What do we know about the long-range side effects of drug therapy on children? (Highlight 14.2, p. 550)

Conduct disorder and oppositional defiant disorder

20. The authors conclude that the terms *conduct disorder*, a predelinquent pattern of behavior, and early stages in the development of an _____ are difficult, if not impossible, to distinguish. (p. 551)

21. An important precursor of the antisocial behavior seen in children with conduct disorder is often what is now called _____ disorder, which usually begins by the age of ____ years, whereas full-blown conduct disorder does not typically begin until the age of _____. (p. 551).

22. Only about ____ percent of children with oppositional defiant disorder go on to develop conduct disorder within a three-year period. The risk factors for both include _____ _____, socioeconomic disadvantage, and _____ behavior in the parents. (p. 551)

23. The essential symptomatic behavior in conduct disorders involves a persistent and repetitive _____ and a disregard for the _____.
List ten characteristics of conduct disordered children: (pp. 551, 554)

24. Evidence has accumulated that a genetic predisposition leading to low _____, mild _____ problems, and _____ temperament sets the stage for early-onset conduct disorder. (p. 554)

25. Although only about ____ to ____ percent of cases of early-onset conduct disorder go on to develop adult antisocial personality disorder, over 80 percent of boys with early-onset conduct disorder do continue to have multiple problems of _____ dysfunction. By contrast, most adolescents who develop conduct disorder in adolescence do not go on to become adult psychopaths or antisocial personalities. (p. 555)

26. Foster home or institutional placement for conduct disorders is ineffective unless the changed environment offers a _____, _____, and _____--yet _____ and _____--setting. (p. 556)

27. Fareta (1981) found that _____ and _____ behavior persisted into adulthood. This and other studies have suggested that conduct-disordered children go on to have _____ as adults. (p. 556)

28. How is behavior therapy used to assist the parents of conduct disordered children? (pp. 556-557)

29. Parents often have difficulty carrying out treatment plans that are part of behavior therapy. If so, other techniques, such as _____ or _____ are used to ensure that the parent is sufficiently assertive to follow through on the program. (p. 557)

Anxiety disorders of childhood and adolescence

30. Separation anxiety disorder is the most common of the childhood anxiety disorders, reportedly occurring with a prevalence of ____ percent of children in a population health study. (p. 557)

31. Children with separation anxiety disorder experience unrealistic fears, oversensitivity, self-consciousness, nightmares, and chronic anxiety. They lack self-confidence, are apprehensive in _____, and tend to be immature for their age. (p. 557)

32. Separation anxiety is more common in boys than in girls. True or False (p. 557)

33. At a four-year follow-up, ____% of children recoered from separation anxiety disorder, although some exhibited _____ _____ problems and continued to have adjustment diffidult over time. (p. 557)

34. A child whose education is disrupted because he or she fails to speak during the first month of school qualifies for selective mutism. True or False (p 558)

35. Selective mutism occurs more frequently in families in which _____ behavior was prominent (Steinhausen & Amadek, 1997). Its severity depends on the particular environmental setting , and it is most commonly associated with _____ _____. (Black & Uhde, 1995). (p. 558)

36. The authors list six general causal factors of anxiety disorders: (pp. 558-559)
   a. Unusual sensitivity, easy conditionability, and a build-up of _____ _____ _____.
   b. Early _____, _____, or _____ which make such children feel insecure and inadequate. Certain life changes such as moving away from friends into a new school can also have an intensely negative effect.
   c. Modeling by an overanxious parent who sensitizes the child to _____ and _____ of the outside world, and thereby communicating lack of confidence in the child's ability to cope – which in turn reinforces the child's feelings of inadequacy.
   d. Detached or _____ parents who fail to provide adequate support in mastering _____ _____ and in gaining a positive self-concept. Other children may be _____-_____ of themselves and feel intensely anxious and devaluated when they perceive themselves as failing to do well enough to earn their parents' love and respect.
   e. Cultures which favor _____, _____, and obedience appear to increase the levels of fear reported.
   f. Exposure to _____ is associated with a reduced sense of security and psychological well-being, as well as a lack of control over reinforcing environmental events.

37. The anxiety disorders of childhood may continue into adolescence and adulthood but this is not usually the case. As they grow up and have wider interactions in school and in peer-group activities, they often benefit from such corrective experiences as making _____ and _____ at given tasks. (p. 559)

38. Psychopharmacological treatment of anxiety disorders in children and adolescents is becoming more common today. However, one factor contributing to caution in using medications is that anxiety is often found to coexist with other conditions, particularly _____. Often there is not the diagnostic clarity required for cautious use of antianxiety medication. (p. 559)

39. Behavior therapy procedures sometimes used in school settings often help anxious children Included here are _____ training and desensitization. Desensitization must be explicitly tailored to _____, and _____ methods (using graded life situations) may be more effective than the use of imagined situations. (p. 559)

Childhood depression

40. What is the point prevalence of major depressive disorder for children and adolescents? (p. 559)

41. Currently, childhood depression is classified according to the _____ DSM-IV diagnostic criteria used in the _____ system, with the only modification being that _____ is often found as a major symptom and can be substituted for depressed mood. (p. 560)

42. Explain some of the current difficulties with pharmacological treatment for childhood depression. (p. 561)

43. What are two important facets of psychological treatment for depression in children and adolescents? (p. 562)

Other symptom disorders: Functional enuresis

44. The term functional enuresis refers to the habitual involuntary discharge of urine after the age of expected continence, which is age ___, that is not _____ caused. What is the difference between primary and secondary functional enuresis? (p. 562)

44. Estimates of the prevalence of enuresis reported in DSM-IV are ___ percent for boys and ___ percent for girls at age 5, and ___ percent for boys and ___ percent for girls at age 10. (p. 562)

45. In an extensive epidemiological study conducted in Holland, Verhulst et al. determined that, between the ages of 5 and 8, the rates of enuresis among boys are _____ to _____ times higher than the rates among girls. (p. 562)

46. Although enuresis may result from a variety of organic conditions, the authors emphasize three psychosocial factors. Complete the requested information in the following list of causes of enuresis: (pp. 562-563)

Causal Factor	Description
1. Faulty learning	Results in a failure to acquire the _____ of reflex bladder emptying.
2. _____	Associated with or stems from emotional problems.
3. Disturbed family interactions	Particularly situations that lead to sustained _____ or _____, or both.
4. Stressful events	Child may _____ to _____ in response to stressful event, such as when a new baby enters the family and become the center of attention.

47. What are the hypothesized underlying mechanisms of imipramine and DDAVP in the treatment of functional enuresis? (p. 563)

48. List some current disadvantages of pharmacological treatment for functional enuresis. (p. 563)

49. What happens to the incidence of enuresis as the child gets older if it is untreated? (p. 563)

50. In a review of the treatment of bedwetting, Houts, Berman, and Abramson (1994) concluded that treated children were _____ at follow-up than nontreated children and that learning-based procedures were _____ effective than were physical treatments. (p. 563)

Other symptom disorders: Functional encopresis

51. Encopresis refers to the absence of appropriate bowel control after age ____. (p. 563)

52. Respond TRUE or FALSE to the following statements about encopresis: (p. 563)
    a. One third of encopretic children are enuretic.   True or False
    b. Six times more boys than girls are encopretic.   True or False
    c. A common time for encopresis is after school.   True or False
    d. Most encopretic children know they need to
       have a bowel movement.   True or False
    e. Many encopretic children suffer from constipation.   True or False

Other symptom disorders: Sleepwalking (somnambulism)

53. Sleepwalking involves repeated episodes in which a person leaves his or her bed and walks
    around without _____ or _____. (p. 563)

54. The onset of a sleeping disorder is usually between _____ and _____ years of age. A
    Swedish study reported that _____ percent of children experience sleepwalking episodes.
    (pp. 563-564)

55. During sleepwalking, the eyes are _____ and obstacles are _____.
    Episodes usually last from ___ to ___ minutes. (p. 564)

56. Causes of sleepwalking are not fully understood, but it takes place during _____ sleep and
    appears related to some _____ situation that has just occurred or is
    expected to occur. (p. 564)

57. The use of conditioning treatments such as pairing awakening with the nightmare that
    triggered sleepwalking in the seven-year old boy is similar to that used to treat _____.
    (p. 564)

Other symptom disorders: Tics

58. A tic is a persistent muscle twitch, usually limited to a _____. (p. 564)

59. Tics occur most frequently between the ages of ___ and ___. (p. 564)

60. An extreme tic disorder involving multiple motor and vocal patterns is called
    _____ syndrome. (p. 564)

61. About one-third of individuals with Tourette's syndrome manifest _____, which is a complex vocal tic that involves the uttering of obscenities. Most cases of this syndrome have an onset before age ___. (p. 565)

Pervasive developmental disorder: Autism

62. Autism afflicts some 80,000 American children and is ___ or ___ times more frequent among boys than girls. Autism is usually diagnosed before _____ months of age and may be suspected in the _____ of life. (pp. 565-566)

63. Complete the following chart summarizing the clinical picture in autistic disorders by writing a brief description of autistic children's behavior in each area: (pp. 566-568)

Area of Behavior	Characteristics
Social deficit	
Use of speech	Speech is absent or severely restricted. Echolalic repetition of a few words may be observed. There are suggestions that some autistic children do comprehend language, but they do not use it to express themselves.
Self-stimulation	
Intellectual ability	Autistic children have difficulty with meaning. Most investigators have viewed these children as retarded. As compared to normal and retarded control children, autistic children displayed impaired memory, as well as a deficit in representing mental states (i.e., deficits in social reasoning), and more impairment in adaptive behavior. These may be due to motivational differences.
Maintaining Sameness	

64. Circle YES, NO, or MAYBE as appropriate to indicate whether each of the following factors is currently thought to be an important cause of autism: (pp. 568-569)

Genetic basis	YES	NO	MAYBE
Chromosome abnormalities	YES	NO	MAYBE
Inborn defect in perceptual/cognitive functions	YES	NO	MAYBE
Personality characteristics of parents	YES	NO	MAYBE

65. The drug most often used in the treatment of autism is _____, but the data on its effectiveness do not warrant use unless a child's behavior is unmanageable by other means. _____ has had moderate effects at reducing the severity of symptoms. Clomipramine has had some observed beneficial effect in reducing aggression levels. (p. 569)

66. Some of the most impressive results in the treatment of autism have been obtained with parents as therapists to treat their own autistic children. YES or NO (p. 569)

67. What is the prognosis for autism in children who show symptoms before age 2? (p. 570)

68. One particular problem with treating autistic children is that they have difficulty _____ _____ to situations outside of the treatment context. (p. 570)

69. How many children who receive treatment attain even a marginal adjustment in adulthood? (p. 570)

Special factors associated with treatment for children and adolescents

70. In what ways do children have difficulty seeking assistance for emotional problems? (p. 571)

71. What does it mean to say a child from a pathogenic home is at a "double disadvantage"? (p. 571)

72. What is meant by the expression, "using parents as change agents"? (pp. 571-572)

73. Give some reasons that placement of a child in a foster home often works out less than ideally for the child. (p. 574)

Child abuse

74. Child abuse reports in the U.S. increased _____% in 1995, with a total number of incidents exceeding _____. An estimated _____ children were killed in 1995 in child abuse incidents. (p. 575)

75. List some of the effects that child abuse may have: (p. 575)
    a. Impaired cognitive ability and memory
    b.
    c. Feel that outcomes of events are beyond their own control
    d.
    e.
    f. Demonstrate less interpersonal sensitivity
    g.
    h. Tend to show more self-destructive behavior than nonabused children
    i. When abused children reach adulthood, they are likely to
       _____.

76. What common factors have been found among families with abusing parents? (p. 576)

77. Describe the various approaches to prevention of child abuse that are available: (p. 576)
    a.

    b.

    c.

    d.

Child-advocacy programs

79. One approach to meeting children's mental health needs is advocacy. Twice in recent years the federal government has established a National Center for Child Advocacy. What happened both times? (p. 577)

80. The authors highlight four causal factors in delinquency: personal pathology, pathogenic family patterns, undesirable peer relationships, general socio-cultural factors, and special stress. Fill in the missing information on the following chart that summarizes the research on the causal factors of juvenile delinquency. (pp. 578-580)

Causal Factors in Juvenile Delinquency

Personal Pathology	
Genetic determinants	Schulsinger (1980) found adopted sociopathic criminals more often had sociopathic biological fathers than non-sociopathic criminals.
Brain damage	Less than _____ percent of delinquents have been found to have brain damage that could lead to lowered inhibitory controls and a tendency toward violent behavior.
Psychological disorders	A small percentage of delinquent acts are associated with _____. Delinquent acts associated with psychotic behavior often involve prolonged emotional turmoil, culminating in an outburst of _____ _____.
Psychopathic traits	Many habitual delinquents appear to share traits typical of psychopathic persons, such as: _____ _____ _____ _____.
Drug abuse	Many delinquents acts--particularly _____, _____, and _____--are committed in order to obtain money to buy expensive drugs, such as heroin.

Pathogenic Family Patterns	
Parental absence or family conflict	Delinquency seems to be more common in homes broken by _____ or _____ than in homes broken by death of a parent.
Parental rejection and faulty discipline	When the father rejects a boy, it is difficult for a boy to _____ with him or use him as a _____ for his own development. Bandura and Walters studied boys whose fathers rejected them, used inconsistent discipline, and were physically punitive. The end result was a _____, _____, _____ youth who lacked normal _____ and tended to act out aggressive impulses.
Limited parental relationships outside the family	Children's acting-out behavior is greater when parents have few friendly contacts outside the home.

Undesirable Peer Relationships	
Delinquency as a shared experience	About _____ of delinquent acts involved one or two other persons, and most of the remainder involved three or four other persons.
Broad social conditions	Inter-related factors that appear to be of key importance include _____, _____, and _____ _____
Gang cultures	What type of feelings does belonging to a gang give a delinquent? _____ _____ _____

81. Behavior therapy techniques--based on the assumption that delinquent behavior is _____, _____, and _____ according to the same principles as other learned behavior--have shown promise in the rehabilitation of juvenile offenders who require institutionalization. (p. 581)

82. The recidivism rate for juvenile offenders depends heavily on the type of _____ _____ and on the particular _____ _____. (p. 581)

◊ CRITICAL THINKING ABOUT DIFFICULT TOPICS

1. In the chapter on substance abuse, you saw that long-term substitution of methadone for opium is sometimes used for treatment, even though methadone and heroin are similar drugs. In the present chapter, you have seen that long-term use of cerebral stimulants such as the amphetamines (e.g., Ritalin) are viewed by many as the treatment of choice (p. 549). Some psychiatrists will see the use of Ritalin as a medication that corrects a "chemical imbalance" and would have no misgivings about very long-term use of the drug. Others have expressed alarm about "the possibility of adverse long-range effects resulting from sustained use during early growth and development . . ." (p. 549, Highlight 14.2, p. 550). What is your own evaluation of this argument? Note that both methadone and Ritalin share many properties of street drugs of abuse (heroin in the case of methadone, amphetamines in the case of Ritalin). Is it okay to take the same drug prescribed as "medicine" under medical supervision but not to take it purchased as a street drug without medical supervision? If so, why--i.e., what important differences do you see between the two? At least some drugs, such as alcohol and the phenothiazines (used to treat schizophrenia), have adverse effects on the brain when used in large doses for long periods of time. Does the concept of correcting a chemical imbalance imply that there should be no adverse effects, since the brain's neurochemistry is being adjusted to a more normal state? How would you resolve these competing views?

Circle the best of the four answers provided and check them according to answers provided at the back of this study guide. Be sure you understand why each answer is correct.

1. Multisite studies in several countries, estimates of childhood disorders ranged from ___ to ___ percent. (p. 543)
   a. 5, 8
   b. 8, 12
   c. 17, 22
   d. 21, 26

2. Compared to a categorical system for classifying childhood and adolescent disorders, a dimensional strategy: (p. 546)
   a. assesses fewer behaviors for each category.
   b. has more diagnostic categories.
   c. ignores presenting symptoms in favor of case studies.
   d. requires more symptoms to make a diagnosis.

3. A researcher gathers his or her symptomatic information through teachers', parents', or clinicians' observations or through a child's _____. (p. 546)
   a. presenting symptoms
   b. school record
   c. peer reputation
   d. statistical profile

4. Which of the following is not a usual characteristic of children with ADHD? (p. 547)
   a. low frustration tolerance
   b. lower in intelligence
   c. great difficulties in getting along with their parents
   d. higher in anxiety

5. In a recent study, Pelham and colleagues (1993) concluded that in the treatment of children with ADHD: (p. 549)
   a. only medication was effective.
   b. only behavior modification was effective.
   c. both medication and behavior modification were effective, but the latter was better.
   d. both medication and behavior modification were effective, but the former was better.

6. Which of the following is the most common developmental sequence for conduct disorder (CD), antisocial personality (ASP), delinquency, and/or oppositional defiant disorder (ODD)? (p. 551)
   a. CD, ODD, ASP
   b. ODD, CD, ASP
   c. CD, ASP, ODD
   d. CD, ODD, delinquency

7. Children diagnosed as suffering from anxiety disorders usually attempt to cope with their fears by: (p. 557)
   a. becoming overly dependent on others.
   b. denying the existence of fearful things.
   c. developing compulsive behaviors.
   d. indulging in "guardian angel" fantasies.

8. Typically, children with anxiety disorders: (p. 559)
   a. become adolescents with maladaptive avoidance behavior.
   b. become adults with idiosyncratic thinking and behavior.
   c. become suicidal when they reach 30.
   d. have experiences that reduce their fears and insecurity.

9. Which of the following childhood disorders is more prevalent among girls than boys? (pp. 547, 557, 562-563)
   a. enuresis
   b. encopresis
   c. childhood anxiety disorders
   d. ADHD

10. Kales and associates have shown that sleepwalking takes place in: (p. 564)
    a. REM sleep.
    b. NREM sleep.
    c. stage 4 sleep.
    d. stage 1 sleep.

11. All of the following are true of infantile autism except: (p. 566)
    a. it afflicts about 6.5 children in 10,000.
    b. it is usually identified before the child is 30 months old.
    c. it occurs much more frequently in boys than in girls.
    d. most cases are found in the upper classes.

12. Autism has been associated with: (p. 568)
    a. parental education.
    b. racial origin.
    c. genetic factors.
    d. a cold and unresponsive mother.

13. The drug(s) used most often in autism is/are _____, but the effects have not been very impressive. (p. 569)
    a. haloperidol
    b. caffeine
    c. barbiturates
    d. anti-anxiety

14. One of the major factors that needs to be taken into account when studying or treating children is: (p. 571)
    a. child advocacy programs are always available.
    b. children are dependent on those around them.
    c. drug therapy is usually warranted.
    d. children are small adults.

15. Treatment without parental consent is permitted in all of the following cases *except*: (p. 571)
    a. immature minors
    b. emancipated minors
    c. emergency situations
    d. court-ordered situations

16. Many habitual delinquents share the traits typical of the _____ personality. (p. 579)
    a. antisocial
    b. obsessive-compulsive
    c. narcissistic
    d. passive-aggressive

17. Haney and Gold found that most delinquent acts were committed: (p. 580)
    a. alone, without any help.
    b. in association with one or two other persons.
    c. with three or four other persons.
    d. with five or six other persons.

18. Alienation from family and the broader society causes juveniles to become more vulnerable to: (p. 580)
    a. incest and related sexual crimes.
    b. negative influences of TV and other media.
    c. the psychological support afforded by membership in a delinquent gang.
    d. solitary acts of violence.

Chapter 15
Clinical Assessment

◊ OVERVIEW

One of the most important activities of the mental health professional is to assess the nature and extent of the problem for which help is being sought. Thus, Chapter 15 is devoted to a discussion of the goals, methods, and issues involved in clinical assessment. For a clinician, the primary goals of clinical assessment include an identification, description, and diagnosis of an individual's presenting symptoms, as well as evaluation of variables that might influence treatment, including potential causal and protective factors. Clinical assessment depends on data from observation and interviews, as well as psychological, often neuropsychological, and, in some cases, neurological tests. Chapter 15 describes what the different types of tests are, how they are constructed, and what types of information can be obtained from them. Additionally, this chapter discusses the increasingly common use of computerized psychological testing for aid in administration, scoring, and even interpretation of data. Given the far-reaching implications of a clinical assessment, it is important for clinicians to be aware of concerns of insufficient validity and bias on the part of both the clinician (e.g., theoretical orientation) and/or the instrument itself (e.g., culture bias). The chapter ends with an evaluation of the relationship between assessment and therapy. Many trained clinicians begin and continue treatment without incorporating conclusions from psychological testing, despite evidence that such testing, in and of itself, can be therapeutic.

◊ CHAPTER OUTLINE

I. The Basic Elements in Assessment
    A. The Relationship Between Diagnosis and Assessment
    B. Taking a Social History
        1. Personality Factors
        2. The Social Context
    C. The Influence of Personal Orientation
    D. Trust and Rapport Between the Clinician and the Client

401

A. Ethical Issues in Assessment

V. Unresolved Issues: On Incorporating Psychological Test Data into Therapy: An Unfulfilled Relationship

VI. Summary

◊ LEARNING OBJECTIVES

After studying this chapter, you should be able to:

1. Describe the basic elements of clinical assessment, including: a) its nature and purpose, b) the relationship between diagnosis and assessment, c) the types of information sought, and d) the different types of data of interest. Further, describe the influence of professional orientation on the assessment process. (pp. 584-587)

2. Explain what is meant by rapport between the clinician and client, and outline the components of a relationship that leads to good rapport. (p. 587)

3. Summarize the various approaches to assessment of physical problems. (pp. 587-590; Highlight 15.1, p. 591)

4. Discriminate between structured and unstructured interviews for the assessment of psychosocial functioning, and evaluate the relative merits of the two. (pp. 590-592)

5. Discuss the use of computerized interviewing, and describe the decision tree approach to classification with software such as "D-Tree." (pp. 592-595)

6. Discuss various approaches to the clinical observation of behavior and identify the advantages of each. (pp. 593, 596)

7. List the features of psychological tests and describe the major intelligence and personality tests. (pp. 596-608)

8. Discuss the controversy over the use of computerized assessment. (p. 598)

9. Describe how psychological assessment is used in the legal system, which tests are commonly used, and why these tests are appropriate. (pp. 608-609)

10. Outline the issues involved in the use of psychological tests for personnel selection and personnel screening. (pp. 610-611)

11. Summarize the process of integrating assessment data into a model for use in planning or changing treatment. (pp. 614-616)

◊ TERMS YOU SHOULD KNOW

clinical assessment (p. 584)

dynamic formulation (p. 585)

electroencephalogram (EEG) (p. 587)

dysrhythmia (p. 588)

computerized axial tomography (CAT scan) (p. 588)

magnetic resonance imaging (MRI) (p. 588)

positron emission tomography (PET scan) (p. 589)

functional magnetic resonance imaging (fMRI) (p. 589)

neuropsychological assessment (p. 590)

Halstead-Reitan battery (Highlight 15.1, p. 591)

Halstead Category Test (Highlight 15.1, p. 591)

Tactual Performance Test (Highlight 15.1, p. 591)

Rhythm Test (Highlight 15.1, p. 591)

personality tests (p. 599)

projective tests (p. 599)

Rorschach Test (p. 599)

Exner Comprehensive Rorschach System (p. 600)

Thematic Apperception Test (TAT) (p. 601)

sentence completion tests (p. 602)

objective tests (p. 602)

Minnesota Multiphasic Personality Inventory (MMPI) (pp. 602-603)

"Minnesota normals" (p. 603)

empirical keying (p. 603)

clinical scales (p. 603)

validity scales (p. 603)

diagnostic standard (p. 603)

descriptive diagnosis (p. 603)

content interpretation (p. 603)

MMPI-2 (pp. 603, 606-608)

MMPI-2 clinical scales: (Table 15.1, p. 606)

hypochondriasis	*paranoia*
depression	*psychasthenia*
hysteria	*schizophrenia*
psychopathic deviate	*hypomania*
masculinity-femininity	*social introversion*

MMPI-2 special scales (p. 606)
    Addiction Proneness Scale   *MacAndrew addiction scale*
    Addiction Awareness Scale   *Marital distress scale*

MMPI-2 validity scales (p. 606)
    Lie Scale   *Defensiveness scale*
    Infrequency Scales   *Response inconsistencies*

factor analysis (p. 607)

computer-based MMPI interpretation (p. 607)

actuarial procedures (p. 607)

faking good versus *faking bad* (p. 609)

Woodworth Personal Data Sheet (Highlight 15.5, p. 610)

personnel selection versus *personnel screening* (Highlight 15.5, p. 610)

◊ NAMES YOU SHOULD KNOW

Gordon Paul (p. 596)

Robert Carson (pp. 598, 608)

Joseph Matarazzo (p. 598)

Hermann Rorschach (p. 599)

J. E. Exner (p. 600)

James Butcher (pp. 600, 602, 603, 606, 607)

Y. S. Ben-Porath (pp. 607, 611, 615)

◊ CONCEPTS TO MASTER

1. Explain the difference between diagnosis and clinical assessment, and list several components that must be integrated into the dynamic formulation. (pp. 585-586)

2. Outline three basic components which are essential in establishing rapport between the clinician and the client. (p. 587)

3. Compare and contrast five important neurological procedures, explaining especially what makes each one valuable. (pp. 580-590)

4. List, describe, and explain the purpose of the five tests included in the Halstead-Reitan battery. (Highlight 15.1, p. 591)

5. Describe the characteristics of a good assessment interview, and list some advantages and disadvantages of the interview method. (pp. 590-592)

6. List and describe several examples of computerized diagnostic interviews and enumerate the strengths and weaknesses of this approach. (pp. 592-593)

7. Explain what is meant by the decision tree approach to classification and evaluate the effectiveness of the "D-Tree" computer program designed to provide DSM-IV diagnosis using the decision tree approach. (Highlight 15.2, p. 594-595)

8. Define and discuss different kinds of clinical observations. How are rating scales used in psychological observation? (pp. 593, 596)

9. Explain the kind of data gathered by psychological tests, and list two types that are commonly used. (pp. 596-597)

10. List and describe three intelligence tests used by clinicians, and explain how this information can be used in assessment. (p. 597)

11. Describe four possible reasons for the reluctance to utilize computer-based assessment procedures. (Highlight 15.3, p. 598)

12. Explain the assumptions behind the use of projective tests, and describe the use of the Rorschach Test and the Thematic Apperception Test (TAT) in clinical assessment. (pp. 599-602)

13. Define *objective tests,* and describe the Minnesota Multiphasic Personality Inventory (MMPI) and its uses in clinical assessment. (pp. 602-603, 606-608)

14. Define the concept of *empirical keying,* and summarize the steps involved in this approach in developing the MMPI. (p. 603)

15. Describe the changes made on MMPI-2, and discuss the effects the changes have had. (pp. 606-608)

16. Compare the advantages of self-report inventories with the criticisms leveled against this method. (p. 607)

17. Explain what is meant by the *actuarial procedures* used to interpret the MMPI-2, and discuss the limitations of this approach. (p. 607)

18. List three tests that are widely used in court testimony, and explain why these rather than other tests are accepted as evidence. (pp. 608-609)

19. Cite some general objectives of personnel screening, and describe the use of some psychological tests to accomplish these goals. (p. 610)

20. List and explain four considerations that should be addressed before implementing a psychological assessment program for pre-employment screening. (pp. 610-611)

21. Summarize the psychological case study of Esteban, noting the various types of clinical assessment that were used to build the dynamic formulation. (pp. 609-614; Highlight 15.4, p. 604-605)

22. Explain the functions of a staff conference in integrating the assessment data and making decisions about the client. (p. 614)

23. Describe five ethical issues that clinicians should be aware of when evaluating test results. (pp. 614-615).

24. Explain the unfulfilled relationship between psychological assessment and therapy, and list three reasons that clinicians often fail to incorporate psychological test data into therapy. (pp. 615-616)

◊ STUDY QUESTIONS

Introduction

1. The goal of clinical assessment is to identify and understand the _____ and _____ of the problem. (p. 584)

2. Data from clinical assessment is used for two purposes. First, it serves as a basis for treatment decisions. A less obvious but equally important function is that of establishing a _____ against which to evaluate progress made during and following treatment. (p. 584)

The relationship beween diagnosis and assessment

3. Although there has been a trend against overdependence on labeling, adequate classification is needed for three reasons: (1) for _____, (2) for treatment planning and managment, and (3) to establish the range of diagnostic problems represented among the patient population in order to know which treatment facilities need to be available. (p. 585)

Taking a social history

4. For clinical purposes, knowledge about an individual's _____, _____ _____, personality characteristics, and environmental pressures and resources is more important than a formal diagnosis. (p. 585)

5. The material gained through assessment is integrated into a consistent and meaningful picture, often called the _____, that should lead to an explanation of why the person is engaging in maladaptive behavior and to hypotheses about the person's future behavior as well. (p. 586)

The influence of professional orientation

6. What assessment techniques would be favored by the following? (pp. 586-587)

   a. Biologically oriented clinician

   b. Psychoanalytically oriented clinician

   c. Behaviorally oriented clinician

   d. Humanistically oriented clinician

Assessment of the physical organism

7. Medical examinations are necessary in some situations to rule out physical abnormalities or to determine the extent to which physical problems are involved. The two types of medical examinations that may be performed include the general _____ examination and the _____ examination, aimed at assessing the _____ (_____) and _____ (_____) integrity of the brain as a behaviorally significant physical system. (p. 587)

8. An EEG is a graphic record of the _____. Significant divergences from the normal pattern of brain impulses can reflect abnormalities of brain function, such as might be caused by a brain tumor or other lesion. (p. 587)

9. What is the major problem encountered with CAT scans? MRI scans? PET scans? (pp. 588-589)

10. Functional MRI measures changes in _____ _____ (i.e., blood flow) of specific areas of brain tissue that in turn depend on _____ activity in those specific regions. Ongoing physiological activity, such as _____, _____, and thoughts, can thus be "mapped" at least in principle, revealing the specific areas of the brain that appear to be involved in their neurophysiological mediation. (p. 589)

11. Neurological tests identify abnormalities in the brain's physical properties. In contrast, neuropsychological assessment identifies gross impairments in _____ and varied psychological _____. (p. 590)

12. The Halstead-Reitan battery consists of a standard set of tests that have been preselected so as to sample in a systematic and comprehensive manner a _____ _____ known to be adversely affected by various types of brain injury. (p. 590)

13. Match the following subtests of the Halstead-Reitan neuropsychology battery with the correct description of its purpose: (Highlight 15.1, p. 591)

Subtest	Purpose
__ Halstead Category Test	a. Determines if an individual can identify spoken words
__ Tactual Performance Test	b. Measures a patient's ability to learn and remember
__ Rhythm Test	c. Measures the speed at which one can depress a lever. Gives clues to the extent and location of brain damage.
__ Speech Sounds Perception	d. Measures attention and sustained test concentration
__ Finger Oscillation Test	e. Measures motor speed, response to the unfamiliar, and the learning of tactile and kinesthetic cues

Psychosocial assessment

14. Psychosocial assessment attempts to provide a realistic picture of the individual in interaction with the _____. (p. 590)

Psychosocial assessment: Assessment interviews

15. There appears to be widespread _____ among clinicians in the accuracy of their own assessment methods and judgments. In order to minimize sources of error and increase reliability, an assessment interview should be carefully structured in terms of goals, comprehensive _____ review, other content to be explored, and the type of relationship the interviewer attempts to establish with the person. The reliability of the assessment interview may also be enhanced by the use of _____ that help to focus inquiry and quantify the interview data. (p. 592)

16. The clinical interview has been criticized as an unreliable source of information on which to base clinical decisions. What type of evidence is used to demonstrate that interviews are unreliable? (p. 592)

17. Give an example of a structured interview for children that has been developed for computer administration. (pp. 592-593)

Psychosocial assessment: Clinical observation of behavior

18. The main purpose of direct observation is to learn more about the person's psychological functioning through the objective description of behavior in various contexts. Ideally, such observations would occur in the individual's _____, but they are typically confined to _____ or _____ settings. In addition, many clinicians ask their patients to report their own behavior, thoughts, and feelings as they occur in various natural settings--a procedure called _____. (p. 593)

19. As in the case of interviews, the use of _____ in clinical observation and self-reports helps not only to organize information but also to encourage reliability and objectivity. (p. 593)

20. What is the most widely used rating scale for recording observations in clinical practice and psychiatric research? What is a similar rating scale designed specifically for depression? (pp. 593, 596)

21. Paul and his colleagues developed a comprehensive behavioral assessment program that they have used experimentally in a number of hospitals. How have they used the observational rating scales? (p. 596)

22. Often it is not feasible to observe a subject's behavior in everyday situations. Describe how observational data are obtained in the following: (p. 596)
    a. When a patient is institutionalized and family observations are desired
    b. When a person has a phobia for snakes
    c. During role playing

Psychosocial assessment: Psychological tests (intelligence and personality tests)

23. Psychological tests are standardized sets of procedures to obtain samples of a subject's behavior that can be compared to the behavior of other individuals, usually through the use of established test _____ or test score _____. (p. 596)

24. Among the characteristics about which the clinician can draw inferences from psychological tests are coping patterns, motive patterns, personality characteristics, role behaviors, values, levels of depression or anxiety, and _____. (p. 596)

25. Individual intelligence tests such as the WISC-R or the WAIS-R require two to three hours to administer, score, and interpret; in many clinical situations, there is not sufficient time or funding to use these tests in every assessment situation. (p. 597)

    a. In what type of cases would an individual intelligence test be indicated?

    b. In which cases would an individual intelligence test be unnecessary?

26. Among other things, computerized assessment packages have been programmed to: a)supply a probable _____, b) indicate the likelihood of _____, c) suggest the most appropriate form of _____, d) predict the _____, and e) print out a summary report concerning the client. Nevertheless, it is the clinician who must assume the major organizing role and _____ _____ _____ for an assessment. (p. 598)

27. Projective tests are aimed at discovering the ways in which an individual's _____ _____ and _____ _____ may lead him or her to organize and perceive _____ information from the environment. (p. 599)

28. Match the following psychological tests with the appropriate description of each test's purpose: (pp. 599-602)

Psychological Test	Purpose
__ Rorschach Test	a. Rating scale based on standardized interview
__ Thematic Apperception Test	b. Intelligence scale for children
__ Minnesota Multiphasic Personality Inventory (MMPI)	c. Intelligence scale for adults
__ WAIS-R	d. Projective test using inkblots
__ WISC-R	e. Projective test using pictures
__ Brief Psychiatric Rating Scale (BPRS)	f. Structured personality test
__ Sentence Completion Test	g. Test that pinpoints topics that should be explored

29. The Rorschach has been criticized because it can be _____ as a result of the subjective nature of test data interpretations. In addition, current treatments generally require _____ descriptions rather than descriptions of deep-seated personality dynamics. (pp. 599-600)

30. The TAT has been criticized for its dated pictures, lengthy administration, and the fact that interpretation is often _____ and limits the _____ and _____ of the test. (p. 602)

31. Objective tests are _____--that is, they typically use questionnaires, self-report inventories, or rating scales in which questions are carefully phrased and alternative responses are specified as choices. They are more amenable to objectively based _____ than projective tests. One virtue of such _____ is that of precision, which in turn enhances the _____ of test outcomes. (p. 602)

32. Place a 1, 2, or 3 in front of the following steps to indicate the sequence in which the step appeared during the construction of the MMPI. (p. 603)

___ Scales are constructed.

___ Items analyses are performed.

___ Items are administered to large groups of normal subjects and psychiatric patients.

33. As used in the MMPI, what is the purpose of a validity scale? (p. 603)

34. How is the MMPI used as a diagnostic standard? (p. 603)

35. What criticisms have been made of the MMPI? (pp. 603, 606)

36. List the following changes made for the MMPI-2 having to do with: (p. 607)

    a. Language:

    b. Questions (items) on the test:

    c. Normative data:

37. Complete the chart below that compares the overall strengths and weaknesses of projective and objective tests. (pp. 599-608)

Test	Strengths	Weaknesses
Projective		Interpretations are subjective, unreliable, and difficult to validate, require trained staff to administer and score
Objective	Cost effective, reliable, objective, administered and scored by computer	

Use of psychological tests in personnel screening

38. The potential for job failure or for psychological maladjustment can be so great in some high-stress occupations that measures need to be taken in the hiring process to evaluate applicants for emotional _____. (p. 610)

39. The use of personality tests in personnel screening has a long tradition. The first formal use of a standardized personality scale in the U.S., the _____ _____ Data Sheet was implemented to screen out draftees who were psychologically unfit for military service. (p. 610)

40. Place the following words in the correct blanks: Personnel selection, personnel screening. (p. 610)

    a. Screening out is called _____. This type of selection is done to alert employers to possible maladjustment that would impact adversely upon the way in which the individual would function in a critical job.
    b. Screening in is called _____. This type of selection is done when the employer believes that certain personality characteristics are desirable for a particular job.

41. Before personality tests are used in personnel screening, the psychologist needs to consider four issues: (a) how much weight the test should be given, (b) whether the job is critical enough to justify the invasion of privacy involved in the use of psychological testing, (c) _____, and (d) whether the assessment will be used in compliance with federal guidelines, such as the Americans with Disabilities Act. (p. 611)

Integration of assessment data

42. In a clinic or hospital setting, assessment data is usually evaluated in a _____ attended by members of the interdisciplinary team who are concerned with the decision to be made regarding treatment. (p. 614)

43. The following factors should be kept in mind when evaluating test results: (pp. 614-615)
    a) potential cultural bias of the instrument or the clinician
    b) theoretical orientation of the clinician
    c) _____
    d) insufficient validation
    e) _____

421

44. There is growing evidence to indicate that the results of psychological tests can, when sensitively shared with clients, bring about remarkable personality change and insight in clients. Personality information given to clients early in intervention can bring about _____ and a lowering of _____. Test feedback alone produced therapeutic results that were comparable or better than therapy without psychological test feedback. (p. 616)

◊ CRITICAL THINKING ABOUT DIFFICULT TOPICS

1. In discussing computerized assessment, the text says there is no substitute for expert clinical judgment (p. 593). Although the text does not discuss the topic explicitly, this issue is a specific instance of the broader and controversial topic of actuarial versus clinical prediction. By and large, clinicians have believed that their expertise allowed them to make accurate predictions, but research results have found their predictions to be inferior to those based on actuarial data. To illustrate this point, imagine yourself in charge of college admissions with five times more applicants than you have openings. How would you go about deciding which applicants to admit? Past evidence has shown that the actuarial approach of using a combination of SAT or ACT scores and high school grades predicts college GPA reasonably well. Do you think you could use your "expert clinical judgment" to improve on these predictions? If so, what variables would you take into account? What errors might you introduce in doing so? What is the reliability and validity of the predictors you would use in the manner in which you would use them?

2. Read the statements regarding the characteristics of assessments used for court testimony (pp. 608-609) and then review the material on the Rorschach (pp. 599-600) to see whether you could make a case for its use in the legal system. In particular, attend to the question of the evidence for its validity, which is critical if it is to be used in the legal system.

Circle the best of the four answers provided and check them according to answers provided at the back of this study guide. Be sure you understand why each answer is correct.

1. In assessing a client's social context, all of the following were described in the text as pertinent *except*: (pp. 585-586)
   a. environmental demands.   c. sources of emotional support.
   b. interpersonal skills.   d. special stressors.

2. A neurological diagnostic aid that reveals how an organ is functioning by measuring metabolic processes is the: (p. 588)
   a. PET scan.   c. EEG.
   b. CAT scan.   d. angiogram.

3. Which of the following is the *most highly regarded* six-hour neuropsychological test? (pp. 590, 591)
   a. Halstead-Reitan   c. Stanford-Binet
   b. Luria-Nebraska   d. Wechsler Adult Intelligence Scale

4. Clinical interviews have been criticized as unreliable and evidence of this unreliability includes the finding that different clinicians often arrive at different formal diagnoses. For this reason, recent versions of the DSM have emphasized an approach that: (p. 592)
   a. employs a hierarchical structure.
   b. employs multidimensional assessments.
   c. requires confirmation by convergent information.
   d. employs "operational" assessment.

5. According to the text, the rating scale specifically targeted for depression that has almost become the standard for selecting clinically depressed research subjects is the: (p. 596)
   a. Beck Depression Inventory.
   b. Schedule for Rating Depressive Temperament.
   c. Leeds Depression Rating Scale.
   d. Hamilton Rating Scale for Depression.

6. Two general categories of psychological tests used in clinical practice are: (p. 597)
   a. intelligence and personality.
   b. philosophy and religion.
   c. speech perception and reaction time.
   d. tactual performance and auditory perception.

7. An instrument used to measure the present level of intellectual functioning in adults is the: (p. 597)
   a. WISC-R.   c. TAT.
   b. WAIS-R.   d. MMPI.

8. Personality tests are often grouped into two categories: (p. 599)
   a. behavioral and psychodynamic.
   b. conscious and unconscious.
   c. projective and objective.
   d. verbal and performance.

9. The aim of a projective test is to: (p. 599)
   a. predict a patient's future behavior.
   b. compare a patient's responses to those of persons who are known to have mental disorders.
   c. assess the way a patient perceives ambiguous stimuli.
   d. assess the role of organic factors in a patient's thinking.

10. Which of the following is a structured personality test? (p. 602)
    a. MMPI   c. Sentence Completion Test
    b. Rorschach   d. TAT

11. A clinical researcher devises a new psychological test that assesses neuroticism. She is concerned with the possibility that some individuals might not answer the questions in a straightforward, accurate way. To determine whether an individual is honest, she should: (p. 603)
    a. factor analyze the responses.
    b. make use of actuarial interpretation.
    c. construct a validity scale.
    d. test the instrument on a group of college students.

12. Behaviorists have criticized the MMPI for being too: (p. 606)
    a. action-oriented.   c. objective.
    b. "mentalistic."   d. superficial.

13. Advantages of computer scoring include all of the following *except*: (p. 608)
    a. sophisticated scoring may be done efficiently.
    b. less chance for error in scoring (reliable).
    c. the computer integrates the descriptions it picks up.
    d. it can give large amounts of information such as probable diagnosis.

14. Which of the following personality tests would *most likely* be used for personnel screening for a dangerous job? (p. 610)
    a. California Psychological Inventory
    b. MMPI
    c. 16 PF
    d. Strong Vocational Inventory

15. All of the following were suggested as possible reasons for the failure to incorporate psychological assessment data in therapy *except*: (p. 616)
    a. training
    b. theoretical bias
    c. cost
    d. insufficient validation

Chapter 16
Biologically Based Therapies

◊ OVERVIEW

Many states have passed laws allowing or requiring pharmacies to post prices for the most frequently used prescription drugs in order to help consumers comparison shop. When such signs were posted, it surprised quite a few people to learn that several of the most frequently used medications were chemicals that alter a person's emotional state and not drugs for "physical disease." Because of this widespread use of psychoactive drugs, an informed person should have some understanding of what such drugs can really and the tradeoffs involved in using them.

Chapter 16 focuses on biological methods for the treatment of mental disorders. Much of the chapter is dedicated to the four major classes of psychotropic medications: antipsychotics (or neuroleptics), antidepressants, antianxiety medications (or anxiolytics) and mood-stabilizers for bipolar disorders. The chapter discusses the history, major effects, side effects, modes of action, and effectiveness of each class. Other biological treatments, such as electroconvulsive therapy and neurosurgery, are also described, as are specific medications for children. There is also mention of potentially divisive issues such as "cosmetic psychopharmacology" as well as whether clinicians may be liable for failure to ensure that medications are given to patients with disorders for which there are known effective medications. (p. 641). The chapter closes with a discussion of the issue of combined treatment of medication and psychotherapy.

◊ CHAPTER OUTLINE

I.   Early Attempts at Biological Intervention
      A. Coma and Convulsive Therapies
          1. Insulin Coma Therapy
          2. Electroconvulsive Shock Therapy
      B. Neurosurgery

II. Psychopharmacological Methods of Treatment
- A. Antipsychotic Drugs
    1. Side Effects with Traditional Antipsychotics
    2. Recent Alternative Atypical Antipsychotic Drugs
- B. Antidepressant Drugs
    1. Monoamine Oxidase (MAO) Inhibitors
    2. Tricyclic Antidepressants (TCAs)
    3. Selective Serotonin Re-uptake Inhibitors (SSRIs)
    4. Atypical Antidepressants
    5. Using Antidepressants to Treat Anxiety Disorders, Bulimia, and Personality Disorders
- C. Antianxiety Drugs
    1. Side Effects of Antianxiety Drugs
    2. Effects on GABA
    3. Buspirone
- D. Lithium and Other Mood-Stabilizing Drugs for the Bipolar Mood Disorders
    1. Lithium
    2. Other Mood-Stabilizing Drugs
- E. Drug Therapy for Children

III. Unresolved Issues: Medication and/or Psychotherapy?

IV. Summary

◊ LEARNING OBJECTIVES

After studying this chapter, you should be able to:

1. Describe early attempts at biological intervention, including coma and convulsive therapies and neurosurgery, and indicate which are currently believed to be effective. (pp. 619-625)

2. Summarize the major psychopharmacological treatments currently in use (antipsychotics, antidepressants, antianxiety drugs, and lithium and other mood-stabilizers), discussing their history, major effects, side effects, modes of action, and effectiveness. (pp. 625-639)

3. Outline the issues associated with the widespread use of "personality-altering" drugs such as Prozac. (p. 633)

4. List the most common sleep medications, and discuss the risks and benefits of their use. (p. 637)

5. Explain the role of medications in treating childhood disturbances and disorders. Review the issues that should be considered when providing children with pharmacotherapy. (See also Chapter 14) (p. 639-640)

4. Discuss the advantages of combining biological and psychological forms of treatment. (pp. 640-641)

◊ TERMS YOU SHOULD KNOW

insulin coma therapy (p. 620)

electroconvulsive therapy (ECT) (p. 620)

bilateral ECT (pp. 620-621)

unilateral ECT (pp. 620-621)

psychosurgery (p. 622)

neurosurgery (p. 622)

prefrontal lobotomy (p. 622)

cingulotomy (p. 623)

capsulotomy (p. 625)

psychopharmacology (p. 625)

psychotropic drugs (p. 625)

antipsychotic drugs (neuroleptics or major tranquilizers) (pp. 625-629)

carbamazepine (Tegretol) (Table 16.2, p. 630; p. 638)

methylphenidate (Ritalin) (p. 640)

◊ CONCEPTS TO MASTER

1. Briefly summarize the early history of attempts at biological intervention, and explain how medical treatment measures for mental diseases has changed. (p. 619)

2. Describe the use of insulin coma therapy, and explain why it has largely disappeared. (p. 620)

3. Describe the discovery and use of electroconvulsive therapy (ECT) and its positive and negative effects on the patient. (pp. 620-622)

4. Explain the controversy about using ECT and the reasons for its continued use. (pp. 621-622)

5. Describe prefrontal lobotomy and its effects on the patient. (pp. 622-624)

6. Compare the psychosurgery of today with its earlier forerunners, and list the disorders for which psychosurgery is still performed albeit as a last resort.. (pp. 622-625)

7. List several antipsychotic compounds, and describe their effects and side effects in the treatment of behavior disorders. (pp. 625-629)

8. List several antidepressant compounds, and describe their effects and side effects in the treatment of mental disorders. (pp. 629-634)

9. Discuss the controversy over the effects and popularity of the drug Prozac. (p. 633)

10. List several antianxiety compounds, and describe their effects and side effects in the treatment of maladaptive behavior. (pp. 634-636)

11. What was the evaluation by the Institute of Medicine of the safety of the benzodiazepines (e.g. Valium, Librium, Dalmane) as sleeping medication? (Highlight 16.2, p. 637)

12. Describe the use of lithium in the treatment of bipolar mood disorders, and list its effects and side effects. (pp. 636-639)

13. List some of the drugs that have been used in treating maladaptive behavior in children, explain some precautions that must be exercised, and describe the benefits of Ritalin in treating children who are distractible and/or hyperactive. (pp. 639-640)

14. Evaluate the overall advantages and disadvantages of using pharmacological therapy for treating behavior disorders, as compared to psychotherapy alone. Describe the effectiveness of integrated pharmacotherapy/psychotherapy approaches. (pp. 640-641)

◊ STUDY QUESTIONS

Early attempts at biological intervention

1. List several treatments in the history of medicine that involve substantial disruption of biological processes (and suffering to the patient). (p. 619)

Coma and convulsive therapies

2. Insulin coma therapy is no longer practiced. Why was it abandoned? (p. 620)

3. Electroconvulsive therapy (ECT) is much more widely used than insulin therapy, mostly because of its effectiveness in alleviating depressive episodes. Describe what happens during ECT. (pp. 620-621)

4. After awakening several minutes after ECT, the patient has _____ for the period immediately preceding the therapy. With repeated treatments, usually administered three times weekly, the patient gradually becomes _____. (p. 621)

5. What is unilateral ECT? (p. 621)

6. Given that unilateral ECT may not be as effective as bilateral ECT, what do many suggest as the preferred sequence of treatment ? (p. 621)

7. List three populations for which ECT is often the treatment of choice. (p. 622)

8. In 1985, the National Institute of Mental Health sponsored a Consensus Development Conference on electroconvulsive therapy.

   a. What four aspects of ECT were evaluated? (p. 622)

   b. The panel recognized a number of potential risks associated with the use of ECT. Are these risks still a problem? (p. 622)

   c. With present techniques, the death rate from ECT is ____ per 10,000 patients. (p. 622)

   d. Complete the following information about the panel's conclusion regarding ECT's effectiveness. (p. 622)
      * ECT is effective for some types of depression, particularly _____ depression, but not for other types of depression, such as _____ disorder.
      * ECT can be effectively used with some types of manic disorders, particularly _____ mania.
      * The evidence for effectiveness with schizophrenia is _____.

   e. The panel concluded that relapse rates following ECT were high unless the treatment was followed up by _____. (p. 622)

Neurosurgery

9. After extended initial enthusiasm, physicians began to recognize that the results of psychosurgery could be very undesirable. What are some of the undesirable results that were found? (p. 623)

10. The advent of _____ caused an immediate decrease in the widespread use of psychosurgery, especially prefrontal lobotomy. (p. 623)

11. According to Valenstein (1986), what factors led to the premature and "desperate" acceptance of psychosurgery? (p. 623)

12. List two modern neurosurgical techniques, and describe a more recent innovative variation on these techniques. (p. 625)

Emergence of pharmacological methods

13. Pharmacology is the science of
_____ and why they do so. (p. 625)

Types of drugs used in therapy

14. Fill in the missing information in the following chart that summarizes the four types of drugs commonly used for mental disorders: (pp. 625-639)

Class of Drugs	Biological Effect	Behavioral Effect	Example
Antipsychotics		Reduce the intensity of schizophrenic symptoms (including delusions and hallucinations) and have a calming effect	Thorazine
Antidepressant-tricyclics	Increase concentration of biogenic amines at synapses		
Antianxiety-benzodiazepines		Selectively diminish generalized anxiety	
Lithium			Resolve 70-80% of manic episodes and may also be useful in depression of bipolar type

Antipsychotic drugs

15. The following is a schematic diagram of the antipsychotic class of drugs that illustrates two of the general types of antipsychotics, official clinical names for these drugs, and the trade names under which they are sold in the drugstore (by prescription only). Fill in the missing trade names. (pp. 625-629; Table 16.1, p. 627)

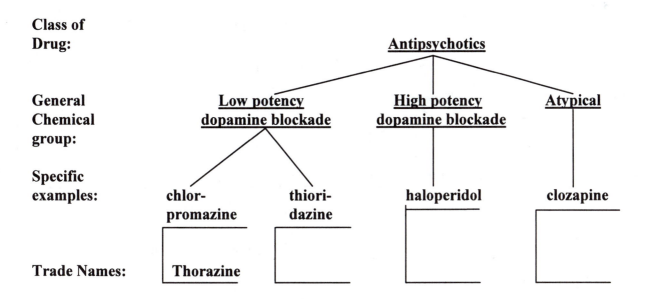

Class of Drug: Antipsychotics

General Chemical group: Low potency dopamine blockade · High potency dopamine blockade · Atypical

Specific examples: chlor-promazine · thiori-dazine · haloperidol · clozapine

Trade Names: Thorazine

16. Compared to anything we have known before, the effects of the antipsychotic compounds in the treatment of schizophrenia are remarkable. At the same time, with persistent use or at high dosages, there are varying degrees of troublesome side effects. What are some typical extrapyramidal symptoms, and what factors interact to determine which side effects develop? (pp. 626-627)

17. What is tardive dyskinesia, and how is it treated? (pp. 627-628)

18. Tardive dyskinesia is more common in women and in people with a nonschizophrenic diagnosis. True or False (p. 628)

19. How do atypical psychotic drugs differ from the older traditional neuroleptics? (p. 629)

20. Why does the use of clozapine require a highly structured blood-monitoring system? (p. 629)

21. The following is a schematic diagram of the antidepressant class of drugs that illustrates the three general types of antidepressants, the official chemical names for these drugs, and the trade names under which they are sold in the drugstore (by prescription only). Fill in the missing information in the blanks. (pp. 629-634; Table 16.2, p. 630)

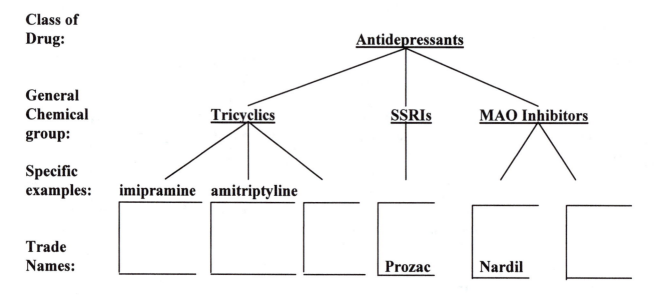

22. Why aren't monoamine oxidase inhibitors widely used today? (p. 629)

23. Imipramine was originally being studied as a possible treatment for _____ (p. 630)

24. When tricyclics are taken for several weeks, what aspects of cellular functioning are altered? (p. 631)

25. The SSRIs are currently considered the preferred class of antidepressant drugs. List two reasons for this. (p. 632)

26. As a result of the very positive effects of Prozac on subjective well-being, patients are often understandably reluctant to give up the drug. This reluctance is reminiscent of the serious

problems with the overuse of _____ eventually produced during the 1970s and 1980s. (p. 633)

27. In his book *Listening to Prozac*, Kramer addresses the disturbing questions raised by the availability of a prescription drug that seems not only to ameliorate depression but in addition, for many persons, to alter their _____. (p. 633)

28. If antidepressants are discontinued when symptoms have just remitted, there is a high probability of relapse. Why? (p. 634)

29. Other than depression, antidepressants are widely used for what psychological disorders? (p. 634)

Antianxiety Drugs

30. The following is a schematic diagram of the antianxiety class of drugs that illustrates the two general types of antianxiety drugs, the official chemical names for the drugs, and the trade names under which they are sold in the drugstore (by prescription only). Fill in the missing information in the blanks: (pp. 634-636; Table 16.3, p. 635)

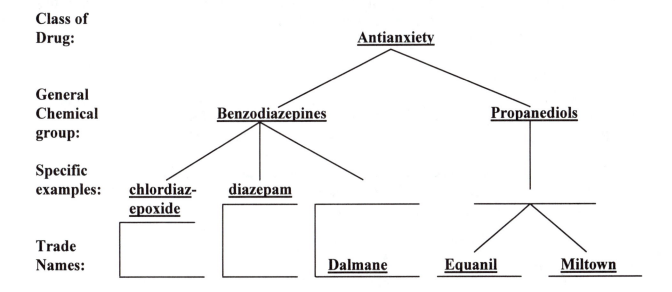

31. All antianxiety drugs have the serious potential of inducing _____ when used unwisely or in excess. (pp. 635-636).

32. The range of application of antianxiety compounds is quite broad. They are used in all manner of conditions in which _____ and _____ may be significant components. (p. 636)

33. Buspirone has been shown to be equally effective as the benzodiazepines in treating generalized anxiety disorder, but patients who have previously taken benzodiazepines tend not to respond as well as ones who have never taken them. According to the text, what is a probable explanation? (p. 636)

34. Why should older people who complain of insomnia not be given sleeping pills? (Highlight 16.2, p. 637)

35. Why is lithium difficult to use? (pp. 637-638)

36. Although lithium was slow to catch on in the United States, there can be no doubt at this point concerning its remarkable effectiveness in at least partially resolving about _____ percent of clearly defined manic states. (p. 638)

37. How much time does lithium require to be effective? (p. 638)

38. What is the biochemical basis of the therapeutic effect of lithium? (p. 638)

39. What two other drugs have been used to treat bipolar disorders successfully? How were they initially used? How effective are they as compared to lithium in the treatment of bipolar depressive episodes? (pp. 638-639)

Drug therapy for children

40. Antianxiety, antipsychotic, and antidepressant medications have all been used effectively with children. True or False (p. 640)

41. What is Ritalin? (p. 640)

Unresolved issues: Medication and/or psychotherapy?

42. All in all, pharmacological therapy has outmoded more drastic forms of treatment and has led to a much more favorable hospital climate for patients and staff alike. However, there are a number of limitations in the use of psychotropic drugs in addition to their undesirable side effects. Complete the following list of limitations: (pp. 640-641)
    a. It is difficult to match drug and dosage to the _____.
    b. It is sometimes necessary to change medications in _____.
    c. The use of medications in isolation from other treatment methods may not be ideal for some psychological disorders, since drugs themselves do not _____ disorders.

43. Describe the Osherhoff vs. Chestnut Lodge case. What issues did the case raise? (pp. 640-641)

◊ CRITICAL THINKING ABOUT DIFFICULT TOPICS

1. In prefrontal lobotomy the frontal lobes of the brain are severed from the deeper centers underlying them. One could hardly imagine a treatment more likely to produce disastrous negative effects, and eventually these negative effects were documented. However, "as is often the case with newly developed therapeutic techniques, initial reports of results tended to be enthusiastic, downplaying complications (including a 1-4 percent death rate) and undesirable side effects" (p. 606). This enthusiasm lasted so long that Moniz, the person who introduced prefrontal lobotomies in 1935, was awarded the Nobel Prize in Medicine in 1949. If such a "treatment" as prefrontal lobotomy is seen in uncontrolled clinical trials as highly successful and if "clinical wisdom" endorsed it for two decades, what does this tell you about all new forms of treatment that are touted as highly promising? How do you think the field of medicine should deal with this problem? Is it possible to avoid false claims while not failing to take advantage of new and effective treatments? How can you as a consumer or as a potential provider attempt to deal with it--or can you?

2. In the Critical Thinking About Difficult Topics section of Chapter 14, you were asked to think about the concept of correcting a "chemical imbalance" through the use of drugs. This term seems to imply that the brain has too little of a given neurotransmitter and that

443

pharmacological treatment can directly increase the amount of that neurotransmitter. However, as you have seen with the drugs of abuse, it is common for the brain to adapt to the presence of drugs (called tolerance) in an effort to oppose or negate their effects. To illustrate that something similar may happen with "medications," consider the following statements from the present chapter:

a. A particularly troublesome side effect of the antipsychotic drugs, which have the property of blocking dopamine receptors, is the development of tardive dyskinesia. Tardive dyskinesia "is believed to be due to the chronic blockade of dopamine in the brain, creating supersensitive dopamine receptors." (p. 627). What this means is that blocking dopamine receptors causes a compensatory increase in dopamine receptor sensitivity. The same may be true for cholinergic receptors when antiparkinsonian drugs are used to reduce the Parkinsonian symptoms produced by the antidopaminergic effects of the antipsychotics.

b. "Although the immediate short-term effects of tricyclics are to increase the availability of norepinephrine and serotonin in the synapses, the long-term effects of these drugs . . . are to produce functional decreases in available norepinephrine and serotonin . . . It is also known that when the tricyclics are taken for several weeks they alter a number of other aspects of cellular functioning, including how receptors function and how cells respond to activation of receptors and the synthesis of neurotransmitters." (p. 631)

c. "Because of their potential for producing dependence, withdrawal from [the antianxiety] drugs can be extremely difficult . . ." (p. 636).

Thus, you can see that, in three very different classes of psychotropic medications, the brain reacts to their presence in complex ways. From this perspective, what does it mean to correct a chemical imbalance by administering drugs? Do these examples (e.g., tardive dyskinesia with antipsychotics, physical dependence with antianxiety drugs) cause you to think adverse effects of long-term consumption may have a significant probability?

3. In his book *Listening to Prozac*, Kramer expresses surprise and concern that an antidepressant drug that should ameliorate symptoms of depression should also alter the person's personality (p. 633). Is this surprising to you? The field of behavioral neurochemistry is concerned with the effects of neurotransmitters on behavior. Investigators in that field automatically assume that manipulating the functioning of a major neurotransmitter will have major effects on behavior. Similarly, temperament theorists have long assumed that there is a biological contribution to temperament. Thus, there is good reason to expect that psychotropic drugs would affect behaviors that we think of as related to temperament. It is easy for those trained

under a disease model to expect "medicines" to treat only "diseases" and not to affect other behavior. Can you try to conceptualize how psychotropic drugs have the primary effect of manipulating brain-behavior relationships while, at the same time, affecting symptomatology of behavior disorders? To do so, you will need to get beyond a simple-minded disease model and think in terms of the biopsychosocial model embraced by the text--in which there is a biological contribution to almost all aspects of behavior.

◊ CHAPTER 16 QUIZ

Circle the best of the four answers provided and check them according to answers provided at the back of this study guide. Be sure you understand why each answer is correct.

1. Electroconvulsive therapy (ECT) was developed as a result of speculation by Von Meduna, a Hungarian physician, that: (p. 620)
   a. electricians who were severely shocked often became epileptic.
   b. epileptics rarely developed schizophrenia.
   c. schizophrenics often had seizures.
   d. survivors of lightening strikes seldom became schizophrenic.

2. Which of the following ECT treatments is associated with fewer distressing side effects, while still maintaining therapeutic effectiveness if higher dose electrical currents are used? (p. 621)
   a. ECT accompanied by muscle stimulants   c. unilateral ECT
   b. bilateral ECT   d. cerebellar ECT

3. Criticisms of the use of ECT for severe depression include all of the following *except*: (pp. 620-622)
   a. it is ineffective.
   b. benefits may be short-lived.
   c. it causes demonstrable brain damage.
   d. it is sometimes used with patients for whom evidence of effectiveness is not convincing.

4. The 1985 NIMH Consensus Panel concluded that relapse rates following electroconvulsive therapy (ECT) were high unless the treatments were followed by: (p. 622)
   a. changes in the patient's psychosocial environment.
   b. maintenance doses of antidepressant medication.
   c. regular psychodynamic therapy sessions.
   d. sedative and muscle relaxant medication.

5. Which of the following caused an immediate decrease in the widespread use of psychosurgical procedures in this country? (p. 623)
   a. a 1951 law banning all such operations
   b. the advent of electroconvulsive therapy (ECT)
   c. the advent of the major antipsychotic drugs
   d. the unusually high mortality rate

6. A modern psychosurgical technique known as *cingulotomy* is used to remove the subjective experience of: (pp. 623-624)
   a. depression.   c. mania.
   b. guilt.   d. pain.

7. Antipsychotic, antidepressant, antianxiety, and lithium compounds are all referred to as _____ drugs. (p. 625)
   a. hallucinogenic   c. narcotic
   b. mind-expanding   d. psychotropic

8. The unique quality of antipsychotic drugs is their ability to: (p. 626)
   a. calm patients down.
   b. put patients to sleep.
   c. reduce patients' anxiety.
   d. reduce the intensity of delusions and hallucinations.

9. Virtually all of the antipsychotic drugs accomplish the same biochemical effect, which is: (p. 626)
   a. blocking dopamine receptors.
   b. blocking the production of noradrenalin.
   c. stimulating the production of endorphins.
   d. stimulating the production of glutamic acid.

10. Which of the following is a trade name for a major antipsychotic drug? (p. 627)
    a. Haldol   c. Desyrel
    b. Valium   d. Sinequan

11. The immediate short-term effects of the tricyclic antidepressants serve to: (p. 631)
    a. reduce central nervous system arousal.
    b. reduce intracranial pressure by absorbing cerebral spinal fluid.
    c. increase the availability of lithium in the central nervous system for absorption.
    d. increase the availability of serotonin and norepinephrine in the synapses.

12. One of the most commonly used tricyclic drugs in the treatment of depression is: (p. 632)
    a. methylphenidate (Ritalin).   c. chlordiazepoxide (Librium).
    b. imipramine (Tofranil).   d. haloperidol (Haldol).

13. Lithium compounds are used in the treatment of: (p. 636)
    a. anxiety.
    b. hyperactivity and specific learning disabilities.
    c. bipolar mood disorders.
    d. hallucinations and delusions.

14. The side effects of lithium include all the following *except*: (p. 638)
    a. lethargy.   c. decreased motor coordination.
    b. memory impairment.   d. gastrointestinal difficulties.

15. In the case of Osherhoff vs. Chestnut Lodge, Osherhoff received a settlement out of court because Chestnut Lodge: (pp. 640-641)
    a. put him on a wait list for 6 months, during which time he continued to suffer major depression.
    b. had not administered drug therapy.
    c. had administered the wrong drug therapy.
    d. had provided psychotherapy by a minimally trained psychotherapist.

◊ OVERVIEW

Chapter 17 describes in some detail the various psychological treatment approaches that are employed to treat the types of problems discussed in earlier chapters. Psychologically based therapies, according to the text, may attempt to change maladaptive behavior, minimize or eliminate stressful environmental conditions, reduce negative affect, improve interpersonal competencies, resolve personal conflicts, modify inaccurate self-thoughts, and/or improve self-imafe. There are a wide variety of techniques available, and often completely different approaches have been developed for the same problem behavior. These various approaches to treatment are all outgrowths ob the different models of psychopathology described earlier.

This chapter covers the major psychological therapies: psychodynamic therapies, behavior therapy, cognitive and cognitive-behavior therapies, humanistic-experiential therapies, as well as group, couples, and family therapies. Despite the large number of therapies, no single approach to psychotherapy has yet proven capable of handling the entire range of problems seen clinically. Consequently, the inclination to identify strongly with one approach or another is decreasing. Today, many therapists are familiar with a variety of techniques chosen from several therapeutic approaches and use them depending on the type of problems the client is having.

◊ CHAPTER OUTLINE

I. An Overview of Psycholofical Treatment
    A. Why Do People Seek Therapy?
    B. Who Provides Psychotherapeutic Services
    C. The Therapeutic Relationship
        1. The Therapeutic Alliance
        2. Other Qualities Enhancing Therapy

II. Psychodynamic Therapies
    A. Freudian Psychoanalysis
        1. Free Association
        2. Analysis of Dreams
        3. Analysis of Resistance
        4. Analysis of Transference
    B. Psychodynamic Therapy Since Freud
        1. Interpersonal Therapy
        2. Object Relations, Self Psychology, and Other Interpersonal Variations
    C. Evaluating Psychodynamic Therapy

III. Behavior Therapy
    A. Guided Exposure
        1. Systematic Desensitization
        2. Flooding
    B. Aversion Therapy
    C. Modeling
    D. Systematic Use of Reinforcement
        1. Response Shaping
        2. Token Economies
        3. Behavioral Contracting
        4. Biofeedback Treatment
    E. Evaluating Behavior Therapy

IV. Cognitive and Cognitive-Behavior Therapy
    A. Rational-Emotive Behavior Therapy
    B. Stress-Inoculation Therapy
    C. Beck's Cognitive Therapies
    D. Evaluating Cognitive-Behavioral Therapies

V. Humanistic-Experiential Therapies
    A. Client-Centered Therapy
    B. Existential Therapy
    C. Gestalt Therapy
    D. Evaluating the Humanistic-Experiential Therapies

VI. Therapy for Interpersonal Relationships
    A. Couples Counseling (Marital Therapy)

◊ LEARNING OBJECTIVES

After studying this chapter, you should be able to:

1. Provide a general overview of (a) the assumptions and goals of psychotherapy, (b) the varied types of individuals who receive psychotherapy, (c) the various categories of providers of psychotherapeutic services and their specialized training, (d) the critical elements of the therapeutic relationship, and (e) qualities that enhance therapy. (pp. 644-648)

2. List and describe the basic goals and techniques of psychoanalysis, as well as developments in psychodynamic therapy since Freud. Evaluate the effectiveness of the psychodynamic approach to the treatment of maladaptive behavior. (pp. 648-654)

3. List and describe the basic goals and techniques of the behavior therapies. Summarize recent developments in the behavior therapies, and evaluate their effectiveness in the treatment of maladaptive behavior. (pp. 654-662)

4. List and describe the basic goals and techniques of the cognitive-behavior therapies. Summarize recent developments in the cognitive-behavior therapies, and evaluate their effectiveness in the treatment of maladaptive behavior. (pp. 662-668)

5. List and describe the basic goals and techniques of the humanistic-experiential therapies. Summarize recent developments in the humanistic-experiential therapies, and evaluate their effectiveness in the treatment of maladaptive behavior. (pp. 668-672)

6. Describe the basic goals and techniques of couples counseling, family therapy, and group therapy. Summarize recent developments in these therapies, and evaluate their effectiveness in the treatment of maladaptive relationships. (pp. 672-675)

7. Summarize the interest in integrating the diverse array of psychological treatments into one overriding theory of psychotherapy, and discuss strategies for combining concepts and techniques from various schools. (pp. 675-676)

8. Discuss the many difficulties associated with attempting to evaluate the effectiveness of psychotherapy. (pp. 676-678)

9. Explain what is meant by negative process , and describe potential deteriorative effects in psychotherapy. (p. 678)

10. Review the issues and evidence surrounding the matching or mismatching of ethnicity in client-therapy pairings, and its potential effects on the therapeutic process. (pp. 679-680)

11. Discuss the methodology as well as the value and limitations of *efficacy* psychotherapy outcome studies. Explain how efficacy studies differ from *effectiveness* psychotherapy outcome studies. (pp. 680-681)

◊ **TERMS YOU SHOULD KNOW**

---

psychotherapy (p. 644)

"YAVIS" phenomenon (p. 645)

therapeutic relationship (p. 646)

behavior therapy (p. 654)

behavior therapists (p. 654)

guided exposure (p. 654)

systematic desensitization (p. 654)

systematic (p. 654)

anxiety hierarchy (p. 655)

marathon desensitization groups (p. 655)

flooding (p. 655)

in vivo (vs. in vitro) exposure (p. 655)

eye-movement desensitization and reprocessing (EMDR) (Highlight 17.2, p. 656)

interoceptive exposure (p. 657)

aversion therapy (pp. 657-658)

covert (or vicarious) desensitization (p. 658)

modeling (p. 658)

contingency management (p. 658)

response shaping (p. 659)

token economies (pp. 659-660)

behavioral contracting (p. 660)

biofeedback (p. 661)

family systems therapy (p. 674)

conjoint family therapy (p. 674)

structural family therapy (p. 674)

multimodal therapy (p. 675)

eclectic (p. 676)

technical eclecticism (p. 676)

regression to the mean (p. 677)

negative process (p. 678)

randomized trials (RCTs) *(or efficacy trials)* (p. 680)

double-blinding (p. 680)

manualized therapy (p. 681)

◊ NAMES YOU SHOULD KNOW

William Schofield (p. 645)

Jerome Frank (p. 647)

Hans Strupp (p. 647)

Joseph Wolpe (p. 655)

Albert Bandura (p. 658)

Gordon Paul (pp. 659, 660)

Edward Blanchard (p. 661)

Aaron Beck (pp. 662, 663, 665-668)

Albert Ellis (p. 663)

Donald Meichenbaum (pp. 663, 664, 665, 667)

Fritz Perls (pp. 671-672)

Virginia Satir (p. 674)

S. Minuchin (p. 674)

Paul Wachtel (p. 676)

◊ CONCEPTS TO MASTER

1. List and explain several reasons why people enter psychotherapy, and describe the types of mental health professionals who are trained in the identification and treatment of mental disorders. (pp. 644-645)

2. Outline the major features of the therapeutic relationship that enhance psychotherapy and promote better treatment outcomes. Note that these are "common" or "nonspecific" factors in the sense that they have little to do with specific techniques or specific theoretical approaches. (pp. 646-647)

3. The patient's "expectation of receiving help" is also important to the outcome of therapy and may operate to some degree as a placebo does in medicine. Explain this statement. (pp. 647-648)

4. List the four basic techniques of psychoanalysis, and explain how they are used in psychodynamic therapy. (pp. 648-650).

5. Summarize the changes in psychodynamic therapy that have taken place since Freud. (p. 650)

6. Evaluate the effectiveness of the psychodynamic approach to the treatment of maladaptive behavior. (pp. 651, 654)

7. Explain how behavior therapists differ from psychodynamic therapists, and describe the principle of guided exposure. (p. 654)

8. Explain the learning principles underlying systematic desensitization, list three steps in its application to maladaptive behavior, and list several variants of this method. (pp. 654-655)

9. Explain the technique of flooding. Compare and contrast in vivo exposure procedures with in vitro (imaginal) methods. (pp. 655-656)

10. Define *aversion therapy*, and give several examples of its use in treating behavioral disorders. (pp. 657-658)

11. Define *modeling*, and explain how it can be used in the treatment of mental disorders. (p. 658)

12. Explain what is meant by systematic use of reinforcement, and describe three general techniques based on this plan. (pp. 658-660)

13. List several ways that behavioral contracting can facilitate psychotherapy. (p. 660)

14. Describe biofeedback, list three steps in the biofeedback approach to therapy, and describe several of its applications to maladaptive behaviors. (p. 661)

15. List and explain three advantages that behavior therapy has over other psychotherapies, and indicate why it cannot be a cure-all. (p. 662)

16. Define *cognitive-behavior therapy*, and discuss the two main themes that characterize all cognitive-behavioral therapies. (p. 662)

17. Why does Ellis believe that many of us behave irrationally and feel unnecessarily that we are failures? List several of Ellis's core irrational beliefs. (pp. 663-664; Table 17.1, p. 664)

18. Describe several techniques used by rational-emotive therapists to treat mental disorders. (pp. 663-664)

19. Describe the three stages of stress-inoculation therapy. (pp. 664-665)

20. Describe Beck's cognitive-behavior therapies, and explain the theory on which they are based. (pp. 665, 667; Highlight 17.3, p. 666)

21. Compare the outcomes of cognitive-behavior therapies with other psychotherapies, and describe some trends in its use. (pp. 667-668)

22. Describe Carl Rogers's client-centered therapy (including its primary objectives and techniques), and indicate the impact it has had on the field. (pp. 668-670)

23. Describe the characteristics of group therapy and psychodrama. (Highlight 17.4, p. 669)

24. "Pure" client-centered therapy is rarely used today, but it has been influential. How are the humanistic therapies of today similar to client-centered therapy, and how are they different? (p. 670)

25. List several important concepts that underlie existential psychotherapy, and describe its application to maladaptive behavior. (pp. 670-671)

26. Explain the main goals of Gestalt therapy, and describe several techniques used by Perls and others to treat mental disorders. (pp. 671-672)

463

27. List some criticisms of the humanistic-experiential therapies, and point out some of their positive contributions to the field. (p. 677)

28. Describe several foci and techniques of couples counseling, and indicate some of its difficulties and outcomes. (pp. 672-674)

29. Describe two types of family therapy, and give some examples of their use to treat maladaptive behavior. (p. 674)

30. Define *eclecticism*. Describe the past opposition that various psychotherapy schools have directed toward each other, and discuss the relaxing of their boundaries. (p. 675)

31. Discuss strategies for integration of the various psychotherapy approaches, and compare and contrast *technical eclecticism* with *theoretical integration*. (p. 676)

32. List five sources of information used to evaluate the effectiveness of psychological treatment, and describe the limitations of each. (pp. 676-677)

33. Discuss the effectiveness of psychotherapy compared with treatment delivered by nonprofessionals and compared with no treatment at all. (pp. 677-678)

34. Define negative or deteriorative effects in psychotherapy, and discuss this problem both generally and in the special case of therapist-client sexual entanglements. (p. 678)

35. Describe the controversy centering around possible conflicts between the role of the therapist and the values of society. (pp. 678-679)

36. Review to what extent the influence the matching or mismatching of ethnicity in client-therapy pairings is associated with differing psychotherapeutic outcomes. (p. 679-680)

37. Compare and contrast efficacy psychotherapy outcome studies with effectiveness outcome studies. (pp. 680-681; Table 17.2, p. 681)

◊ STUDY QUESTIONS

Introduction

1. The belief that people with psychological problems can change--can learn more adaptive ways of perceiving, evaluating, and behaving--is the conviction underlying all psychotherapy. Psychotherapy often proves to be _____ _____ in the long run than alternate modes of intervention. (p. 644)

2. There are several general goals of psychotherapy. Following are four of the goals; fill in the missing three: (p. 644)
   a. Changing maladaptive behavior
   b. Changing environmental conditions that may be causing or maintaining the maladaptive behavior
   c. Improving interpersonal skills
   d. Resolving conflicts among motives
   e.
   f.
   g.

3. It has been estimated that there are several _____ "therapeutic" approaches in existence, ranging from psychoanalysis to Zen meditation. (p. 644)

Why do people seek therapy?

4. Describe the most obvious clients for psychotherapy. (p. 644)

5. What types of individuals are likely to be reluctant or resistant clients? (p. 645)

6. Clients who do the best in psychotherapy are often "YAVIS" types. Explain what is meant by "YAVIS" and why such patients do best in psychotherapy. (p. 645)

Who provides psychotherapeutic services

7. List several professional groups who provide psychotherapeutic services (p. 646)

8. What is the "team approach?" Describe the importance of providing treatment facilities in the community (p. 646)

The therapeutic relationship

9. Describe the client's major contribution to the therapeutic relationship. (pp. 646-647)

10. The establishment of an effective psychotherapeutic _____ _____ between client and therapist is seen by most investigators and practitioners as the bedrock of psychotherapeutic gain. (p. 646)

11. Describe the importance of communication to the therapeutic relationship. (p. 647)

12. Motivation to _____ is probably the most crucial element in determining the success or failure of psychotherapy. (p. 647)

13. Almost as important as the preceding is a client's _____ of receiving help--often sufficient in itself to bring out some improvement. (p. 647)

14. To at least some extent, effective therapy depends on a good _____ between client and therapist. Hence, a therapist's own _____ is necessarily a factor of some importance in determining therapeutic outcomes. (p. 647)

Psychodynamic therapies

15. Psychodynamic therapy is a psychological treatment approach that focuses on individual personality dynamics from a _____ perspective. As developed by Freud, classic psychoanalysis is an intensive, long-term procedure for uncovering repressed memories, thoughts, fears, and conflicts presumably stemming from problems in early _____ _____--and helping the individual come to terms with them in light of the realities of adult life. (p. 648)

468

16. There are four basic techniques of psychoanalysis: free association, dream interpretation, analysis of resistance, and analysis of transference. Briefly explain how the analyst uses each technique: (pp. 648-650)

Technique	How It Is Used
Free association	
Analysis of dreams	
Analysis of resistance	
Analysis of transference	

17. How do most modern analysts (e.g., Mann) differ in emphasis from strict Freudian psychoanalysis? (p. 650)

18. In what ways are psychodynamic interpersonally-oriented therapies similar to and different from classical psychoanalysis? (p. 651)

19. Indicate whether each of the following statements represents a valid criticism of psychodynamic therapy. Circle the correct response: (p. 651)
   a. It is time consuming and expensive.   True or False
   b. It is based on a questionable theory of human nature.   True or False
   c. It neglects the patient's current problems.   True or False
   d. There is inadequate proof of its effectiveness.   True or False

20. For whom is psychodynamic therapy the treatment of choice? (p. 651)

21. How do the authors view the general results of brief psychodynamic psychotherapy efficacy studies? (pp. 651, 654)

22. The behavioral perspective views the maladjusted person as one who has (a) failed to acquire competencies needed for _____, or (b) learned faulty _____ or _____ patterns that are being maintained by some kind of reinforcement, or (c) both. Instead of exploring past traumatic events or inner conflicts, behavior therapists attempt to modify problem behaviors directly by _____ or _____ maladaptive reactions, or by manipulating environmental contingencies. (p. 654)

23. One can remove ("_____") a classically conditioned response by repeated presentations of the pertinent stimuli in the absence of "_____," which in this case would be some dreadful event whose imminence is signaled by the occurrence of the inciting stimuli. (p. 654)

24. _____ _____ is the technique behavior therapists have developed to ensure the unlearning of the anxiety reaction. (p. 654)

25. Systematic desensitization is designed to eliminate behaviors that are being _____ reinforced but can be used for other types of problems. (p. 654)

26. Systematic desensitization consists of three steps. What are they? (p. 655)

27. What is a *marathon desensitization group*? (p. 655)

28. What is *eye movement desensitization and reprocessing* (EMDR)? (p. 656)

29. List the conclusions of the reviews of EMDR research literature. (p. 656)

30. What factors make flooding procedures relatively more bearable, even without diminished effectiveness? (p. 657)

31. Explain *interoceptive exposure*, and describe its effectiveness. (p. 657)

32. Aversion therapy involves modification of behavior by _____, which can be of two types. What are these types? (p. 657)

33. Describe three variants of aversion therapy, and list several maladaptive behaviors for which aversion therapy has been used as a treatment. (p. 658)

34. There is little likelihood that a previously gratifying but maladaptive behavior pattern will be permanently relinquished unless _____ forms of _____ are learned during the aversion therapy. (p. 658)

35. Modeling involves learning skills through _____. (p. 658)

36. Modeling may be used to promote the learning of simple skills, such as _____ in a profoundly retarded child or being more effective in _____ for a shy, withdrawn adolescent. (p. 658)

37. Briefly describe each of the following techniques: (pp. 659-660)

    a. Response shaping

    b. Token economy

38. What are the advantages of using tokens as reinforcers for appropriate behavior? (p. 659)

39. What is the ultimate goal in token economies as well as other programs involving initially exreinsic reinforcement? (p. 660)

40. A behavioral contract often specifies a client's _____ as well as the responsibilities of the other person to provide tangible rewards in return. (p. 660)

41. Briefly list some of the ways a behavioral contract can facilitate therapy. (p. 660)

a. The structuring of the treatment relationship can be explicitly stated.

b.

c.

d.

e. Clear treatment goals can be defined.

f.

42. Biofeedback consists of three steps. What are they? (p. 661)

a.

b.

c.

43. Tension headache victims generally do not respond well to biofeedback. True or False. (p. 661)

44. What control or comparison group is essential in evaluating the effectiveness of biofeedback? When such comparisons are made, how effective is biofeedback found to be? (p. 661)

45. Respond true or false to the following statements about behavior therapy. (p. 662)

a. The treatment is precise.	True or False
b. Behavior therapy is particularly successful in the treatment of Axis II disorders.	True or False
c. Behavior therapy techniques are important in the treatment of sexual dysfunction.	True or False

46. How have behavioral therapists changed their thinking so that many are now labeled "cognitive-behavioral therapists"? (p. 662)

47. At present, there are several alternative approaches to cognitive-behavioral therapy, but two main themes seem to characterize them all. Complete the following: (p. 662)
    a. The conviction that cognitive processes influence affect, motivation, and behavior
    b.

48. The chart below summarizes three different cognitive-behavioral therapies. Fill in the requested information: (pp. 663-665)

Therapeutic Approach	Description
Rational-emotive therapy	a. This approach was developed by _____. Today, it is one of the most widely used therapeutic approaches. (p. 663)
	b. To eliminate irrational beliefs, the RET therapist disputes these false beliefs through _____ _____ and also uses _____ _____ techniques to bring about changed thoughts and behaviors. (pp. 663-664)
Stress-inoculation therapy	a. Stress-inoculation training usually involves three stages. Briefly describe what happens at each of the stages: (pp. 664-665) 1. Cognitive preparation 2. Skill acquisition and rehearsal 3. Application and practice
Beck's cognitive-behavior therapies	a. This therapy was originally developed for the treatment of _____. (p. 665)

	b. A basic assumption of this approach is that problems like depression result from a person's negative views about himself or herself, the world, and the future. Such behavior typically includes features such as the following. Briefly describe each one: (p. 665) Selective perception Overgeneralization Magnification Absolutistic thinking
	c. Describe how Beck's approach to changing irrational thinking differs from Ellis' RET. (p. 665)
	d. Cognitive restructuring may involve other techniques as well. Briefly describe each one, and explain its importance to therapy: (p. 665) Schedule of daily activities Discovery of dysfunctional assumptions or depressogenic schemas

49. Do data on RET indicate that it is more effective than exposure-based therapies in the treatment for severe anxiety disorders and depression? (p. 667)

50. Stress-inoculation therapy has been successfully used with a number of clinical problems, especially _____, _____, _____ behavior, mild forms of _____, and the consequences of _____ _____. (p. 667)

51. How do Beck's type of cognitive-behavioral treatments for depression compare with drug treatment? (p. 667)

52. Many empirical studies in the past decade have compared cognitive-behavioral methods with other treatment approaches for a variety of other clinical disorders. The most dramatic recent results have been in the treatment of _____ disorder and _____ disorder. (p. 668)

Humanistic-experiential therapies

53. These approaches have developed in reaction to behavioral and psychodynamic therapies, which are believed to fail to take into account either the _____ or the _____ of human beings. (p. 668)

54. Proponents of the humanistic-experiential therapies see psychopathology as stemming in many cases from problems of _____, _____, _____, and a failure to find meaning and genuine fulfillment. (p. 668)

55. Humanistic-experiential therapies are based on a major assumption. What is it? (p. 668)

56. How do behavioral therapists differ from humanistic therapists with respect to responsibility for the direction and success of therapy? (p. 668)

57. The chart below summarizes the major approaches to psychotherapy that are humanistic-experientially oriented. Fill in the requested information: (pp. 668-671)

Therapeutic Approach	Description
Client-centered therapy	a. This therapy was originated by _____ in the 1940s as an alternative to psychoanalysis. In this therapy, the psychoanalytic view of primacy of the irrational instinct and the idea that the proper role of the therapist is to be the director of therapy are rejected. (p. 668)
	b. The primary role of client-centered therapy is to resolve "incongruence." What is this incongruence, and how does it come about? (p. 668)
	c. How does the client-centered therapist resolve incongruence? (p. 668)
	d. What is the typical sequence of a patient's attitudes and behavior during treatment, according to Rogerian client-centered therapy? (p. 670)
Existential therapy	a. Existentialists are deeply concerned about the predicament of humankind, the breakdown of _____ _____, the _____ and _____ of individuals in contemporary society, and the lack of _____ in peoples' lives. (pp. 670-671)
	b. Existential therapists do not follow rigid procedures, but they all emphasize the _____ of each individual, and his or her "way of being in the world." (p. 671)

	c. In contrast to the behavioral therapist and the psychoanalyst, the existential therapist _____ his or her feelings and values with the client. (p. 671)
Gestalt therapy	a. This therapy was originated by _____ as a means of teaching clients to recognize the _____ _____ and emotions they had been _____ from awareness. (p. 671)
	b. The main goal of Gestalt therapy is to increase an individual's _____ and _____. (p. 671)
	c. Gestalt therapy sessions focus on the more obvious elements of a person's behavior. The sessions are often called _____ training. (p. 671)
	d. What is "taking care of unfinished business"? (p. 671)

58. What format is most often employed in group therapy? (Highlight 17.4, p. 669)

59. Complete the following list of the three major criticisms that have been made of humanistic-experiential therapies. (Ironically, the points of criticisms are seen by proponents of humanistic-experiential therapies as the strengths of their approach.) (p. 672)

a. Lack of a highly systematized model of human behavior and its specific aberrations

b.

c.

60. These therapeutic techniques focus on relationships rather than individuals and emphasize the role of faulty communication in causing maladaptive behavior. The following chart summarizes the major forms of interpersonal therapy. Fill in the missing information: (pp. 672-675)

Therapeutic Approach	Description
Couples counseling	a. Is seeing both members of a couple usually more effective than working with only one? (p. 672)
	b. How do happily married couples differ from unhappily married couples? (p. 673)
	c. How are videotapes useful in couple counseling? (p. 673)
	d. How effective are marital therapies at resolving crises according to Cookerly (1980)? (p. 673)
Family therapy	a. How did family therapy originate? (p. 674)
	b. Who does the family therapist view as the "patient" to be directly involved in therapy if lasting improvement is to be achieved? (p. 674)

	c. The most widely used approach to family therapy is _____ developed by Satir. This therapy emphasizes improving family communication, interactions, and relationships among family members. (p. 674)
	d. Another approach is called "structural family therapy" and was developed by _____. This therapy assumes that if the family context changes, then the individual members will change. Thus, an important goal is to change the family organization so that family members will behave _____ and less pathogenically toward each other. (pp. 674-675)
	e. The therapist operates as an agent for altering the interaction among the family members, which has characteristics of _____, _____, and poor conflict resolution skills. (p. 675)
	f. Structural therapy has been used successfully with anorexia, _____, childhood _____ disorders, and _____ addiction. (p. 675)
	g. Which approach to family therapy has been found to be most effective by Gurman et al. (1986) and by Shadish and colleagues (1993)? (p. 675)

Integration of psychotherapy approaches

61. How did early behaviorists view psychoanalysis? (p. 675)

62. How did psychoanalysts view behaviorism? (p. 675)

63. How did both psychoanalysts and behaviorists view humanistic-existential approaches? (p. 675)

64. One approach to attempt to combine therapy approaches is to identify _____ _____ shared by all or most varieties and work from there to understand how these _____ _____ produce the therapeutic effects. What is another strategy? (p. 676)

65. The liberal borrowing of tactics and strategies from the various therapies (i.e., using whatever "works") is sometimes called _____ _____. (p. 676)

Evaluation of success in psychotherapy

66. The chart below lists some of the sources of information that can be used to gauge the outcome of psychotherapy and also note the bias inherent in each source. Fill in the missing information: (p. 677)

Source	Bias
Therapist	a. Wants to see him/herself as competent and successful b.
Patient	a. b.
_____ _____	a. May be more objective than ratings by those directly involved in the therapy. b.

67. Changes in preselected and specifically denoted behaviors that are _____ _____ appear to be the safest measures of outcome. (p. 677)

68. Some forms of psychopathology, such as _____ and _____ episodes and some instances of _____, appear to run a fairly brief course that is not influenced one way or another by psychotherapy. (p. 678)

480

69. Most researchers today would agree that psychotherapy is more effective than _____ _____. (p. 678)

70. Underline the correct phrase: The largest proportion of the gain in treatment occurs (in the beginning, in the middle, close to the end) of psychotherapy according to Howard et al. (1986). (p. 678)

71. In perhaps _____ percent of client-therapist relationships, the client ends up worse off than before treatment. (p. 678)

72. When client and therapist become embroiled in a mutually antagonistic and downward spiraling course, the rupture in therapeutic alliance has been termed _____ _____. (p. 678)

73. Are sexual relationships between therapists and clients considered ethical? (p. 678)

74. Each time a therapist decides that one behavior should be eliminated or substituted for another, they are making a _____ _____. (p. 679)

75. The significance of client-therapist ethnic match for Mexican-American clients in the Los Angeles area depends on what variable? (p. 679)

Unresolved issues

76. What is the basic design of a randomized clinical trial? (p. 680)

77. A significant and persistent frustration in psychosocial therapy outcome research has been the difficulty of finding a credible psychosocial analogue to a _____ _____. (p. 680)

78. What are characteristics of typical *efficacy* studies of psychosocial treatment? (p. 681)

79. How do these characteristics differ in effectiveness from *effectiveness* studies? (Table 17.2, p. 681)

◊ CRITICAL THINKING ABOUT DIFFICULT TOPICS

Consider the following statements from the text and keep them in mind in attempting to answer the questions that follow.

- "Most of us have experienced a time or situation when we were dramatically helped by 'talking things over' with a relative or friend. Formal psychotherapy as practiced by a mental health professional has much in common with this type of familiar experience." (p. 644)

- "Individuals who seem to have the best prognosis for personality change, according to repeated research outcomes, . . . are Young, Attractive, Verbal, Intelligent, and Successful. Ironically, those who tend to do best in psychotherapy are those who seem objectively to need it least." (p. 645)

- "Motivation to change is a crucial element in determining the quality of the therapeutic alliance and hence the level of success likely to be achieved in the therapeutic effort. Almost as important is a client's expectation of receiving help . . . Just as a placebo often lessens pain for someone who believes it will do so, a person who expects to be helped by psychotherapy is likely to be helped, almost regardless of the particular methods used by a therapist." (p. 647)

- "Even under the best of circumstances, however, there is always the possibility that improvement will be attributed to the particular form of treatment used, when it is in fact a product of placebo effects, other events in a client's life, or even of spontaneous change." (p. 677)

- "In view of the many ways that people can help each other, it is not surprising that often considerable improvement occurs without professional therapeutic intervention. Relevant here is the observation that treatment offered by professional therapists has not, in general, been clearly demonstrated to be superior in outcome to nonprofessionally administered therapies." (pp. 677-678)

1. The text offers the rather modest summary statement that "Most researchers today would agree that psychotherapy is more effective than no treatment" (p. 678). How many of the quotations above suggest that a significant portion of this effectiveness has little or nothing to do with the treatment provided, but rather have to do with the client's characteristics (e.g., abilities, motivations, and expectancies) and response to the fact of being treated? If so, how do we know that the specific procedures in psychotherapy are at all effective?

2. Each of the approaches to psychotherapy (e.g., systematic desensitization, client-centered, cognitive-behavioral therapy for depression) reviewed in this chapter asserts that specific aspects of that approach are important to the outcome of therapy. On the other hand, many components are seen in any form of psychotherapy and thus are "common factors" that have nothing to do with specific procedures for that particular form of therapy. It has been argued that these common factors account for most of the success in psychotherapy. How many of the quotations above refer to these nonspecific or common factors? How can we know that a form of therapy is effective because of its specific features?

3. The text does not discuss the topic of the "attention-placebo" control group--perhaps because this is a complex topic. In such a control group the client meets with a therapist for a short time (e.g., fifteen minutes) on a regular basis. The client believes this interaction is treatment and, indeed, the therapist expresses interest in and support for the client, but nothing resembling formal psychotherapy is attempted. On the whole, this type of control group shows a significantly better outcome than do untreated clients. Thus, like psychotherapy, attention-placebo is more effective than no treatment. What does this finding imply for the design of studies on the effectiveness of specific forms of psychotherapy? If Brand X psychotherapy is not better than attention-placebo, what would you conclude about the importance of its specific techniques?

4. A closely related issue in the psychotherapy literature concerns whether therapy involves technical skills. The implication of such skills is that only a trained person could deliver them effectively and that therapy provided by such trained individuals would be more effective than therapy offered by others. How many of the quotations above challenge the notion that the effectiveness of psychotherapy is attributable to technical skills acquired during training?

5. Read carefully the discussion on page 677 of the limitations of all sources of evaluation of the outcome of psychotherapy. In view of these limitations and the quotations above, how can we ever determine whether psychotherapy is effective? Can we argue that the sources of error are random and equal across groups in controlled clinical trials, making it possible to compare treatments with no treatment and with each other?

6. It is not uncommon to hear a psychotherapist assert, "I know from my own experience that psychotherapy works and that I have helped many patients." Develop a response to the therapist indicating that such a response reflects a failure in his or her education. That is, explain why it is extremely difficult to know why an individual client improves and why it is necessary to evaluate the effectiveness of therapy with controlled clinical trials involving random assignment of clients to groups (to control for client factors) and to include an attention-placebo control group (to control for common or nonspecific factors).

◊ CHAPTER 17 QUIZ

Circle the best of the four answers provided and check them according to answers provided at the back of this study guide. Be sure you understand why each answer is correct.

1. Individuals who seek therapy because they feel overwhelmed by sudden highly stressful situations typically respond best to: (pp. 644-645)
   a. existential approaches that reduce alienation.
   b. long-term psychodynamic analysis.
   c. short-term, directive, crisis-oriented treatment.
   d. therapies that employ confrontational methods.

2. Which type of patient may make substantial gains in personal growth in psychotherapy? (p. 645)
   a. those with physical problems who were referred by a physician
   b. those who have experienced long-term psychological distress
   c. severely disturbed psychotic individuals
   d. those described in terms of the so-called YAVIS pattern

3. According to the text, which of the following is *not* a major contribution to the therapeutic relationship? (p. 646)
   a. client's motivation.   c. client's expectation of receiving help.
   b. clinician's personality   d. client's emotional reactivity.

4. A son of a critical father comes to therapy one day and with no provocation is extremely hostile in his remarks to the therapist. The therapist might consider that _____ is occurring. (pp. 649-650)
   a. free association
   b. countertransference
   c. transference
   d. manifest content

5. Contemporary psychodynamic approaches to therapy tend to place an emphasis on: (p. 650)
   a. early repressed sexuality.
   b. interpersonal functioning.
   c. long-term treatment.
   d. childhood events.

6. Which of the following is the central ingredient and key element in treating many forms of anxiety disorders? (p. 655)
   a. exposure
   b. relaxation training
   c. positive reinforcement
   d. conditioning

7. All of the following are steps in Wolpe's approach to systematic desensitization *except*: (p. 655)
   a. asking the client to imagine anxiety-producing situations while relaxing.
   b. constructing a hierarchy of anxiety-producing situations.
   c. placing the client in anxiety-producing life situations.
   d. training the client to relax.

8. Aversion therapy reduces maladaptive behavior by following it with: (p. 657)
   a. a request for the client to avert his or her eyes from the stimulus.
   b. negative reinforcement.
   c. punishment.
   d. stimuli diverting the client's attention.

9. Which of the following is *not* an example of contingency management (i.e., systematic use of reinforcement)? (pp. 658-660)
   a. token economy
   b. behavioral contracting
   c. response shaping
   d. modeling

10. Which of the following statements regarding biofeedback is true? (p. 661)
   a. Biofeedback is a more elaborate means of teaching relaxation.
   b. Biofeedback is more effective than relaxation training.
   c. The effects of biofeedback are often generalized outside the laboratory.
   d. Carefully controlled research on biofeedback has often supported earlier impressions of widespread clinically significant improvement.

11. Which of the following is an example of a core irrational belief, according to Ellis? (p. 664; Table 17.1, p. 664)
    a. "When the fear comes, just pause."
    b. "One must have perfect and certain self-control."
    c. "It will be over shortly."
    d. "Keep the focus on the present."

12. According to Aaron Beck (1979), individuals maintain false beliefs even in the face of contradictory evidence because: (p. 665)
    a. they are reinforced for doing so.
    b. of biologically-based drives to do so.
    c. of a strong regressive pull to be a "child" or a "parent" rather than an "adult."
    d. they engage in selective perception and overgeneralization.

13. Not only was Carl Rogers rated as one of the most influential psychotherapists of his time, but he was also a pioneer in: (p. 670)
    a. advocating health insurance for mental illness.
    b. carrying out empirical research on psychotherapy.
    c. initiating, broad spectrum mental health program.
    d. reorganizing mental hospital procedures.

14. *Regression to the mean* is a limitation of which of the following sources of estimation of a client's gains in therapy? (p. 677)
    a. impressions of change by the therapist
    b. reports of change by the client
    c. reports of change by the client's family and friends
    d. comparisons of pre and post-treatment personality test scores

15. The rate of improvement in treatment offered by professional therapists compared to nonprofessionally administered therapies: (pp. 677-678)
    a. is about twice as high.   c. is about the same.
    b. is about 50% higher.   d. is actually worse.

◊ OVERVIEW

Previous chapters have catalogued the many forms of mental disorders and have briefly described various treatment programs, most of which focus either directly on the patient or involve only immediate family members. Chapter 18, by contrast, describes programs and research that are focused at the broader societal level in order to attempt to prevent maladaptive behavior from occurring in the first place. This chapter tackles some of the more controversial legal and ethical issues surrounding psychopathology. For example, what consitutes sufficient grounds to commit a person to a mental institution? What are a patient's rights? How is "dangerousness" defined and assessed? What should a therapist do when told that a patient is planning to harm another person? Does insanity at the time of a crime preclude or absolve guilty intent? The chapter also discusses how the U.S. government, professional and volunteer agencies, and world organizations are involved in improving mental health. Finally, Chapter 18 discusses the neglect of patients' needs associated with managed health care and deinstitutionalization, as well as challenges for the future, the need for societal planning, and the importance of individual contributions.

◊ CHAPTER OUTLINE

I. Perspectives on Prevention
    A. Universal Interventions
        1. Biological Measures
        2. Psychosocial Measures
        3. Sociocultural Measures
    B. Selective Interventions
        1. An Illustration of Selective Prevention Strategies
            a) Education Programs
            b) Intervention Programs for High-Risk Teens
            c) Parent Education and Family-Based Intervention Programs

V. Unresolved Issues: On the Crisis in Mental Health Care
    A. Mental Health Treatment - Who Decides What Kind and How Long?
    B. Time-Limited Therapy

VI. Summary

◊ LEARNING OBJECTIVES

After studying this chapter, you should be able to:

1. Define *universal intervention*, and explain how universal intervention includes biological, psychosocial, and sociocultural efforts. (pp. 685-687)

2. Define *selective intervention*, and describe and illustrate selective intervention programs, using the example of teen alcohol and drug abuse prevention. (pp. 687-690; The Cutting Edge, p. 691)

3. Define *indicated intervention*, describe two types of crisis intervention, and describe and illustrate three types of indicated intervention, using the example of an airplane crash or other major disaster. (pp. 690-695)

4. Describe efforts to resocialize patients both in mental hospitals and in aftercare programs, including methods for making a mental hospital a therapeutic community. Compare the effectiveness of these approaches. (pp. 695-697)

5. Outline the procedures involved in civil commitment and the safeguards for patients' rights and due process in involuntary commitment. (pp. 697-700; Highlight 18.1, p. 699)

6. Discuss the problems of assessing and predicting "dangerousness" and explain the obligations of the clinician under the "duty-to-warn" legal doctrine. (pp. 700-703)

7. Review the various legal rulings relevant to the insanity defense and discuss the problems and controversies associated with this concept. (pp. 703-708; Highlight 18.2, pp. 704-705)

8. Trace the history of deinstitutionalization of chronic mental patients and summarize the current responses to this phenomenon. (pp. 708-711)

9. List and describe the various U.S. government, professional, voluntary, private industrial, and international organizations involved in mental health efforts. (pp. 711-714)

10. Describe challenges for the future and what can be done on an individual level about some of the broad societal issues discussed. (pp. 714-715).

11. Discuss the problems associated with managed health care. (pp. 716-717)

◊ TERMS YOU SHOULD KNOW

universal intervention (pp. 685-687)

selective intervention (pp. 685, 687-690)

indicated intervention (pp. 685, 690-695)

risk factors (p. 685)

protective factors (p. 685)

crisis intervention (p. 690, 692)

Project Northland (The Cutting Edge, p. 691)

short-term crisis therapy (p. 692)

hot line (p. 692)

debriefing sessions (pp. 694-695)

therapeutic community (p. 695)

milieu therapy (pp. 695, 696)

social learning program (pp. 695, 696)

aftercare programs (pp. 696-697)

halfway house (p. 697)

forensic psychology (pp. 697-698)

voluntary hospitalization (p. 698)

involuntary commitment (p. 698)

right to treatment (Highlight 18.1, p. 699)

freedom from custodial confinement (Highlight 18.1, p. 699)

right to compensation for work (Highlight 18.1, p. 699)

right to live in a community (Highlight 18.1, p. 699)

right to less restrictive treatment (Highlight 18.1, p. 699)

right to legal counsel at commitment hearings (Highlight 18.1, p. 699)

right to refuse treatment (Highlight 18.1, p. 699)

hold order (p. 700)

dangerousness (pp. 700-702)

risk assessment (p. 701)

false negative (p. 701)

"overcontrolled" hostile person (p. 702)

duty-to-warn doctrine (Tarasoff decision) (p. 702)

insanity defense (NGRI plea) (pp. 703-708)

actus rea vs. *mens rea* (p. 703)

M'Naughten rule (p. 706)

irresistible impulse (pp. 706-707)

Durham rule (product test) (p. 707)

ALI standard (substantial capacity test) (p. 707)

IDRA (p. 707)

guilty but mentally ill (GBMI) (p. 708)

deinstitutionalization (pp. 708-711; also p. 695)

Health Maintenance Organizations (HMOs) (pp. 710; 716-717)

National Institute of Mental Health (NIMH) (pp. 711-712)

National Association for Mental Health (NAMH) (p. 712)

National Association for Retarded Citizens (NARC) (pp. 712-713)

employee assistance programs (EAPs) (p. 713)

World Health Organization (WHO) (pp. 713-714)

World Federation for Mental Health (p. 714)

managed health care (pp. 716-717)

open-panel systems vs. *closed-panel systems* (p. 716)

capitation (p. 716)

◊ CONCEPTS TO MASTER

1. Define the current conceptualization of prevention, and list the three categories of prevention, according to the IOM report. (p. 685)

2. Define *universal intervention,* and describe strategies for biological, psychosocial, and sociocultural universal intervention efforts. (pp. 685-687)

3. Define *selective intervention,* and describe six selective intervention programs that have shown promise in prevention of teen alcohol and drug abuse. (pp. 687-690)

4. List and explain three broad government strategies for preventing alcohol and drug abuse that have proven insufficient. Describe Project Northland, and discuss its effectiveness. (pp. 688, 690, The Cutting Edge, p. 691)

5. Define *indicated intervention* and *crisis intervention*. Describe two types of crisis intervention, explain how they differ in the immediacy and duration of services, and indicate what types of personnel are involved. (pp. 690-692)

6. Describe the three types of indicated intervention services that have been shown to be effective in dealing with the psychological problems related to air disasters. (pp. 694-695)

7. List and explain three general therapeutic principles that guide the milieu approach to treatment. (p. 695)

8. Compare the relative effectiveness of three treatment approaches in mental hospitals, and describe some criticisms of the most effective of these approaches, as well as the authors' logical response to such criticism. (p. 696)

9. Define *aftercare* programs, and describe "The Lodge" and its relative effectiveness. (pp. 696-697)

10. List four conditions that must be met before involuntary commitment to a mental institution can occur, and describe the legal process that follows, including the stringent safeguards to ensure patients' rights and due process. (pp. 698-700; Highlight 18.1, p. 699)

11. Describe the findings regarding violence and mental disorder, and discuss the following three problems associated with predicting dangerousness: the ambiguity of the concept of "dangerous," the role of situational circumstances, and the pressure to err on the conservative side. (pp. 700-701)

12. Describe some methods for assessing a patient's potential for dangerousness, and explain the difficulty in assessing dangerousness in an overcontrolled offender. (pp. 701-702)

13. Discuss the Tarasoff case, and explain the implications of the Tarasoff decision on a therapist's duty to warn persons that a patient is planning to harm. (pp. 702-703)

14. Explain what is meant by the insanity defense in criminal cases, and describe five established precedents defining this plea. (pp. 703-707)

15. Summarize the controversy surrounding altered states of consciousness (e.g., psychotropic medications) and personality (e.g., dissociative identity disorder) as grounds for the insantiy defense. What are some of the problems encountered with such a plea? (Highlight 18.2, p. 704)

16. Discuss variations from state to state in law regarding the insanity defense, note problems with the basic concept, and explain the role of "guilty but mentally ill" in this context. (pp. 707-708)

17. Define *deinstitutionalization.* Summarize the factors that drove deinstitutionalization, and describe the unforeseen problems that arose as a result. (pp. 708-710)

18. .Describe the current facilities that partially serve chronic mental patients. (pp. 710-711)

19. List and describe four major functions of the National Institute of Mental Health (NIMH). (p. 711)

20. List several professional organizations in the mental health field, and explain three key functions that they perform. (p. 712)

21. Describe some of the major functions of the National Association for Mental Health (NAMH). (p. 712)

22. List and describe six areas of job design and conditions of work in which serious problems may exist. (p. 713)

23. Describe the functions and contributions of WHO and the World Federation for Mental Health. (pp. 713-714)

24. Describe several opportunities that individuals have to contribute to the advancement of mental health, and list some basic facts that should help them to succeed in those endeavors. (p. 715)

25. Describe the following aspects of HMOs: the use of "panels," capitation-based methods of payment, negotiating reduced prices directly with the provider, the use of a "gatekeeper" to limit the provision of services and the use of less trained people to provide psychotherapy. (pp. 716-717)

Introduction

1. Why is the topic of prevention in the mental health field still based largely on hypotheses about what works rather than on substantial empirical research? (p. 685)

2. What new specification was provided in the Institute of Medicine (IOM) report on long-term prevention research programs? (p. 685)

3. What are the three subcategories of prevention efforts, according to the IOM report? (p. 685)

Universal intervention

4. Universal intervention involves research into the conditions that foster mental disorders. It also involves the eradication of negative conditions and institution of circumstances that foster mental health. Fill in the missing information on the following chart that illustrates various universal intervention measures: (pp. 686-687)

Type of Universal Intervention	Example
Biological (p. 686)	Biologically based universal intervention begins with developing _____ lifestyles. Many of the goals of health psychology can also be viewed as universal intervention. To the extent that physical illness always produces some sort of _____ _____ that can result in problems such as depression, good health is prevention with respect to good mental health.

Psychosocial (pp. 686-687)	The first requirement for psychosocial health is that a person develop the skills needed for effective _____ _____, for expressing _____ constructively, and for satisfying _____ with others. The second requirement is that a person acquire an accurate _____ on which to build his or her identity. Third, psychosocial well-being also requires _____ for the types of problems a person is likely to encounter during given life stages.
Sociocultural (p. 687)	Sociocultural prevention is focused on making the _____ as "nourishing" as possible. Examples of sociocultural prevention include a broad spectrum of social measures ranging from public _____ and _____ to economic planning and social legislation directed at ensuring adequate health care for all citizens.

Selective intervention

5. List three strategies proposed by the government to tackle drug abuse. (p. 688)

6. List six selective intervention programs that have shown promise in the treatment of drug abuse.(pp. 689-690)

7. Name and describe the prevention program that has been adapted for an alcohol abuse prevention project in Russia. (The Cutting Edge, p. 691)

Indicated intervention

8. Crisis intervention is an attempt at indicated intervention that aims at delivering prompt treatment. Complete the list of ways by which prompt services are given. (p. 692)
   a.

   b. Telephone hot line

9. The sole concern of *short-term* crisis therapy is the current problem with which the individual or family is having difficulty. How long does such therapy last? (p. 692)

10. Explain why both face-to-face and telephone hot line crisis intervention are discouraging for the therapist. (p. 692)

The mental hospital as a therapeutic community

11. Describe the following aspects of a therapeutic community: (p. 695)
    a. Staff expectations

    b. Do-it-yourself attitude

    c. Group cohesiveness

12. _____ was initiated to prevent the often negative experiences many psychiatric patients had when confined to a mental hospital for long periods of time. (p. 695)

13. To keep the focus on returning patients to the community and on preventing a return to the institution, hospital staffs try to establish _____ with patients' families and communities and to provide them with _____ _____ about the patient's recovery. Between ___ and ___ percent of psychotic patients labeled as psychotic can be discharged within a few weeks or at most a few months. (p. 696)

14. Paul and Lentz (1977) performed an evaluation of the relative effectiveness of three treatment approaches for chronic hospitalized patients: milieu therapy, social-learning treatment program, and traditional mental hospital treatment. Respond to the following questions about this study: (p. 696)

   a. Briefly describe each of the three treatments that were compared:

     Milieu therapy

     Social-learning treatment

     Traditional mental hospital treatment

   b. Describe how the study was carried out.

   c. Who were the subjects?

15. The results of the Paul and Lentz study were quite impressive. Both milieu therapy and social learning therapy produced significant improvement in overall functioning and resulted in more successful hospital releases than the traditional hospital care. However, the _____ _____ was clearly superior to the more diffuse program of _____. The relative improvement rates for the different treatments were that ___ percent of the social-learning program, ___ percent of the milieu therapy group, and less than ___ percent of the traditional treatment group remained continuously in the community. (p. 696)

16. Many studies have found that as many as ___ percent of schizophrenic patients have been rehospitalized within one year of their discharge. (p. 696)

17. Aftercare programs reduce the likelihood of rehospitalization. Describe halfway houses and community based treatment facilities. (pp. 696-697)

18. Although some patients continue to have mental health problems and many encounter problems of gaining the _____ and _____ of community residents, efforts to treat severely disturbed patients in the community are often very successful. (p. 697)

The commitment process

19. In most cases, people are sent to state mental hospitals voluntarily. However, there are four conditions on which a person can be formally committed. Complete the following list of them: (p. 698)
    a. Dangerous to himself or herself
    b.
    c. Unable to make responsible decisions about hospitalization
    d.

20. What is the first step in the process of committing a person involuntarily? (p. 698)

21. Commitment is a civil court proceeding that varies slightly from state to state. In a typical procedure, a court order must be obtained for commitment. If there is imminent danger, however, the law allows emergency hospitalization without a formal commitment hearing. In such cases a physician must sign a statement. The person can then be picked up—usually by the police—and detained under a _____, usually not to exceed 72 hours. (pp. 698-699)

Assessment of "dangerousness"

22. One study reported that homicidal behavior among former patients was increased eight-fold with the diagnosis of _____, and ten-fold with the diagnoses of _____ or _____. (p. 700)

23. What three critical dilemmas did the case of the murder of Eva B. illustrate regarding attempts to identify and predict dangerousness? (pp. 700-701)

24. What is the foremost problem in adequately appreciating the difficulties involved in conducting a violence risk assessment? Explain. (p. 701)

25. Violent acts are difficult to predict because they are determined as much by _____ circumstances as they are by the personality traits of the individual. Mental health professionals typically err on the conservative side when assessing violence proneness. (p. 701)

26. What is the equation for an aggressive act? (p. 701)

27. The two major sources of personality information for the prediction of dangerousness are data from _____ and the individual's _____. (p. 702)

28. What is an overcontrolled hostile person, and in what way does this relate to the assessment of dangerousness? (p. 702)

29. Compare the original Tarasoff decision with the revised opinion of the California Supreme Court in 1976. (p. 703)

30. When does a clinician have a "duty-to-warn" or "duty to protect"? (pp. 702-703)

The insanity defense

31. How frequently is the insanity plea used? (p. 706)

32. How does the time served by the criminal sent to a psychiatric hospital compare to time served by criminals sent to prison? (p. 706)

33. The established precedents that define the insanity defense are listed below. Briefly describe each one. (pp. 706-707)

a. The M'Naughten Rule

b. The irresistible impulse

c. The Durham Rule

d. Diminished capacity

Deinstitutionalization

34. What has happened to the number of persons hospitalized in state and county mental hospitals since 1950? What accounts for the changes? (p. 708)

35. Complete the list below of five unforeseen problems that have arisen in the effort to deinstitutionalize the mentally ill? (p. 709)

   a. Many residents of mental institutions had no families or homes to go to.
   b.
   c.

   d. Many patients had not been carefully selected for discharge and were ill-prepared for community living.
   e. Many of those who were discharged were not followed-up sufficiently to ensure successful adaptation.

36. Rossi (1990) estimated that ___ percent of homeless individuals suffer from chronic mental disorder. Goldfinger et al. (1996) reported that ___ percent of the homeless people in the study abused various substances. (p. 710)

37. Deinstitutionalization notwithstanding, some ___ percent of all the dollars spent on mental health care are spent for hospitalization. (p. 710)

38. As a result of the need for alternative care facilities following deinstitutionalization and of financial incentives provided by Medicare, _____ persons make up 51 percent of the nursing home population at present. (p. 711)

Organized efforts for mental health

39. The extent of mental disorders was brought to public attention during World War II. How? (p. 711)

40. What types of activities does the NIMH do? (p. 711)

41. Does the federal government directly supervise: (p. 712)
    a. local community services?
    b. state mental hospitals?

42. What happened to the mental health programs in the 1980s compared to the 1960s and 1970s? (p. 712)

43. What is the role of voluntary agencies in regard to mental health needs? (pp. 712-713)

44. Many companies have introduced numerous psychological services, often referred to as _____. In contrast, employers have been slower to deal with issues of _____ and work _____ as means of maximizing worker mental health. (p. 713)

45. It has been estimated that over _____ million people worldwide are affected by mental disorders. (p. 713)

46. An important contribution of the WHO is its _____, which enables clinicians and researchers in different countries to use a uniform set of diagnostic categories. (p. 714)

Challenges for the future

47. How do the authors feel about the need for social planning? (p. 715)

48. List some constructive courses of action open to each citizen to work for improved health in society. (p. 715)

49. Indicate whether each of the following is true or false by circling the appropriate response: (p. 715)
   a. From time to time, everyone has serious difficulty coping with problems.   True or False
   b. During such a crisis, professional assistance may be needed.   True or False
   c. Such difficulties can happen to anyone if the stress is severe.   True or False
   d. Early detection and treatment is important to prevent chronic conditions.   True or False

Unresolved issues

50. In the decisions concerning access to psychotherapy and at times the type of mental health treatment to be provided, the HMO representative or "gatekeeper" to reimbursement is often a medical _____ who is untrained in psychiatric disorders or psychosocial interventions.   In some systems of care, the gatekeeper might be a _____ professional with no training in medicine. (pp. 716-717)

51. Lazarus (1996) pointed out that _____ psychotherapy has been virtually eliminated for all but a small number of wealthy private clients. Most managed care groups approve only short inpatient stays (less than ten days) and_____ to _____ sessions of outpatient mental health treatment at a time. (p. 717)

52. Few if any of the decisions regarding the amount and type of services provided in managed mental health care programs are guided directly by _____ criteria. (p. 717)

507

◊ CRITICAL THINKING ABOUT DIFFICULT TOPICS

1. Question 2 in the Critical Thinking About Difficult Topics section for Chapter 2 asked you to think about the concepts of free will versus determinism as they arise in discussions of abnormal behavior. Can you see the same issue arising in some aspects of the insanity defense? For example, in invoking the "irresistible impulse" rule it is argued that in some cases persons "had lost the power to choose between right and wrong" and "were compelled beyond their will to commit the act" (pp. 706-707). Does this imply that "free will" applies to the actions of most of us? If so, do you think that view of human behavior is compatible with the deterministic framework usually adopted in psychology?

2. Your text describes the current conflict between: 1) attempts to save money in managed care and 2) the assertion that the resultant mental health care is of poor quality (pp. 716-717). Can you think of ways in which you could contain costs while maintaining the quality of mental health services? One approach that has been suggested is to restrict mental health care to "empirically validated treatments" – i.e., to forms of treatment that have been demonstrated in research to be effective for patients with specific diagnoses. Do you think this is a satisfactory solution? Are there any pitfalls in such an approach?

◊ CHAPTER 18 QUIZ

Circle the best of the four answers provided and check them according to answers provided at the back of this study guide. Be sure you understand why each answer is correct.

1. Over the years most efforts toward mental health have been largely geared toward helping people only after they have already developed serious problems. An alternative to this is: (p. 685)
   a. crisis intervention.
   b. *in vivo* treatment.
   c. prevention.
   d. retrospective research.

2. All of the following groups are at high risk for mental disorders *except*: (p. 685)
   a. elderly people living alone.
   b. married people between 25 and 35.
   c. recently divorced people.
   d. the physically disabled.

3. Any effort aimed at improving the human condition, at making life more fulfilling and meaningful, may be considered part of _____ prevention of mental or emotional disturbance. (p. 686)
   a. universal
   b. selective
   c. indicated
   d. secondary

4. Adequate preparation for potential problems likely to be encountered by anyone during a given life stage is a requirement for _____ health, at the _____ level of prevention: (p. 686)
   a. biological, universal
   b. psychosocial, universal
   c. biological, selective
   d. psychosocial, selective

5. All of the following are sociocultural efforts toward universal intervention of mental disorders *except*: (p. 687)
   a. economic planning.
   b. penal systems.
   c. public education.
   d. social security.

6. Project Northland's selective interventions included all of the following *except*: (The Cutting Edge, p. 691)
   a. parent-education programs.
   b. peer leadership.
   c. community-wide activities.
   d. mass media campaigns.

7. Allen Jones is a middle-aged factory worker, husband, and father of five children. He has never previously been involved in psychotherapy until his home is destroyed in a tornado. While he attempts to find housing for his family, he discovers that his wife wants a divorce. He immediately becomes quite depressed and is unable to follow through on his house-seeking. Allen Jones is a prime candidate for: (pp. 690, 692)
   a. day hospitalization.
   b. crisis intervention.
   c. psychoanalysis.
   d. milieu therapy.

8. Milieu therapy is: (pp. 695-696)
   a. the temporary substitution of one treatment mode by another until adequate resources can be acquired to provide the treatment of choice.
   b. a general term for any form of preventive treatment.
   c. the establishment of a hospital environment itself as a therapeutic community.
   d. the integration of any two distinct forms of treatment.

9. Which of the following treatment approaches was found by Paul and Lentz (1977) to be the most effective? (p. 696)
   a. social learning treatment
   b. peer group influence programs
   c. traditional hospital care
   d. milieu therapy

10. Typically, the first step in committing an individual to a mental hospital involuntarily is: (p. 698)
   a. appointing a physician and a psychologist to examine the client.
   b. filing a petition for a commitment hearing.
   c. holding a commitment hearing.
   d. notifying the police.

11. Which of the following patient rights was *limited*, according to a 1990 U.S. Supreme Court ruling? (Highlight 18.1, p. 699)
   a. right to compensation for work
   b. right to refuse ECT and psychosurgery
   c. right to receive treatment
   d. right to refuse psychotropic medication

12. One dilemma in attempting to rehabilitate previously violent psychiatric patients is that the mental health workers must exhibit some degree of _____. (p. 701)
   a. patience
   b. stability
   c. professionalism
   d. trust

13. A clear implication of the Tarasoff decision is that a therapist must: (pp. 702-703)
   a. inform the police when a client has made global threats.
   b. warn a person whom his or her client has specifically threatened to harm.
   c. warn anyone whom he or she believes might be in danger from a client.
   d. warn the authorities when a client threatens suicide.

14. Studies have confirmed that individuals acquitted of crimes by reason of insanity typically spend _____ time in psychiatric hospitals as (than) individuals convicted of crimes spend in prison. (p. 706)
   a. less
   b. about the same amount of
   c. about the same amount or more
   d. much more

15. Under which of the following precedents did the law hold that individuals might not be responsible for their acts, even though they knew what they were doing was wrong, if they had lost the power to choose between right and wrong? (pp. 706-707)
a. the M'Naughten Rule (1843)
b. the irresistible impulse (1887)
c. the Durham Rule (1954)
d. federal Insanity Defense Reform Act (1984)

16. Between 1970 and 1992, the patient population at state mental hospitals was reduced by ____ percent. (p. 708)
a. 73 c. 23
b. 53 d. 10

17. Most often, in an HMO, the gatekeeper who determines which mental health treatments will be offered is a: (p. 716)
a. psychiatric social worker c. medical generalist or business professional
b. Ph.D. psychologist d. psychiatrist

ANSWER KEY FOR CHAPTER QUIZZES

◊ CHAPTER 1

1. c. is "away from the normal"
2. a. deviant from social expectations
3. b. adaptivity of the behavior in furthering individual and group well-being
4. b. reliable
5. d. configural
6. d. specifies the exact behaviors that must be observed
7. b. elimination of prototypal classification
8. d. comorbidity
9. c. the person's present condition
10. b. Axis II
11. d. all of the above
12. d. Axis IV
13. a. disorders secondary to gross destruction and malfunctioning of brain tissue
14. b. acute
15. d. all of the above
16. a. lifetime prevalence
17. b. high socioeconomic status and older age
18. b. hypotheses
19. d. random selection
20. a. analogue
21. c. prospective

CHAPTER 2

1. b. the Edwin Smith papyrus
2. d. There are basically four types of body fluids
3. b. the influence on thinking and/or behavior of "natural appetites" and the desire to eliminate pain and attain pleasure
4. a. the anatomy of the central nervous system
5. b. death of Galen in 200 A.D.
6. d. Avicenna
7. d. Yin and Yang
8. c. King James I of England
9. b. Malleus Maleficarum
10. a. demons, etc. did not cause mental disorders
11. b. St. Mary of Bethlehem mental hospital
12. b. intimidate patients
13. a. The Geel Shrine, Belgium
14. d. in a humanitarian fashion
15. c. Benjamin Rush
16. d. the result of severe psychological stress
17. c. general loss of faith among the general population
18. c. neurasthenia
19. a. inhuman treatment accorded the mentally ill
20. d. infecting the sufferer with malaria
21. b. hysteria
22. c. catharsis
23. d. whether the outcome (reinforcer) is dependent on the animal's behavior

◊ CHAPTER 3

1. d. contributory cause
2. c. receptor site
3. a. re-uptake
4. a. the proband
5. b. id
6. b. neurotic anxiety

7. d. separation-individuation
8. d. basic trust
9. b. operant conditioning
10. c. differential reinforcement
11. d. its overconcern with symptoms
12. a. attributional style
13. a. accommodation
14. b. detachment
15. c. permissive-indulgent
16. a. parents' income
17. b. correlational in nature
18. c. developing a unified point of view

◊ CHAPTER 4

1. d. eustress
2. b. frustration
3. b. approach-avoidance conflict
4. d. they measure reactions to specific environmental events
5. c. mourning
6. a. protect the self from damage and disorganization
7. b. less available for coping with others
8. c. elevated levels of urinary noradrenaline
9. a. emotional arousal, increased tension, and greater alertness
10. c. 12 months
11. b. shock phase
12. d. the conditions of battle that tax a soldier's stamina
13. d. There might be other adjustment problems involved.
14. b. were more prepared by prior experience with stressors, stoicism training, and commitment to a cause
15. a. both psychotherapy and medications
16. b. is exceedingly difficult

◊ CHAPTER 5

1. d. phobias
2. b. reduction in anxiety
3. c. immunization
4. c. toy rabbits
5. b. specific social phobia
6. d. brevity, intensity
7. b. tricyclic antidepressant
8. a. mimic the physiological cues that normally precede a panic attack
9. d. carbon dioxide inhalation and lactate infusion
10. c. anxious apprehension
11. b. GABA
12. a. compulsion
13. d. avoidant and dependent
14. b. exposure treatment, response prevention

◊ CHAPTER 6

1. c. 21%
2. b. denial and rejection of the dead person
3. d. cyclothymic disorder
4. a. at least one episode of mania
5. d. deflated self-esteem
6. c. a depletion of norepinephrine and/or serotonin
7. d. response contingent positive reinforcement is not available
8. b. there is no control over aversive events
9. d. acetylcholine depletion
10. b. the disorder is bipolar in nature
11. d. all of the above are equally effective
12. c. one year
13. d. recovery
14. a. 40, 30

◊ CHAPTER 7

1. a. somatization disorder
2. c. "I deserve your attention and concern"
3. b. ability to talk only in a whisper
4. c. conversion disorder
5. a. a conscious plan to use illness as an escape
6. a. escaping from their personal identity
7. c. generalized
8. d. dissociative identity disorder
9. b. traumatic childhood abuse
10. c. theories of emotional functioning

◊ CHAPTER 8

1. d. psychogenic physical disorders
2. a. repressed anger
3. b. anorexia nervosa, binge eating/purging subtype
4. b. binge eating disorder
5. a. lack of conformity and oppositional style
6. b. over-encouragement of autonomous strivings
7. c. humoral and cellular
8. a. bacterial infection
9. b. aerobic exercise
10. c. there is direct neural control of immunological agents
11. d. lack of metabolic retention of sodium
12. a. angina pectoris
13. d. decelerated speech and motor activity
14. a. blue collar men
15. c. migraine headaches
16. c. preventing pathogenic life-style behaviors

CHAPTER 9

1. d. maladaptive ways of perceiving, thinking, and relating
2. a. 3
3. b. II
4. d. clinicians often do not receive sufficient training in the diagnosis of personality disorders
5. b. schizotypal
6. a. avoidant
7. a. passive-aggressive
8. c. only prospective studies have been possible so far
9. c. borderline
10. c. higher for males than for females
11. a. deficient aversive emotional arousal
12. d. reactivity of the behavioral inhibition system
13. b. emotional family disturbance before the parent left
14. d. ineffective discipline and supervision
15. d. antianxiety drugs

◊ CHAPTER 10

1. b. psychoactive substance dependence
2. c. 12
3. a. 0.1
4. a. alcohol amnestic disorder
5. d. personal maladjustment
6. c. is associated with the common use of alcohol as a means of coping with stress
7. d. aversive conditioning
8. d. 54
9. c. less effective than all others
10. c. small, apparently irrelevant decisions
11. c. endorphins
12. a. antisocial
13. d. stimulant
14. b. LSD
15. c. decrease in size, but not number, when an adult loses weight
16. a. being born to an alcoholic parent

◊ CHAPTER 11

1. d. transvestism
2. c. an adolescent male who is shy and feels inadequate in relations with women
3. a. are young adult males
4. d. transvestic fetishism
5. a. homosexuality
6. b. homosexual transsexuals
7. d. the manner in which child abuse "experts" elicited children's testimony
8. d. 44, 2.5
9. a. do not consider themselves victimized
10. b. of lower intelligence
11. b. impulsive, antisocial behavior
12. a. dysfunction
13. d. climaxing too early
14. b. one-half
15. a. yohimbine

◊ CHAPTER 12

1. a. .2
2. d. older in females than males
3. d. cognitive slippage
4. b. confused sense of self
5. a. undifferentiated
6. b. catatonic
7. d. schizophreniform disorder
8. c. higher concordance rates for identical twins
9. d. 100
10. a. high-risk studies
11. d. Dopamine-stimulating drugs cause hallucinations
12. b. a loss of brain tissue mass
13. c. cognitive slippage
14. a. 10 percent

---

CHAPTER 13

1. a. mental retardation
2. b. circumscribed
3. d. human brain
4. c. loss of function
5. c. III
6. d. delirium.
7. c. 40
8. a. prevention
9. a. simple deterioration
10. c. 6
11. b. Down syndrome
12. b. continuing recurrence of small strokes
13. c. events immediately preceding the injury
14. b. dementia
15. b. ability to succeed at schoolwork
16. d. Mild
17. c. 25
18. a. fertilized egg
19. c. normal environmental stimulation
20. b. overall classroom climate
21. b. specific

◊ **CHAPTER 14**

---

1. c. 17, 22
2. d. requires more symptoms to make a diagnosis
3. a. presenting symptoms
4. d. higher in anxiety
5. d. both medication and behavior modification were effective, but the former was better
6. b. ODD, CD, ASP
7. a. becoming overly dependent on others
8. d. have experiences that reduce their fears and insecurity
9. c. childhood anxiety disorders

10. b. NREM sleep
11. d. most cases are found in the upper classes
12. c. genetic factors
13. a. haloperidol
14. b. children are dependent on those around them
15. a. immature minors
16. a. antisocial
17. b. in association with on or two other persons
18. c. the psychological support afforded by membership in a delinquent gang

◊ CHAPTER 15

1. b. interpersonal skills
2. a. PET scan
3. a. Halstead-Reitan
4. d. employs "operational" assessment
5. d. Hamilton Rating Scale for Depression
6. a. intelligence and personality
7. b. WAIS-R
8. c. projective and objective
9. c. assess the way a patient perceives ambiguous stimuli
10. a. MMPI
11. c. construct a validity scale
12. b. "mentalistic"
13. c. the computer integrates the descriptions it picks up
14. b. MMPI
15. d. insufficient validation

◊ CHAPTER 16

1. b. epileptics rarely developed schizophrenia
2. c. unilateral ECT
3. a. it is ineffective
4. b. maintenance doses of antidepressant medication
5. c. the advent of the major antipsychotic drugs

6. d. pain
7. d. psychotropic
8. d. reduce the intensity of delusions and hallucinations
9. a. blocking dopamine receptors
10. a. Haldol
11. d. increase the availability of serotonin and norepinephrine at synaptic sites
12. b. imipramine (Tofranil)
13. c. bipolar mood disorders
14. b. memory impairment
15. b. had not administered drug therapy

◊ CHAPTER 17

1. c. short-term, directive, crisis-oriented treatment
2. d. those described in terms of the so-called YAVIS pattern
3. d. client's emotional reactivity
4. c. transference
5. b. interpersonal functioning
6. a. exposure
7. c. placing the client in anxiety-producing life situations
8. c. punishment
9. d. modeling
10. a. Biofeedback is a more elaborate means of teaching relaxation
11. b. "One must have perfect and certain self-control."
12. d. they engage in selective perception and overgeneralization
13. b. carrying out empirical research on psychotherapy
14. d. comparisons of pre- and post- treatment personality test scores
15. c. is about the same

◊ CHAPTER 18

1. c. prevention
2. b. married people between 25 and 35
3. a. universal

4. b. psychosocial, universal
5. b. penal systems
6. d. mass media campaigns
7. b. crisis intervention
8. c. the establishment of a hospital environment itself as a therapeutic community.
9. a. social learning treatment
10. b. filing a petition for a commitment hearing
11. d. right to refuse psychotropic medication
12. d. trust
13. b. warn a person whom his or her client has specifically threatened to harm
14. a. less
15. b. the irresistible impulse (1887)
16. a. 73 percent
17. c. medical generalist or business professional

NOTES

NOTES

NOTES

NOTES

NOTES

NOTES

NOTES